Uniting a Divided City

Uniting a Divided City

Governance and Social Exclusion in Johannesburg

Jo Beall
Owen Crankshaw
Susan Parnell

Earthscan Publications Ltd
London • Sterling, VA

First published in the UK and USA in 2002
by Earthscan Publications Ltd

ISBN: 1 85383 916 7 paperback
      1 85383 921 3 hardback

Typesetting by PCS Mapping & DTP, Gateshead
Printed and bound in the UK by Creative Print and Design (Wales), Ebbw Vale
Cover design by Danny Gillespie

For a full list of publications please contact:

Earthscan Publications Ltd
120 Pentonville Road, London, N1 9JN, UK
Tel: +44 (0)20 7278 0433
Fax: +44 (0)20 7278 1142
Email: earthinfo@earthscan.co.uk
Web: **www.earthscan.co.uk**

22883 Quicksilver Drive, Sterling, VA 20166-2012, USA

A catalogue record for this book is available from the British Library

Library of Congress Cataloging-in-Publication Data

Beall, Jo, 152-.
    Uniting a divided city : governance and social exclusion in Johannesburg / Jo Beall,
Owen Crankshaw, Susan Parnell.
       p. cm.
    Includes bibliographical references and index.
    ISBN 1-85383-921-3 – ISBN 1-85383-916-7 (pbk.)
    1. Johannesburg (South Africa)–Social conditions. 2. Johannesburg (South
Africa)–Politics and government. 3. Social change–South Africa–Johannesburg. 4.
Urban renewal–South Africa–Johannesburg. 5. Community development–South
Africa–Johannesburg. 6. Municipal services–South Africa–Johannesburg. 7.
Marginality, Social–South Africa–Johannesburg. I. Crankshaw, Owen. II. Parnell, Sue.
III. Title.

HN801.J64 B43 2002
306'.096822'1–dc21

                               2002008533

Earthscan is an editorially independent subsidiary of Kogan Page Ltd and publishes in
association with WWF-UK and the International Institute for Environment and
Development

This book is printed on elemental chlorine-free paper

Contents

PART 1   WAYS OF UNDERSTANDING DIVIDED CITIES

PART 2   THE CHANGING SPATIAL STRUCTURE OF THE CITY

PART 3   INSTITUTIONAL RESPONSES TO URBAN CHANGE

PART 4   LIVING IN A DIVIDED CITY

List of Figures

List of Tables

CHAPTER 9

CHAPTER 10

Acknowledgements

This book is the outcome of research conducted over four years and undertaken for several different projects. The key project on which the book draws is a study of Johannesburg, undertaken within the context of a three-year-long research programme on Urban Poverty, Partnerships and Governance, conducted across ten cities of the South. We are grateful to ESCOR, which funded the research, and to members of the ESCOR Steering Committee for their sage guidance, in particular Michael Mutter of the Infrastructure and Urban Development Division of the UK's Department for International Development, who was also very supportive of *Uniting a Divided City*. Nick Devas of the University of Birmingham, who coordinated the programme, contributed greatly to our understanding of the Johannesburg experience, as did the other members of the UK Research Team: Philip Amis, Richard Batley, Ursula Grant, Diana Mitlin, Fiona Nunan, David Satterthwaite, Cecilia Tacoli and Elizabeth Vidler. We also benefited from the generous engagement of the other city research teams, particularly Solomon Benjamin and R Bhuvaneswari from Bangalore, Felisa Etemadi of Cebu, David Korboe and Rudith King on Kumasi, the late Rose Gatabaki-Kamau on Mombasa, who sadly died before the completion of the programme, and Marcus Melo and Celina Souza, who shared their work on Brazil. We are most grateful to them all.

Following on from the ESCOR project, the Greater Johannesburg Metropolitan Council (GJMC) decided to include a focus on social exclusion as part of its poverty mapping. The book draws on major contributions by the three authors to the *Social Exclusion and Social Capital in Johannesburg* study that was commissioned by the city in 2001. The book also draws on research undertaken as part of an Open University audio-cassette presentation on Johannesburg. We are grateful to Tim Allen of the London School of Economics, who coordinated and presented the Open University series, and to Simon Lawson, who produced the programme 'Smart Johannesburg', for their challenging perspectives on Johannesburg in a global context. Additional research funds from the London School of Economics and the University of Cape Town helped us to assemble a wide range of comparative material, process South African survey and census material and conduct in-depth research across eight case-study areas in Johannesburg.

Turning research reports into a manuscript required the three authors to spend an extended period of time together, an opportunity afforded us by a generous award from the Suny Toyota International Centre for Economic Research and Development at the London School of Economics. Such a wide array of funding for both contextualized and grounded policy-oriented research is only rarely available to social scientists, and we are acutely aware of the privileged opportunity we were afforded. This was not least because of the fascinating time frame of our work, which occurred when South Africa sought to consolidate its democratic transition.

Within the city of Johannesburg, we received remarkable cooperation and willingness to reflect frankly on the challenges of transforming city governance. Special thanks are due to Jayne Eagle, Jan Erasmus, Kenny Fihla, Ketsoe Gordhan, Roland Hunter, Majur Maganal, Pascal Maloi, Laila McKenna, Rashid Seedat and Mellisa Whitehead. The interim phase of local government restructuring was deeply challenging in Johannesburg, and so we have a long list of thanks to all of those who helped us – whether directly or indirectly – explore the intricacies of the South African transition and to access the rapidly changing face of post-apartheid Johannesburg. We are particularly grateful for the insights of colleagues in South Africa: Kevin Allan, Graeme Gotz, Kirsten Harrison, Sophie Oldfield, Alan Mabin, Lali Mohlabane, Edgar Pieterse, Ari Sitas, Alison Todes and Astrid von Kotze. We also thank Dominique Wooldridge for her enthusiastic collaboration in various aspects of our extended involvement when researching Johannesburg and for permission to use one of her wonderful photographs. Thank you, also, to Mary Hart, Shireen Hassim, Steve Gelb, Abba Omar, Leteifa Mobara, Chris and Jayne Rogerson, Mary and Richard Tomlinson, and the numerous Johannesburg family and friends who provided open house on our frequent visits to the city.

This study would not have been possible without rigorous field research. We received assistance from several non-governmental organizations (NGOs) and are especially grateful to Hassen Mohamed of Planact, Thembi Mapetla of HelpAge International, and Moeketsi Lephuting from the Group for Environmental Monitoring for assisting with access to communities and community-based organizations (CBOs), as well as to Kirsten Harrison who organized and undertook much of the research in Yeoville. Members of staff and students at the University of the Witwatersrand were most helpful in providing contacts and making interpreters and research assistants available to us. Our work was also dependent upon long-term research assistance, and this came in the form of reliable and good-natured professionalism from Reathe Taljaard and her team from Progressus. We are particularly grateful to Brenda Malongete, Luck Mumba and Peter Nchabeleng, who between them conducted focus group discussions in a number of African languages as well as in English, Afrikaans, French and Portuguese.

Uniting a Divided City could not have been written without the facilitation, back-up and support of our 'home fronts' of London and Cape Town. This was provided by Sharon Adams and Saskia Kuiper at the University of Cape Town and Remmy Ahmed, Silvia Posocco and Julia Shaw at the London School of Economics. Phillip Stickler drew the maps. Moral support, friendship and an endless supply of good food were provided by those who visited and sustained us in France, as we sat doggedly at our laptops. To Malcolm Alexander, Charlie Beall, Ann Perry, Gordon Pirie, Anthony Swift, Mike Toller and Rosé Bank, a warm and heartfelt thank you.

Jo Beall, Owen Crankshaw and Susan Parnell
January 2002

List of Acronyms and Abbreviations

ANC	African National Congress
BAAB	Bantu Affairs Administration Board
BID	business improvement district
BLA	Black Local Authority
CASE	Community Agency for Social Enquiry
CBD	central business district
CBO	community-based organization
CDF	Community Development Forum
CDS	City Development Strategy
CEO	chief executive officer
CJP	Central Johannesburg Partnership
COSATU	Congress of South African Trade Unions
DAC	Development Assistance Committee (of the OECD)
DFA	Development Facilitation Act
DFID	Department for International Development (UK)
DLG	Developmental Local Government
DP	Democratic Party
DME	Department of Mineral Affairs and Energy
DWAF	Department of Water Affairs and Forestry
EMSS	Eastern Municipal Sub-Structure
ESCOR	Economic and Social Research Unit
ESKOM	Electricity Supply Commission
GASEWA	Gauteng Self-Employed Women's Association
GDP	gross domestic product
GEAR	Growth, Employment and Redistribution (macro-economic policy programme)
GGP	gross geographic product
GIS	geographic information system
GJMC	Greater Johannesburg Metropolitan Council
GJTMC	Greater Johannesburg Transitional Metropolitan Council
ICHUT	Inner-City Housing Upgrading Trust
ICO	Inner-City Office
ICVS	International Crime Victim Survey
IDP	Integrated Development Plan
IDT	Independent Development Trust
IFP	Inkatha Freedom Party
ILO	International Labour Organization
IMF	International Monetary Fund

ISC	interim steering committee
ISCOR	Iron and Steel Corporation
ISS	Institute of Security Studies
IT	information technology
JCC	Johannesburg City Council
JDA	Johannesburg Development Agency
JSE	Johannesburg Stock Exchange
km	kilometre
KZN	KwaZulu-Natal
LED	local economic development
LDO	Land Development Objective
LIDP	Local Area Integrated Development Plan
LOGON	Local Government Learning Network
MLC	Metropolitan Local Council
MTC	Metropolitan Trading Company
NEDLAC	National Economic, Development and Labour Council
NGO	non-governmental organization
NHF	National Housing Forum
NIMBY	not in my backyard
NMC	Northern Metropolitan Council
NMLC	Northern Metropolitan Local Council
NMSS	Northern Metropolitan Sub-Structure
NPRS	national poverty reduction strategy
OECD	Organisation for Economic Co-operation and Development
POWA	People Opposing Women Abuse
PWV	Pretoria–Witwatersrand–Vereeniging Region
R	South African Rand
RDP	Reconstruction and Development Programme
RSC	Regional Services Council
SACP	South African Communist Party
SADC	Southern African Development Community
SALGA	South African Local Government Association
SAMWU	South African Municipal Workers Union
SANFED	Sandton Federation of Ratepayers
SANCO	South African National Civic Organization
SANGOCO	South African Non-Government Organization Coalition
SAP	South African Police
SEWU	Self-Employed Women's Union
SMDF	Strategic Metropolitan Development Framework
SMME	Small, Medium and Micro Enterprise
SMSS	Southern Municipal Sub-Structure
sqm	square metres
UDC	urban development corporation
UDF	United Democratic Front
UMP	Urban Management Programme
UNCED	United Nations Conference on Environment and Development

UNDP	United Nations Development Programme
UN-Habitat	United Nations Human Settlements Programme (formerly known as UNHCS – United Nations Centre for Human Settlements)
USAID	US Agency for International Development
USN	Urban Sector Network
WMSS	Western Municipal Sub-Structure
YCDF	Yeoville Community Development Forum
YCPF	Yeoville Community Policing Forum

Part 1

Ways of Understanding
Divided Cities

Chapter 1

Introduction to a Divided City

INTRODUCTION

For many people, Johannesburg has become the imagined spectre of our urban future. Global anxieties about catastrophic urban explosion, social fracture, environmental degradation, escalating crime and violence, as well as rampant consumerism alongside grinding poverty, are projected onto a city the fate of which has implications and resonance way beyond its borders. No doubt, the experience of Johannesburg is also very particular, not least because of its origins in gold production built on the sweat equity of black migrant workers and its reputation as the quintessential apartheid city. Nevertheless, it is no coincidence that Johannesburg evokes frequent comparison with cities across the North and South. For example, Teresa Caldeira (2000, p1) positions her recent study of São Paulo as a city of walls, alongside 'cities as distinct as ... Los Angeles, Johannesburg, Buenos Aires, Budapest, Mexico City and Miami'. Specifically, she equates the discourses of fear and practices of segregation associated with transitions to democracy in Latin America, the decline of socialism in Eastern Europe and the influx of immigrants into cities of North America with those fears and responses accompanying the end of apartheid in South Africa.

Unlike many other cities, however, Johannesburg was provided with the extraordinary opportunity of reinventing itself, of fundamentally reforming its policies and planning practices and of radically reconfiguring its social and political institutions in the wake of South Africa's celebrated transition from an apartheid regime to a liberal democracy in 1994. The establishment of post-apartheid urban governance in Johannesburg was guided by an exemplary national constitution that values human rights, and was accompanied by no shortage of political will at the local level. However, like cities elsewhere in the world, decision-makers in Johannesburg have been constrained by the need to balance harsh fiscal and administrative realities with growing demands for social justice. New understandings of local government in Johannesburg have been quickly shaped by the imperative of developing rapid and pragmatic approaches to service delivery, urban economic development, spatial restructuring, environmental sustainability and institutional reform. This has left open the questions of whether a balance could be achieved between equity and efficiency goals and whether early commitments to participatory processes and responsive

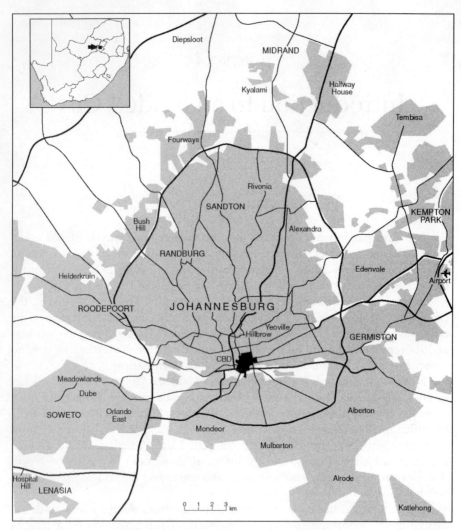

Figure 1.1 *A locational map of Johannesburg*

government could be maintained. It is these concrete problems and the solutions used to tackle them that form the empirical focus of *Uniting a Divided City*, which explores the conditions that frame, and the processes that underpin, Johannesburg's transformation from an inequitable and racially divided city in a pariah state to a cosmopolitan metropole and magnet for the sub-continent (see Figure 1.1).[1]

The broader reach and analytical contribution of the book stem from the fact that the extent and complexity of urban poverty, inequality and social exclusion in Johannesburg have been habitually underestimated and inadequately accounted for by those trying to understand and intervene in the urban experience. This has put the city under the spotlight because, in looking for a positive rather than a negative scenario of a socially just, democratic and sustainable urban future, international analysts, policy-makers and practitioners are closely monitoring the experience of post-apartheid Johannesburg as it tries to steer and manage complex political, social and economic change (Mabin, 1999). In this sense, the experience of Johannesburg has become a litmus test for uniting divided cities and the future of *iGoli*, or 'the city of gold', has significance for urban governance everywhere.

Uniting a Divided City is unusual in three important respects. First, it is based upon an exceptional assemblage of empirical data and analysis, since it is the product of extended research conducted by the three authors between 1997 and 2001.[2] Second, it combines a detailed knowledge of the particularities of the Johannesburg context with a broader understanding of how the city fits into international trends and debates. Last, the interdisciplinary nature of the collaboration has given rise to the opportunity of drawing upon a range of research methods and analytical entry points, making possible the compilation of insights that arise out of ethnography, qualitative sociological and organizational research, as well as social survey analysis.[3] From the vantage points of sociology, geography and development studies, our different skills and perspectives have provided us with a multifaceted lens through which to identify and interrogate what is both specific and more widely resonant about social change and urban governance in Johannesburg.

Such methodological and disciplinary diversity, of course, begs the question: what dimensions and processes hold such an endeavour together? The first is an abiding interest on all our parts in urban social change. The second is a belief that policy, and policy-relevant academic work, needs to be deeply grounded in nuanced and historically sensitive social analysis. Third, we share a common conceptual starting point. This resides in a commitment to understanding the articulation of structure, agency and the variety of institutions that make up social systems. We are ultimately concerned with how these play themselves out in cities, while recognizing that they do not necessarily originate or end in the urban context. As such, our analysis of the divided city is one that stretches from a consideration of its economic structure to a concern with the social structures that infuse human relationships; from the formal and informal organizations and collectivities that constitute a city's governance, to the micro-level institutions that are constitutive of the everyday lives of its citizens.

ORGANIZATION OF THE BOOK

In Chapter 2, we reflect on how Johannesburg comes to represent a typical 21st-century city and then seek to explain this characterization in relation to some key intellectual and disciplinary reference points. We begin with a reflection on global urban development and the growth of urban poverty as seen through the literature on Third World cities.[4] Second, we make reference to debates on social polarization and differentiation in urban centres of the North. Third, we consider debates on urban governance, urban management, decentralization, participation and planning. Fourth, we look at how the interplay of structure, agency and institutions manifests itself in the micro politics of everyday life, with reference to the literature on urban livelihoods, social capital and state–society relations. Finally, we review the literature on social exclusion, pointing out its value as a conceptual framework that has had resonance in both the North and the South, and which allows for a fusion of analytical and operational approaches to divided cities.

Part 2 analyses structural dimensions at the macro level and is concerned with the economic and demographic conditions that frame the divided city. Chapter 3 looks at Johannesburg as a post-industrial city, while Chapter 4 considers the spatial consequences of post-Fordist economic change. Part 3 is concerned with the opportunities at the local level, presented by liberal democratic political reconstruction, and the challenges for urban government and urban management. As such, it constitutes analysis at the meso level and is divided into two chapters. Chapter 5 looks at apartheid and post-apartheid local government in the context of centralizing tendencies and decentralizing imperatives. Chapter 6 looks at city finances and the instrument of the budget under conditions of fiscal austerity; is the budget a vehicle for accommodation and does it reflect multiple interests in the city?

Part 4 looks at the issue of urban governance from below and constitutes the micro-level analysis of the book. It focuses on how ordinary citizens and organized civil society embrace, eschew or are excluded from participatory planning and inclusive governance in Johannesburg. Based on case-study research conducted across several areas of the city,[5] the chapters are organized around the following themes. Chapter 7 is concerned with the development partnerships in the inner city, which is increasingly characterized by cosmopolitan and transitional populations. It reviews the success stories when the city's partnership is with business alongside the problems associated with reaching out to residents. Chapter 8 is based upon research conducted in the relatively newly formed informal settlement of Diepsloot, taking what is widely recognized as a best practice scenario of participatory planning and interrogating its prospects for democratic and inclusive urban planning in such communities over the longer term.

Chapter 9 turns the spotlight on the older and more established neighbourhoods of Soweto, where increasing social differentiation has particular outcomes in terms of access to, and consumption of, urban services and, ultimately, the nature of civic engagement. Chapter 10 deals with communities that, for reasons of insecurity, choose to exclude themselves. These so-called 'gated communities' include an ethnically defined migrant workers' hostel in Soweto, given wide berth because it is perceived as dangerous but whose residents also cut themselves off from life in Soweto more broadly. They also include the closed residential living arrangements of bounded compounds or townhouse complexes, located in middle-class areas of Johannesburg. Formerly the exclusive preserve of whites, they are increasingly home to a deracialized professional and post-Fordist middle class, as issues of safety and security haunt people across Johannesburg's social and racial spectrum. The book concludes with a discussion that revisits the notion of a divided city and the lessons Johannesburg holds for the prospect of inclusive urban governance.

Chapter 2

Reverberations from a Divided City

JOHANNESBURG AS A 21ST-CENTURY CITY

The transition from apartheid in Johannesburg has meant that power in this divided city is more contested than ever before. Notwithstanding the acceptance of promising redistributive frameworks of reconstruction, poverty and inequality in Johannesburg are far from being reduced. Erstwhile anti-apartheid activists and 'comrades' have very rapidly had to make the transition from opposition and struggle politics to the grind of organizational change. Equally, long-standing city officials from the apartheid era have had to adapt to very different visions for the city. Ongoing urbanization, regional immigration, national emigration and economic sluggishness serve to compound the problems of reconstruction and the contradictions bequeathed by the previous dispensation. The task facing the new Greater Johannesburg Metropolitan Council (GJMC) is not aided by the presence of a powerful commercial and residential elite who, while not overly demanding of the local state, are reluctant to contribute any further to the needs of the poor. Against a backdrop of fiscal stasis, issues of poverty reduction and redistribution are still under negotiation. The harsh realities of intra-racial inequalities that were hidden beneath the racial hierarchy of apartheid are beginning to reveal themselves. This means that it is imperative that Johannesburg's political leaders and managers begin to move beyond the racial discourse of the political struggle against apartheid in order to confront the changing structural base of inequality within the city, as well.

For many in South Africa, Johannesburg is the test case of urban reconstruction. We would go further and argue that the Johannesburg case has wider significance for how we understand divided cities across the world. Johannesburg can be seen as axiomatic of a 21st-century city in a number of ways. First, Johannesburg is an unequal city. Although a very large percentage of its population is poor, it has a substantial middle and upper-middle class, competing in global financial and trade markets and adhering to international norms of urban consumption and culture. Their expectations of what constitutes a well-run city permeate the aspirations of the GJMC and must be set against the demands of the city's disadvantaged populations. Balancing the state's commitment to global competitiveness alongside poverty reduction, when the current political and policy juncture (and not only in South Africa) means that both objectives carry moral weight, is an essential component of urban governance in Johannesburg.

Second, Johannesburg is a city whose economic base is in transition. The economic transformation of Johannesburg goes well beyond the decline of traditional mining and manufacturing sectors in the mid-1970s, although these patterns are evident in the city. Economic change in Johannesburg is also about deliberate economic restructuring, which saw a shift from import substitution to export-led growth from the late 1970s. In the post-apartheid era, it is also about the search for an economic future for the city and its environs, based upon the development of a high-tech hub for the regional and sub-Saharan African market. While neo-liberal economic reform has been forced on many cities of the South through the imposition of International Monetary Fund (IMF) and World Bank structural adjustment programmes, such direct intervention has been unnecessary in South Africa, which embarked on its own process of economic liberalization in synchrony. Less deliberate but equally constitutive of economic transition in Johannesburg is growing economic informality. Incorporating and managing, rather than controlling and marginalizing, the unregulated economies of the poor is an imperative of 21st-century governance, and one that increasingly is not confined to cities of the South.

Third, Johannesburg is a cosmopolitan centre. Its diverse population hails from across South and Southern Africa, the African sub-continent, Europe and Asia. Many of its citizens maintain strong rural or small-town links. Johannesburg is a multilingual, religiously diverse and polycultural city. As the authorities in Johannesburg are aware, negotiating difference is a crucial aspect of combating social exclusion and managing urban social cohesion. Fourth, unlike most internationally atypical cities of the North, Johannesburg's population is expanding. More akin to cities in Africa, Asia and Latin America, it lies at the centre of a rapidly urbanizing region and must face the challenges of sustainable urban growth. Among these challenges are the provision of services alongside the simultaneous maintenance of the urban fabric and the rural hinterland.

Fifth, Johannesburg is a city in which the public and private sectors are renegotiating their relationship and that is seeing a drift towards privatization, not just of infrastructure and services, but also affecting land development regulations, building codes and social services. The impact of privatization on the poor of Johannesburg and issues of conditions of employment, affordability for residents and overall social justice are emerging as central challenges to democratic urban governance. Sixth, public–private–community relations are being renegotiated. The ruling African National Congress (ANC) party in South Africa has been unapologetically centralist; but a combination of pragmatic imperatives, political sleight of hand and international influence is seeing elements of decentralization penetrating urban planning in Johannesburg.

Finally, in terms of the responses of citizens to urban change, Johannesburg straddles a potential divide between the opportunities presented by an impressive legacy of popular democracy and the constraints imposed by the political and civic disengagement of an increasingly fragile and disillusioned populace. In the urban context, this means that the inclusive forces of active advocacy, accountable government and participatory planning processes have to compete with the divisive forces of political apathy. They must also compete with a frequently uncivil society – problems familiar to other cities where local elections fail to attract voters and where the streets and public spaces are no longer inclusive public spaces.

These seven general tensions that underpin urban social exclusion and the challenges of contemporary urban governance provide some sense of why Johannesburg, although having been caught up in the specificities of post-apartheid transition, increasingly represents the more general challenges of governing a divided city. In turn, these seven tensions infuse our analysis of structure, agency and institutions as they operate at the macro, meso and micro levels.

WAYS OF SEEING DIVIDED CITIES

Whether read from the macro, meso or micro scales, cities are not only sites of economic development, vibrant centres of social and cultural creativity or sites of political innovation. They are also places of disadvantage and division and can be divided along a range of axes, including class, race, ethnicity, gender, generation and length of urban residence. Reconstructing divided cities can likewise take place along very varied and sometimes quite different axes. In this section, we review three main bodies of literature that have been drawn upon to understand social fracture in an urban context, such as occurs in Johannesburg, straddling as it does the processes of urban change evident in both the North and the South. The first is the literature on Third World cities, which focuses primarily on issues of urban poverty. The second relates to inequality and derives mainly from debates happening in the North. These are concerned with issues of differentiation and social polarization within cities as a result of the spatial and social changes deriving from shifts from Fordist to post-Fordist production processes globally. It is an engagement with these debates that primarily informs Part 2 of the book, which lays out how we see and analyse the structural underpinnings of Johannesburg as a divided city.

Urban Poverty in Cities of the South

A necessary, but by no means sufficient, starting point for understanding divided cities in the South is the literature on 'Third World cities' (Drakakis-Smith, 1995). This invariably starts from the premise that the critical issue to be addressed is urban poverty. Indeed, our original joint studies on Johannesburg (Beall, Crankshaw and Parnell, 1999; 2000) were part of a broader comparative research programme on urban poverty and governance in cities of Africa, Asia and Latin America, which situated itself within this broad frame of reference (Devas et al, 2001). Consideration of the issue of urban poverty in cities of the South has been clearly important for at least two reasons. First, until relatively recently, Third World cities were seen to consume a disproportionate share of national investment, exemplified by Lipton's (1977) 'urban bias' thesis. Concomitantly, poverty was understood primarily as a rural phenomenon and development initiatives were overwhelmingly concerned with rural investment. Comparatively little attention was paid to social differentiation within urban centres or the fact that for the urban poor, proximity to goods and services did not necessarily mean access. One reason for this neglect was that it was widely believed that urban poverty was a temporary phenomenon that would disappear with modernization. However, it soon became clear that the visible symptoms of urban social disadvantage, such as overcrowding, burgeoning informal settlements and expanding informal economies, were not disappearing but increasing (Gilbert, 1992). These patterns were equally observable in South Africa during the early development decades, despite strict influx control laws and other draconian efforts to keep urbanization under control and poverty in the rural areas.

Second, international data illustrate that massive changes are taking place in the levels and patterns of urbanization on a global scale. Table 2.1 shows that the global urban population is set to double from 2.6 billion in 1995 to 5.1 billion in 2030, by which time three out of five people in the world will be living in cities. The South's share of the world's urban population has risen roughly in line with its population share. In other words, the South's share of city dwellers has increased mainly because the South's share of the world's total population has increased from 68 per cent in 1955 to 79 per cent and rising in 1995 (see Table 2.1). This suggests that population growth within cities is the single most important factor in urban growth, although in some contexts the influence of rural–urban migration should not be underestimated (Potts, 1995; Simon, 1992). Migrants to cities are predominantly young and this inevitably contributes to the high rates of natural increase in urban centres. Dramatic as these projections are, fears of urban implosion are misplaced and it is unlikely that the urban population will continue growing indefinitely. In fact, global urban growth rates have been declining and are expected to continue to do so (UNCHS, 1996). Similarly, according to the most recent census and the demographic projections of the Johannesburg Metropolitan Council, South Africa's and Johannesburg's population figures are not as high as once anticipated.

Along with increasing urbanization, the number of people in poverty in Third World cities (as measured by conventional income-based poverty lines) has been growing. Projections suggest that soon the majority of the absolute poor will be living in urban centres in the South (UNCHS, 1996). We recognize that arbitrary definitional categories that divide rural and urban poverty into a dualistic spatial classification can be unhelpful, not least because they divert attention from the structural causes of poverty operating at the national or international levels (Wratten, 1995). We also are concerned that a focus on urban poverty does not lead to the neglect of the billions of rural dwellers living in poverty throughout the world. However, it is also the case that poverty manifests itself in different ways in urban and rural areas, even when it is caused by similar factors.

Table 2.1 *Urban population estimates, 1955–2030*

| | Population (100,000) | | | | | | | |
| | Actual | | | | | Forecast | | |
	1955	1965	1975	1985	1995	2005	2015	2030
World	872	1185	1543	1997	2574	3227	3962	5117
More developed regions	501	625	733	808	877	927	972	1015
Less developed regions	371	560	809	1189	1697	2301	2991	4102
Africa	41	66	104	162	251	379	548	864
Asia	293	426	593	847	1192	1595	2043	2736
Latin America and Caribbean	86	133	196	271	350	426	499	599

Source: adapted from UNDP (1997)

Youthful populations in cities are coterminous with high levels of unemployment. However, urban poverty is equally associated with poor living conditions. For example, Satterthwaite (1997) has estimated that in 1990 at least 600 million people in the urban centres of Latin America, African and Asia lived in housing of such poor quality that it constituted a threat to their health and lives. Urban household consolidation and urban livelihood systems are very different from those pursued in the countryside (Beall, 2002a), and urban labour markets and the position of the poor within them constitute an important determinant of poverty in urban areas (Amis, 1995). The urban poor also experience vulnerability for different reasons, closely linked to the fact that they live in an almost entirely monetized economy. Vulnerabilities associated with the operation of both formal and informal land and housing markets are a particular feature of urban social disadvantage. In some cities, insecurity of tenure for the poor is compounded by unhealthy and insecure living conditions, such as appalling overcrowding, contaminated water, poor or absent sanitation, lack of services and the threats posed by marginal and unstable physical locations (floods, landslides, industrial pollution) and by crime, corruption and violence, including on the part of the authorities and law and order agencies (Beall, 2000a).

As the ranks of the urban poor grow apace, so the imperative of addressing urban poverty has risen higher on the policy agenda both for national and city governments and for international development agencies. This has filtered through to thinking in post-apartheid Johannesburg, although the continued overwhelming emphasis on rural poverty in international development circles has had greater purchase in terms of national government in South Africa (Crankshaw and Parnell, 1996). In line with international trends, many post-apartheid studies of social disadvantage in South Africa suggest that poverty remains a predominantly rural issue and one that overwhelmingly impacts on women (Budlender, 1998; May, 1999). These analyses have been accompanied by vociferous calls from President Thabo Mbeki's ANC government for the country to combat rural poverty (Hadland and Rantao, 1999). This rural bias is understandable given the structural legacy of the migrant labour system and the apartheid policies that saw Africans as temporary sojourners in urban areas and that fostered the practice of abandoning the working poor at the end of their productive lives to rural reserves or '*bantustans*' (the name given to apartheid's 'self-governing homelands', most of which, until 1994, were not even included in official definitions of what constituted the Republic of South Africa).

However, a denial of urban poverty ignores the indefatigable agency of millions of black South Africans who defied the pass laws, withstood the bulldozers and resisted the myriad institutions of apartheid that sought to keep them out of the cities until the various apposite laws were abolished in 1986. It fails to take into account the formal and informal institutions that bind South Africans across the rural–urban divide, through household survival strategies and group support and identity founded on oscillating migration, remittances, inter-generational child care and the iterative transfer and adaptation of rural and working-class culture. The bias towards emphasizing rural poverty and poverty-reduction solutions suggests an uncritical acceptance of the preoccupations of international development agencies with the context of rural development, and a denial of growing evidence that urban poverty has been increasing steadily in South Africa since the late 1970s (SANGOCO, 1998).

A focus on poverty of any sort is a recent phenomenon in South Africa. In the past, there was not even a language of poverty in use. The apartheid government couched their interventions in terms of 'separate development', and opposition ranks were chiefly concerned with combating racial oppression or class exploitation, which was seen as inextricably linked with racial oppression (Bozzoli, 1987), rather than poverty as such. What the poverty lens offers contemporary South African debates is a fresh perspective on problems that were frequently seen as the unique consequences of apartheid policies. However, if we are to move beyond an analysis of 'context' to include an understanding of the causal links and the social systems of cities, we need to move towards relational explanations for poverty and inequality. In this regard, we suggest that earlier liberal and radical analyses of apartheid South Africa were perhaps both nearer the mark than the corpus of work on 'the Third World city'.

To the extent that these issues have been taken up in the Third World cities literature, contemporary analyses of urban poverty and inequality see neo-liberal macro-economic reforms as having a particularly negative impact on the less well off in urban areas. IMF- and World Bank-induced structural adjustment programmes have cut deep into urban per capita incomes, which have reverted to 1970 levels and, in some countries, to 1960 levels (World Bank, 1991, p45). Social analyses of the urban impact of structural adjustment programmes suggest that urban dwellers are more integrated within cash economies and have particularly suffered as a result of policy initiatives, such as the lifting of subsidies (for example, food and transport) and the introduction of user charges for services (Kanji, 1995; Moser, 1996; Moser et al, 1993). Reductions in real wages, along with slow employment growth and retrenchments in the public sector, have swelled the ranks of the informal economy in many cities of the South.

South Africa did not come under an externally imposed structural adjustment programme, but neither did it need to. The twilight years of apartheid already saw moves towards private solutions to what were formerly public responsibilities, as well as the beginnings of economic structuring. In the post-apartheid period, the short-lived Reconstruction and Development Programme (RDP) that accompanied the period of the transitional government was soon replaced by the far more neo-liberal economic framework of Growth, Employment and Redistribution (GEAR) (Marais, 1998). While neo-liberal policies have seen a growth in urban poverty, they are also accompanied by increased social differentiation and extremes of wealth and poverty on a global scale.

Inequality in Cities

Increasing inequality has been fundamentally linked to changes in global production accompanying the shift from Fordist to post-Fordist regimes of accumulation (Marcuse and van Kempen, 2000). Changes in ownership, management and production have seen management and the labour process fragmented across continents. The related and much contested concept of 'globalization' refers to the process by which capital flows, labour markets, commodity markets, information, raw materials, management and organization are fully interdependent throughout the world. Castells (1998, p162) argues that in understanding the processes and mechanisms by which national economies become progressively integrated within a global capitalist economy, we need to recognize that:

> *Globalization proceeds selectively, including and excluding segments of economies and societies in and out of the networks of information, wealth and power that characterize the new dominant system.*

Translated to the urban context, it has been argued that this has given rise to key urban centres or world cities that have become 'sites of immense concentrations of economic power' and that coordinate and control the new international division of labour (Sassen, 1994, p120).

The most established body of literature on changing patterns of inequality at the city level deals largely with trends in the advanced industrial countries of the North and relates to urban deindustrialization. This notion is used to refer to the long-term absolute decline of manufacturing employment in core cities and the accompanying loss of manufacturing jobs, compensated for in successful cases by the growth of service-sector employment. Sassen's (1991) social polarization thesis contends that one of the effects of macro-economic restructuring, involving the contraction of manufacturing and the growth of the financial and service sectors, has been a new polarization between emergent high-income and low-income occupational strata, and new class alignment (Sassen, 1991, p13). Whereas Fordist regimes are associated with strong trade unions, high wages and full-time permanent employment, post-Fordist regimes are associated with weak trade unions, low wages and 'flexible' employment practices. This shift, therefore, has seen high returns for the skilled and professional classes and declining conditions of service for low-paid workers in many cities.

Compelling though this argument is, critics have pointed out that this is a potentially determinist view and that urban social problems are not the exclusive, nor the inevitable consequence, of globalization (Dieleman and Hamnett, 1994). When applied to South Africa, where the legacy of racial oppression cannot be denied, it is also ahistorical. As Seekings and Nattrass (forthcoming) argue, inequality in South Africa can no longer be explained by race alone. This is particularly important in the context of South African cities, such as Johannesburg, where there are high levels of intra-racial inequality, suggesting that there are other social and economic forces at work. Moreover, the analysis errs towards path-dependency, and as Hall and Hubbard (1996, p159) observe:

> *Cities are not the helpless pawns of international capital but have the capability to mediate and direct their own destiny by exploiting their comparative advantages over other cities... Cities and their agents are active constituents, both 'mirror' and 'mould' of global processes.*

This said, the agency operative in some of the more marginal cities of the Third World, and in those that appear to be the losers in the global cities league tables, is severely circumscribed. In these circumstances and where national states, let alone local governments, have limited control over their economies and citizens over their polities, commitment to urban social investment is sorely tested and contested, even when the benefits are widely recognized. Nonetheless, it is a truism to state that no thesis developed out of one situation, no matter how carefully, can be generalized to all others. The question for us is: how well does it stand up to the empirical test of Johannesburg?

Under apartheid, South Africa was a country exhibiting levels of inequality in wealth and access to services among the highest in the world (Wilson and Ramphele, 1989, p4). At a city level, a combination of policies and legislation dating from the early 20th century consistently denied native Africans vital components of well-being and a secure base in urban areas where, in principle at least, they were not allowed to live permanently.[1] This history confirms the legacy of Johannesburg's past in contributing to contemporary levels of inequality. The fact that Johannesburg has a majority black population today is testimony to the ultimate failure of these policies. Metropolitan Johannesburg is a city approaching 3 million people, although it is part of an urban conurbation with a population of 7.3 million. Nevertheless, as the industrial and commercial heartland of South Africa, it is also home to many of the country's rich and well-educated population; as a result, *average* urban wages and overall levels of urban infrastructure do not reflect the extent of intra-urban patterns of inequality.[2] Historical legacies notwithstanding, the relationship between poverty and inequality in contemporary Johannesburg is also very much tied up with national macro-economic policy, which in recent decades has encountered difficulties in positioning itself vis à vis the global economy.

Many of the post-Fordist characteristics of urban inequality described above could easily apply to Johannesburg, while its demographic transitions are more characteristic of cities of the South. As we show in Chapter 3, as with many industrialized cities elsewhere, Johannesburg has seen a decline in manufacturing. The consequent growth of urban unemployment has meant that the new GJMC inherited a situation in which a greater number of people had to survive in the city without a regular formal source of income than ever before. In Johannesburg, this has served to compound existing patterns of inequality and social disadvantage (Beavon, 1997; Tomlinson, 1999). Johannesburg is now seeking to globally niche itself as 'Smart Johannesburg' or 'Smart Gauteng', based on the growth of services and a high-tech economy (Beall and Lawson, 1999).[3] This is serving to entrench inequality and has had a dramatic impact upon the shape of the city, with the inner city being deserted for the Palo Altoesque commercial corridor that bridles the main highway between Johannesburg and Pretoria. Here, too, there are strong parallels with the literature on the spatial configuration of post-Fordist cities of the North, as we show in Chapter 4.

WAYS OF GOVERNING DIVIDED CITIES

Part 3 of this book shifts from an analysis of structure to a concern with the formal institutions of city government. Local authorities are often ill prepared for the enormous and increasing demands that are placed upon them. With Johannesburg as no exception, they are poorly equipped to provide or even maintain the existing infrastructure necessary for local economic development and for meeting the service needs of heterogeneous urban residents. This is at a time when international development institutions have turned increasing attention to questions of how the state functions (World Bank, 1997). Expectations of local government in South Africa as the hands and feet of post-apartheid reconstruction place an even greater political expectation on municipal and metropolitan performance in redressing urban inequality. Political conditionality, widely referred to as 'good governance' or 'human rights' in development rhetoric, has gained ascendancy in relative proportion to international resources and foreign aid budgets becoming more limited. It also accompanied difficulties that were experienced by international lending institutions to implement growth-oriented policies in a context of inefficiency, malfeasance and a general disregard for the rule of law (Moore, 1993).

Urban Governance and Urban Management

Governance is a broad term used to refer to the economic, political and administrative processes by which a country's affairs are managed (World Bank, 1994). 'Good governance' is a popular notion that has emerged to describe efforts to improve the accountability, transparency and competence of government. While there is not yet consensus as to what constitutes good governance, there is general agreement that bad governance is good for no one, especially the poor (Narayan et al, 2000, p198). The Development Assistance Committee (DAC) of the Organisation for Economic Co-operation and Development (OECD) has published guidelines on governance that reflect the thinking of member states and suggest a broader interpretation of governance to include participation and democracy (OECD, 1997). South Africa's position on governance was well articulated by Cheryl Carolus, speaking on behalf of the ANC at the 1994 Fourth United Nations Conference on Women in Beijing:

> *We believe that it is important to shift from the concept of 'government' toward that of 'governance'. Fundamental to this is the notion that the smooth running of our society is possible only through partnership and a vibrant civil society. This means moving away from statism.* (Friedlander, 1996, p37)

This statement is not meant to imply an agenda of 'rolling back the state'; rather, it is an aversion to domination by the state to the exclusion of other 'role players', to use favoured South African parlance. According to McCarney (1996a, p5) an understanding of governance in the urban context helps shift thinking away from state-centred perspectives by including, within its purview, civic associations, private-sector organizations, community groups and social movements, 'all of which, in fact, exert an indelible impact on the morphology and development of urban centres'. In other words, the concept of urban governance allows us to consider local government as more than just a bureaucratic, technical or administrative function; instead, it is one part of a relational interaction with other organized constituencies and interest groups acting in the city.

The concept of 'urban governance' has come quick in the wake of the concept of 'urban management', which made it into the urban development lexicon a decade earlier and which was strongly influenced by the dominance of neo-liberalism (Stren, 1993, pp131–132). The fundamentals of an urban management approach continue to have considerable purchase (Post, 1997, p348), not least by virtue of their promotion by the Urban Management Programme (UMP), which was set up during the late 1980s through the combined efforts of the World Bank, United Nations Development Programme (UNDP) and the United Nations Centre for Human Settlements (Habitat) (UNCHS), now the United Nations Human Settlements Programme, known as UN-Habitat. This is not a bad thing if concern with efficiency and effectiveness is combined with democratic processes and participatory planning, and does not sidestep the neglected issue of urban politics, which often occurs.[4] This is less the case in the recent planning literature, both for the South (Douglass and Friedmann, 1998; Watson, 2001) and the North (Fainstein, 1994; Healey et al, 1995).

Integrated Planning and the Politics of Decentralization

In the context of global economic change and moribund national polities, it has been suggested that we are witnessing a 'double movement of globalization, on the one hand, and devolution, decentralization or localization, on the other' (Swyngedouw, 1992, p40), or what he calls 'glocalization'. While such a perspective suggests that local actors and city governments might have greater agency and manoeuvrability, as Vidler (1999, p8) points out, 'to observe that the supranational and subnational levels have increased in importance says little about the relationship between them'. Moreover, as the political and economic importance of cities has grown, local government has assumed a role that is at once larger and smaller than it used to be. Notwithstanding the declining significance of state engagement in service provision and social welfare that is associated with the rise of neo-liberal policies at a global scale, the responsibilities of city government have increased. Stoker (2001) identifies this trend as a move away from municipalities' conventional responsibilities for service delivery to a wider remit, including public–private partnerships and a concern with enabling strategies that foster engaged participation by citizens.

Among the many tasks that are now the responsibility of municipalities are the development of urban-growth strategies that are commensurate with poverty reduction and the strategic management and coordination of multiple development partners, a role for which local authorities are not always well equipped (Batley, 1996). Furthermore, managing inequality was once the exclusive domain of central government policy, and it was at the national level that resources were most effectively redistributed. Now this task increasingly falls to city governments across the world (Devas and Rakodi, 1993; Douglass and Friedmann, 1998; Dunn, 1994). Aside from overseeing social welfare, economic performance and infrastructure, municipalities and metropolitan governments are also having to take the lead in environmental protection through Local Agenda 21, a directive that came out of the United Nations Conference on Environment and Development (UNCED) held in Rio in 1992 (the Earth Summit). And if the world cities challenge and the portmanteau agenda of UN-Habitat are anything to go by, cities also need to be vigilant in promoting social inclusion (Beall, 2000b; Taylor, 1999). Enhanced resources do not always match these multiple agendas, so that cities are increasingly handicapped by capacity constraints and are the recipients of unfunded mandates.

The promotion of decentralization, especially in post-conflict, or newly democratized, nations has been widely noted (Heller, 2000; Stoker, 2001). As part of this general trend, United Nations agencies, the World Bank and international donors now regularly recommend the adoption of city development strategies (CDSs) alongside national poverty reduction strategies (NPRSs) as a condition of their technical assistance. This trend reveals a broadly held consensus on the importance of the local (city) scale of decision-making. It also reflects the contradictory pattern that is seen in many parts of the world of minimizing state-led development at the national scale, while at the same time increasing state responsibility at the local government scale. Contemporary South Africa has not adopted a formal policy of decentralization. On the contrary, in order to manage ethnic and regionally based political opposition, the ANC fought for a highly centralized political system at the national negotiating forums of 1994. As such, South Africa has been able to resist what Tendler (1997) calls 'decentralization fever'. This phenomenon spreads through the infectious enthusiasm of the multilateral development institutions (World Bank, 1997) because local government does not receive international aid on a scale that obliges it to adhere to the detailed conditionalities that are normally imposed by the international financial architecture.

Nevertheless, through the discourses of 'popular democracy' and 'integrated development planning' rather than 'decentralization', the experience of South Africa has shown remarkable parallels with international trends. Johannesburg and Cape Town have both embarked on city development strategies with the assistance of the UMP (Robinson, forthcoming). While CDS-style planning bodes well for thinking about, and addressing, poverty, inequality and redistribution at a city scale, it is not yet clear what the governance implications of such external engagement with these cities will be, and whether it will ultimately create tension with the national state. Moreover, in practice it may be difficult to track the impact of an external push for devolution in South Africa. However, with or without an explicit decentralization policy, deracialized and democratic local government in South Africa has had to take on a dramatically expanded role, albeit on terms that are driven by national legislation, regulations and funding (Heller, 2000; Oldfield, 2001).

As in other cities across the world where decentralization has been driven by national governments, or where donors have insisted on decentralization and the integration of planning as a prerequisite for loans, grants or development assistance, Johannesburg has changed both the scope of its concerns and the way it does business. The most obvious manifestation of the expanded role of city government in South Africa is the introduction of new functions, such as environmental management, promoting gender equity and even housing provision. In line with international planning norms, post-apartheid legislation demands that local councils not only extend their remits but that they do so in a coordinated and integrated fashion, and in a participatory manner (USN, 1998). The focus on local democracy and participation also draws from earlier debates on community participation and participatory development (Abbott, 1996; Dudley, 1993; Narayan et al, 2000; Stiefel and Wolfe, 1994; Uphoff, 1992; Wade, 1987). Indeed, the inclusion of participatory integrated-development planning as a municipal requirement in South African law became one of the driving forces of decentralization in South Africa (Parnell and Pieterse, 1998; Watson, 2001). This, in turn, became the quintessential reference point for planners, internationally, who were keen to find best practice examples of inclusive, post-modern planning approaches (Healey, 1995; Bollens, 1999).

Local government decentralization and the rise of integrated planning practices have raised fresh theoretical interest in the complex systems that are used to regulate and govern cities. A central focus is what has been perceived as the shift from modernist, statist approaches to the organizing principles of a more 'post-modern urbanism', read as inclusive, holistic, flexible and collaborative (Friedmann, 1998; Dear, 2000). In the African context, this has prompted research that teases out complex state–civil society relationships, emphasizing informal structures of power alongside more formal institutions, highlighting the incapacity of the state to respond to citizens through conventional development initiatives (Simon 1999; Robinson, forthcoming).

Similarly, in the planning community – a discipline imbued with traditions of scientific projection, regulation and control – more recent theoretical emphasis has been not on outcomes alone, but also on processes that foster connections, negotiations and consensus-seeking solutions to urban problems (Watson, 1998). Internationally, Healey's work (1995) on institutionalist planning has been seminal, both in influencing some of the more inclusive and consultative planning frameworks promoted in the context of development in the South (Moser, 1993; Safier, 1992), and also in debates about participatory planning that today span the North–South divide. Writing with practitioners in mind, Healey seeks ways of linking the performance criteria of different and new aspects of government (for example, environmental responsibilities) to a spatial plan. Healey also promotes the search for political spaces in which professionals and residents can negotiate appropriate urban futures within the ambit of professional planning practice.

Against this background, integrated planning – dubbed by Dear (2000) as 'proto-postmodern' – is associated with incorporating the views of all affected parties in order to make connections between different state- and private-sector actions and ambitions in the urban arena. We would argue against the tendency to label as post-modernist, any interventions or forms of practice that are holistic, participatory and reflexive, and that recognize difference and diversity (Beall, 1997a). However, we concur with Watson (1998) that it does apply to planners who have been more concerned to learn from unfolding urban realities than to direct urban change (Watson, 2001). As such, it is not clear that post-modernist approaches to planning are adequate to the task of catering for complex futures. Dear warns that this move away from state-led planning of earlier periods is unleashing a mutant form of practice that is not yet well understood (Dear, 2000, p127).

Despite a paradigm shift among academic planners and unquestionable evidence of a shift in the practice of urban design and management towards more inclusive, consultative and participatory processes, the experience of Johannesburg suggests that many planners remain tied to older traditions (Bollens, 1998). Although 'blueprint' planning has less and less purchase, even in municipal planning departments, its underlying modernist values persist. Internationally, they can be seen in the persistence of project planning over programmatic and sector-wide approaches, as well as the drive to meet development targets of reducing poverty by the year 2015 (DFID, 1997) and addressing universal basic needs and shelter for all (UNCHS, 1996). In South Africa, the ongoing debates about minimum standards and zoning are powerful indicators of old school preoccupations, including the continued pre-eminence that is given to outcomes over processes. Indeed, some argue that the ending of apartheid has heightened the modernist expectations of historically disenfranchised people, and that the post-apartheid project of urban reconstruction is, quintessentially, driven by notions of modernity (Mabin, 1998).

In addition to concerns with process, the impact of new planning theory has been most evident in South Africa in relation to the call to expand the scope of municipal action beyond the customary realm of infrastructure and service provision. Arising from the new planning agenda, municipalities have become additionally responsible for local economic development and the vexed question of trying to relate this to urban-scale management in a context where municipalities have to be cognisant of both the informal and the global economies. Moreover, they are expected to do so in ways that optimize the interests of all citizens (Amin and Graham, 1999). Equally taxing are more general concerns about the imperative of linking urban governance to other tiers of government, while maintaining local autonomy and upholding the views of local participants in planning processes. These issues have been taken up variously by planners and political scientists, both in South Africa and more generally. Therefore, the simultaneous turn to integration in planning and decentralization in government is not necessarily associated with a narrowing of the scope of local administrative concerns. Although the post-Fordist era of local government is associated with the state shedding its responsibility for providing services, the commitment to participation and integrated development has typically created fresh areas of local state responsibility, if not capacity. Johannesburg provides a fairly typical example of these apparently contradictory trends in the expanding and contracting role of government.

SOCIAL INSTITUTIONS IN DIVIDED CITIES

Part 4 of this book sees our focus shift to how governance works at the micro level. This encompasses social relations within households and neighbourhoods, community organization and collective action. In particular, we are interested in the interactions between citizens and the city, what Evans (1996a) calls 'synergy' across the public–private divide. In this section, therefore, we extend our understanding of institutions to include not only organizations but also social and informal institutions. In new institutional economics and public choice theory, institutions are understood in terms of the motivations and decisions of utility-maximizing individuals within a collectivity, whether it be a firm or any site of collective action (Clague, 1997).[5] We also use the concept of institutions to imply more than organizations and their structure, but use it in a more sociological sense as a manifestation of behavioural regularity. In this sense, families can be institutions, as are organizations and conventional patterns of social interaction, such as regularized class, gender and race or ethnic relations.[6] Giddens (1979, p66) understands institutions as both organizations and the more generalized 'generative rules and resources that are produced and reproduced in interaction'. Both occur within frameworks of structured inequality, and it is with this understanding that we use the term here.

This perspective makes it possible to understand the changes in the economic structure and the political organization of the city, alongside fine-grained analyses of the human endeavours and social relationships of Johannesburg's most marginal and most privileged residents. It enables us to deal with the many contradictions posed by this unique and resonant divided city. Such contradictions include the citizens who embraced, in unprecedented numbers during 1994, a non-racial, non-sexist liberal democracy, but who still engage in social relations that are gender oppressive and informed by racism and xenophobia. This perspective on institutions has also been important in understanding the social relations and organizational dynamics (at the community level, and between citizens of Johannesburg and the local state) that give rise to what Hirschman (1970) has called the options of 'exit', 'voice' and 'loyalty' for those involved, or what Brett (1996) understands as 'exit', 'voice' and 'reciprocity'.

What comes through very strongly in our analyses in Part 4 is a strong sense that those with little power are less able to choose and shape the institutions within, and through which, they live. In this sense, our approach to understanding the politics of everyday life diverges somewhat from recent urban sociology and anthropology, which to our mind stops short of adequately and explicitly locating micro studies within broader structural explanations. Recent examples might include the literature on urban survival strategies in the face of failed promises of modernity (Ferguson, 1999; Scheper-Hughes, 1992).[7] This critique holds, too, for the livelihoods literature, which has for some time now dominated studies of rural development (Carney, 1998; Chambers and Conway, 1992) and which has only recently penetrated urban development debates (Rakodi and Lloyd-Jones, 2002). When households or communities are the units of analysis (Beall and Kanji, 1999; Moser, 1998), a livelihoods framework can work fairly well for the urban context, although a focus on gender relations, ironically, tends to get lost (Beall, 2002a). However, when scaled up to city level, this framework often fails because insufficient attention has been paid to the processes of governance, or what have been dubbed 'political assets' (Beall and Lingayah, 2001). Moreover, the task of integrating a gender perspective within the analysis and practice of local government is far from complete. While a livelihoods perspective can contribute to this, it is necessary to move beyond the household and community levels, as well, in order to focus on gender issues in urban governance and politics (Beall, 1996; OECD, 1995).

Engaged Citizens and Responsive Government

Our structure–agency–institutions lens keeps us at arm's length from the now much-vaunted conceptual framework for understanding state–society relations: that of social capital. Generally defined as norms of trust, reciprocal relationships and networks of repeated interaction, all of which we explore, we distance ourselves somewhat from the concept of social capital as it has been employed. To describe something that links people and improves their collective being in the world in utility-maximizing ways (Coleman, 1990). Moreover, it has been argued, in what Harriss and de Renzio (1997) describe as a tautological leap, that significant stocks of social capital can lead to increased civic engagement and more responsive government (Putnam, 1993). At the level of international development, the concept has had marked resonance (World Bank, 1997); the reasons for this have been well rehearsed in the resounding critique provided by Fine (1999). The concept has also been taken up in South Africa (May et al, 1999), including in relation to urban debates where it is an operational concept in the 'White Paper on Local Government' (Harrison, 2001). As such, it would be difficult for us to discuss governance in post-apartheid Johannesburg without engaging with it. Moreover, as Campbell and Mzaidume (2001) have argued, it is a useful heuristic tool.

Our major reservation in relation to the concept of social capital is that it is conceptually strong around issues of agency, while remaining theoretically weak on structure. As Levi (1996) has argued, power structures in a particular social setting can promote or constrain human agency, and it is insufficient to simply characterize these, as does Putnam (1993), in terms of vertical and horizontal networks. Some organizations, networks or social institutions look the way they do because the actors within them have power over others. In the context of South Africa, this would hold for institutionalized racism during the apartheid era. However, as we show in the chapters in Part 4, it also dictates informal access to information, resources and political decision-making arenas, as well as to formal organizational structures of urban management.

Secondly, Putnam stands accused of over-romanticizing horizontal associations and appears to make no distinction between, for example, neighbourhood associations, soccer clubs or trade unions. By treating all horizontal networks as organizational equivalents, and by paying attention only to the fact that groups exist rather than to what people actually do together and what determines their exit, voice or loyalty (Hirschman, 1970), the assumption is that all are equally capable of making effective demands on government – or, indeed, find it necessary to do so. As we show in Chapter 10, people find ways of opting out and seeking what they need on their own account, when neglected by government or failed by policy. The means by which this is done are not always constructive or helpful to the wider urban good. As Fox (1996, p1091) points out for Mexico, it is 'covered with strong horizontal associational webs at the most local level', but has 'appalling systems of governance'. Part 4 of this book shows South Africa to have a rich and varied civil society; but as demonstrated in Chapter 7 on the inner city, this does not always translate into the willingness or capacity to engage the local state.

A third criticism of the social capital concept relates to the fact that simply by coming together, networks and organizations do not automatically promote trust and reciprocity, particularly outside of exclusive groups (Beall, 1997b; Harriss and de Renzio, 1997). As we show for Johannesburg, social networks can be very excluding and can lead to some getting access to resources and opportunities at the expense of others. South Africa has put in place fine structures for state–civil society engagement. However, as shown by the case of integrated planning in the informal settlement of Diepsloot, discussed in Chapter 8, there are no guarantees that the 'social capital' underpinning or engendered by this process is inclusive or sustainable. Exclusive groups can also be decidedly anti-social (Beall, 2000b). This is particularly the case in Johannesburg, as is typified by the inclusiveness of criminal syndicates and the existence of violent gangs that terrorize many neighbourhoods. Moreover, as Putzel (1997) has argued, social capital often has a 'dark side' and can induce political apathy and withdrawal as much as civic engagement. We take issue, therefore, with Putnam's (1993, p176) claim of the connections between 'strong society, strong economy; strong society, strong state'. Our findings on Johannesburg suggest that while robust horizontal networks of association might make for strong communities under particular circumstances (for example, during the anti-apartheid struggle), only in some circumstances does this enhance participatory and integrated planning. These, in turn, are no guarantee of enhanced popular democracy.

More apposite to our findings is Evans's (1996a; 1996b) analysis of state–society relations. He makes the point, drawing on Ostrom's (1996) notion of 'coproduction', that state–society synergy is based, in part, on complementarity between government and citizens. In other words, public and private institutions have contrasting properties and propensities. However, they are also based partially on 'embedded autonomy', which he says characterizes the day-to-day ties and interactions that connect citizens and public officials across the public–private divide and the loyalties that build up around them. This suggests that institutional relationships are complex, and that the boundaries between formal and informal institutions cut across multiple axes and are infinitely porous. Linking these ideas to relations of power, we examine the constraints and opportunities of building trust and synergy in urban governance in contemporary Johannesburg, and we return to these themes in our conclusion on uniting divided cities.

MAKING THE CONNECTIONS: SOCIAL EXCLUSION IN DIVIDED CITIES

In pulling these different levels together, and in tracing the causes, impact and responses to social polarization in Johannesburg, we are drawn to the concept of social exclusion for three main reasons. Firstly, it has purchase in debates that straddle North and South (Clert, 1999). Secondly, from our perspective, the concept of social exclusion usefully accommodates our chosen analytical lens of structure, agency and institutions. Thirdly, a social-exclusion perspective helps to provide the transition from simply analytical to operational concerns. In other words, it helps link preoccupations with understanding the urban condition to those addressing urban social change. As originally conceived, the concept of social exclusion derived from a concern in France with the relationship between members of society and the nation state (Lenoir, 1974). More recently, it has been claimed that social democratic policies are no longer viable in the face of global economic integration and neo-liberal deregulation (Gray, 1996). Social exclusion has also been most commonly applied, in the European context especially, to policies concerned with integrating those excluded from formal labour markets and from state welfare benefits.

The diffusion of the concept of social exclusion beyond Europe can be linked to the United Nations Summit on Social Development in Copenhagen in 1995 (the Social Summit), which accepted and propagated the concept in the Copenhagen Declaration and its programme of action, and the subsequent take-up of the agenda by the International Labour Organization (ILO) (Clert, 1999). A side effect of this broader application comprised efforts to understand the more complex and intangible patterns of inclusion and exclusion that accompany globalization processes, as well as the polarization between countries incorporated within, and bypassed by, the global economy (Gore and Figueiredo, 1997). Immediate criticisms included the observation that, at an international level, dependency theories talked of a core and periphery in the global economy long before the notion of globalization took hold and that, within national and city boundaries, the concept of marginalization had served the South well, particularly Latin America (Rodgers et al, 1995). The most important criticism, particularly in response to early conceptualizations of social exclusion, was that the concept has limited value in national contexts where the vast majority of the population falls outside of formal labour markets, and where access to state-provided welfare benefits has been the luxury of a very privileged few. South Africa has much in common with countries of the South, where informality in income earning and social protection is the norm rather than the exception.

Thus, social exclusion is a very contested concept, not least of all because of the considerable slippage between its colloquial and analytical, or policy-driven, meanings and application. Following Beall and Clert (2000), we identify three broadly distinct and identifiable approaches to social exclusion. Firstly, there is a neo-liberal perspective that sees social exclusion as an unfortunate but inevitable side effect of global economic realignment. This perspective emerges from debates on the moral and cultural causes of poverty and social disadvantage, evident in the underclass debate because it concerns itself with the issue of welfare dependency. In South Africa, the problem of welfare dependency is not widespread: this perspective is therefore not taken up here. A second position argues either that social exclusion represents little more than an unhelpful relabelling of poverty or, more radically, acts to distract attention from inequality generated by the workings of the economic system (Bessis, 1995; Willis, 2000).

A third perspective, dubbed by Beall (2002b) as 'transformationalist', argues that social exclusion is a dimension of social disadvantage related to, but distinct from, material poverty or economic inequality. As such, social exclusion can occur among people and groups who are not significantly distinguished from one another economically. For example, in Chapter 9, where we discuss consumption of services in Soweto, we show how both landlords and tenants are economically disadvantaged, but relational issues circumscribe access to services by tenants. Contrasting poverty and inequality, on the one hand, and social exclusion, on the other, can be most clearly demonstrated in the case of prejudice based on ethnic identity or race (Beall, 2002b). For instance, in the past apartheid ensured that blacks were economically disadvantaged, politically oppressed and socially excluded. Today, as we show in Chapter 7 on the inner city, many African migrants to Johannesburg are economically relatively advantaged, but are excluded by fierce xenophobia. In other words, social exclusion is relational, implying not only that a person or persons are being excluded, but that someone or something is doing the excluding (de Haan, 1998).

At the same time, we show, too, that social exclusion can be self-imposed, chosen by communities who, for a range of often pragmatic and livelihood reasons, opt to disengage from the mainstream society or polity in which they live (Beall, 1997a). Sibley (1995; 1998) has pointed to the spatial dimensions of social exclusion; work on gated communities (Caldeira, 2000; Davis, 1990) shows how often self-exclusion is spatially defined, both for the wealthy who barricade themselves within fortress enclaves, and for the criminalized poor who are increasingly prevented from using public spaces. These patterns take on contrary forms in a city such as Johannesburg, where elites are choosing to segregate themselves, but where the excluded masses are increasingly claiming certain, if not all, of the city's public spaces. Identity-based constructions of social exclusion and the ways these link with gender (Beall, 2002b; Jackson,

1999; Kabeer, 2000) also have resonance in a city where levels of rape and violent crime are inordinately high, and where women dare not venture out after dark and parents are intensely fearful on behalf of their young.

In policy terms, Beall (2002b) argues that a 'transformationalist' approach to social exclusion can serve to put a brake on neo-liberal policy imperatives. For instance, public policy can address poverty through targeting vulnerable groups or can address inequality through progressive taxation, without addressing institutional and institutionalized processes of social exclusion. By contrast, a social exclusion perspective requires addressing the formal and informal institutions that accompany and reinforce poverty or inequality. It might be argued, in this regard, that (for the case of Johannesburg) many of the political and administrative reforms discussed in Part 3 of this book deal precisely with these concerns. However, the evidence we marshal in Part 4 leads us to conclude very firmly that the analytical and operational framework implied by a social-exclusion perspective should not lead to a prescriptive approach to social inclusion. Defining what constitutes inclusion, who should be included, as well as the terms of inclusion is a business far too fraught and reminiscent of apartheid planning to be recommended. Rather, we suggest that the concept of social exclusion is used as a means by which society can be analysed and policy can be operationalized at the macro, meso and micro levels, in ways that enable and promote a much more fluid politics of coalition, particularly at the local level. What remains to be seen is whether, in doing this, Johannesburg will be allowed to enjoy the relative stability of cities in the industrialized countries and the many cities of the South with whom it is likely to compete in the global economy.

Part 2

The Changing Spatial Structure of the City

Chapter 3

Beyond Racial Fordism: Changing Patterns of Social Inequality

INTRODUCTION

Johannesburg lies at the heart of the largest urban conurbation in sub-Saharan Africa.[1] At the last count, the population of Johannesburg itself was about 2.3 million and the urban region, as a whole, was 7.3 million. This urban region has now been given the political status of a province and has been named 'Gauteng', a popular local name meaning 'place of gold'. An almost entirely urban province, Gauteng is home to one third of the national urban population of 21.8 million. As the heart of this large conurbation, the city of Johannesburg is not typical of Gauteng, but it nonetheless mirrors the general employment trends and characteristics of the province. As such, Johannesburg is a very unequal city: it houses the wealthiest households in the country and many poor, but not the poorest, households. Johannesburg is also a racially unequal city.

As the industrial and commercial heart of South Africa, Johannesburg was at the centre of struggles for, and against, the apartheid policies of influx control, residential segregation and job reservation. Johannesburg was probably the city where the contradictions of apartheid were felt most keenly and where reforms to racist practices were first attempted, long before they were legalized. So, although Johannesburg exhibits apartheid patterns of racial oppression and exploitation, the city is also beginning to show us what the new, post-apartheid, pattern of inequality is going to look like. To quote Seekings and Nattrass (forthcoming):

> *In post-apartheid South Africa, inequality is driven by two income gaps: between an increasingly multiracial middle class and the rest; and between the African urban working class and the African unemployed and marginalized poor.*

Understanding Johannesburg society in these terms is important for the overall argument made in this book because, unlike much of the work undertaken on cities of the South, we are not concerned only with urban poverty. We are also committed to understanding the causes and effects of inequality. This chapter turns its attention to an exploration of these developments. It explores the relationship between employment and population trends, and the changing nature of structural inequality in the divided city of Johannesburg.

FROM RACIAL APARTHEID TO SOCIAL POLARIZATION IN JOHANNESBURG

With few exceptions, the literature on social inequality in Johannesburg has been concerned primarily with the question of racial inequality. As such, there is now a comprehensive body of scholarship on the geographical and social character of racial inequality. However, a striking feature of this literature is that it seldom compares patterns of racial inequality in Johannesburg with similar patterns found in cities elsewhere in the world. At least part of the reason for this lack of curiosity about how Johannesburg society compares with those of other cities is the assumption that race relations in South Africa are somehow exceptional. This assumption probably has its roots in prevailing explanations for racial inequality in urban South Africa. In essence, studies of racial inequality in South African cities place a great deal of emphasis on the role of the state in discriminating against black South Africans. Since such state institutionalized racism was a feature virtually unique to South African cities during the late 20th century, this is entirely explicable. However, it nonetheless poses problems for the task of comparing Johannesburg with other cities, even racially divided ones.

If we step back from the narrow question of how government policy shaped racial urban inequality and instead ask more general questions about the changing character of South African cities, there are many points of comparison that can be made with cities all over the world. This does not imply that the question of racial inequality should be dropped from our understanding of Johannesburg society – on the contrary. However, it does suggest that it is possible to explain racial inequality in cities such as Johannesburg, both now and in the recent past, in terms of social and economic processes that extend beyond racist state policy and practice. This is a particularly important task because South African cities are no longer in the grip of the apartheid state, although its reach will undoubtedly have lasting effects. As Nattrass and Seekings (2001) argue, inequality in South Africa can no longer be explained by race alone. High levels of *intra*-racial inequality, especially among the African population, mean that there are other social forces at work. The question is: what are these social forces? It is to this question that we now turn.

In addressing this issue, we refer to an established body of literature that is primarily, but not exclusively, concerned with cities of the North, which interprets recent trends in urban inequality in terms of concepts such as 'globalization', 'social polarization' (Sassen, 1991), 'post-industrial society' (O'Loughlin and Friedrichs, 1996) and 'Fordism' and 'post-Fordism' (Abu–Lughod, 1999; Badcock, 2000; Kesteloot, 2000). Although many contributions to this debate have focused on 'world cities' such as London, New York and Tokyo (Abu–Lughod, 1999; Fainstein et al, 1992; Sassen, 1991), cities that have much in common with Johannesburg, such as Rio de Janeiro, Calcutta and Singapore, have also been usefully analysed in these terms. By way of an introduction to our analysis of social inequality in Johannesburg, we therefore examine some of these concepts and their relevance for Johannesburg.

Social polarization is a term that has been used to describe the emerging patterns of inequality in many cities in the advanced capitalist countries. Although there is some debate as to the usefulness of the concept (Hamnett, 1994), it is generally used to describe the occupational and income changes associated with the deindustrialization of many cities. In these debates, de-industrialization refers to the long-term absolute decline of manufacturing jobs and the concomitant rise of service-sector employment. An important consequence of deindustrialization is that the labour demand of the service sector is increasingly for higher educational and professional qualifications that cannot be met by the supply of unemployed workers who have been discarded by the declining manufacturing sector. This labour market failure (or 'mismatch'), it is argued, has resulted in relatively high levels of unemployment among the manual working class of these cities. Furthermore, the occupational profile of service-sector employment is claimed, by some, to be more polarized than that of the manufacturing sector. This is because the service sector is characterized by the employment of relatively more professionals than the manufacturing sector, and because most manual jobs in the service sector are less skilled than those in the manufacturing sector. It is also argued that tertiary-sector employment does not offer unskilled workers the same opportunities for occupational advancement over their lifetimes. Whereas the manufacturing sector offered unskilled entry-level jobs that allowed some opportunity for upward occupational mobility, the service sector in general, only offers dead-end, entry-level jobs (Kasarda, 1990; Wilson, 1987).

Deindustrialization has also been interpreted in much broader terms as simply one of the features of post-Fordist society (Castells, 1989; Harvey, 1989). In addition to the growing importance of service-sector employment, scholars have argued that conditions of service in remaining manufacturing jobs have declined with the rise of new 'flexible' forms of manufacturing production. In this way, this body of literature draws a distinction between a 'Fordist' regime of accumulation, symbolized by factory-based, production-line manufacture, and a post-Fordist regime of accumulation, where the international networked professional and the contract worker are emblematic. Whereas Fordist labour markets are associated with strong trade unions, high wages and full-time permanent employment, post-Fordist ones are associated with weak trade unions, low wages and 'flexible' employment practices, such as casual, temporary and informal employment, home-working and sub-contracting. The role of the state is also argued to be quite different in Fordist and post-Fordist regimes. In the former, the state played a strong regulatory role through its involvement in public welfare and investment in public services, such as transport and utilities. By contrast, post-Fordism has seen the gradual decline of the state's role in welfare provision and the introduction of 'neo-liberal' policies that favour a market economy, a non-interventionist state and social delivery through multi-sector partnerships.

Important subsidiary themes in this literature are concerned with certain social developments that have accompanied, or have been caused by, this important structural change. One important feature of cities in advanced capitalist countries is that they have been host to immigrants from countries of the South. These cities have therefore experienced dramatic changes, not only in the occupational and income structure of their labour markets, but also in the racial and ethnic composition of their residents. Moreover, these ethnic and racial differences have usually corresponded to new occupational divisions, since it is the newcomers to these cities who have taken up employment in low-wage service-sector jobs. An important feature of these emerging racial and ethnic divisions of labour in cities is that they usually entail some level of residential segregation. In most cities of the US, for example, certain inner-city districts have become highly segregated ghettos where there is a concentration of low-income service-sector workers and unemployed workers who have been discarded by deindustrialization.

Why should we turn our attention to debates on urban inequality in advanced capitalist countries to interpret social inequality in Johannesburg? Our reason for doing so is that almost all of the characteristics of urban inequality described above could easily apply to Johannesburg. As with cities all over the world, Johannesburg experienced a post-war economic boom that lasted until the oil crisis of the mid-1970s. For Johannesburg, as for many other cities, this was a period of rapid employment growth. Since then, however, Johannesburg has been in a phase of relatively low growth of economic output and employment. Furthermore, this period has been characterized by the dramatic decline of the manufacturing sector since at least 1980. Nevertheless, over this same period, tertiary-sector employment continued to expand. And although much of the employment growth in the service sector during this time was due to government employment, private-sector employment also showed substantial growth. In this respect, Johannesburg follows the pattern of advanced industrial countries, and not that of developing countries. Whereas most industrialized cities of the North underwent some degree of deindustrialized from as early as the 1950s, cities in many developing countries saw an increase in manufacturing employment from the early 1970s (Wieczorek, 1995).[2] Cities of the South that have experienced patterns of deindustrialization that are similar to those in Johannesburg are Rio de Janeiro (Rebeiro and Telles, 2000) and São Paulo (Caldeira, 2000).

One could legitimately argue that deindustrialization in Johannesburg is driven by quite different social processes from those that are causing de-industrialization in advanced capitalist countries. For example, it seems unlikely that the collapse of Johannesburg's manufacturing sector is due to the flow of capital into more profitable regions or countries, as is probably the case for most cities in the North. As the economic hub of a highly unequal domestic market and a relatively impoverished Southern African regional economy, there are likely to be very pressing demand-side issues, as well. It is also true that a greater skills mismatch in Johannesburg's changing labour market has meant a much higher unemployment rate than occurs in the cities of advanced capitalist countries. However, these factors are caveats or qualifiers, rather than contradictions to our broader analysis. Regardless of the local specificities involved in the patterns of urban inequality, their basic contours remain the same.

THE CHANGING POLITICAL ECONOMY OF JOHANNESBURG

Over the last half century, demographic and social changes in Johannesburg have been shaped by dramatic structural changes in the political economy of the city. Against a backdrop of, for the most part, rapid and continuing urban growth, these changes can be best understood in terms of two contrasting periods and modes of capitalist growth. The first period, which has been characterized as a period of 'racial Fordism' (Gelb, 1991), lasted roughly from the end of World War II to the onset of the world oil crisis in the mid-1970s.[3] This was a prosperous phase for Johannesburg and the country as a whole, characterized by relatively high rates of growth in employment and in the gross domestic product (GDP). It was also a period in which South Africa was protected from the vagaries of international economic trends by the counter recessionary qualities of gold production, a much more important factor in the country's national economy than in subsequent decades. Although this was less important for Johannesburg itself, which, by the middle of the 20th century, saw manufacturing rather than gold production as the mainstay of its economy, the overall stability of the national economy was important in the city's development.

The second period, which can be characterized broadly as a period of post-Fordist growth, covers the period from the mid-1970s to the present. In South Africa and in Johannesburg, this was a period of slower economic growth; in the face of a growing population, this meant a much slower overall rate of growth of the per capita GDP. Although there are no estimates of Johannesburg's per capita gross geographic product (GGP) prior to 1968 and after 1994, the estimates for the period from 1970 to 1991 show a negative average annual rate of growth of per capita GGP of minus 0.6 per cent.

The high rate of growth in Johannesburg between 1946 and 1980 was the result of strong growth in most sectors of economic activity. The only sector in economic decline during this period was the gold-mining sector, which saw its share of total employment within Johannesburg fall from 23 per cent in 1946 to only 1 per cent in 1996 (see Figure 3.1). This decline of gold mining was not due to any changes in the demand for gold, but to the fact that the city's gold fields were being worked out. Over this period, mining employment moved out of Johannesburg to the new gold fields being opened up some 300 kilometres (km) to the south-west. Since 1980, the slow-down in the rate of growth in per capita GGP was associated with a slower rate of employment growth, which was driven largely by the decline of employment in the manufacturing sector. Between 1980 and 1996, employment in the manufacturing sector fell from 24 per cent of all employment to only 13 per cent (see Figure 3.1).

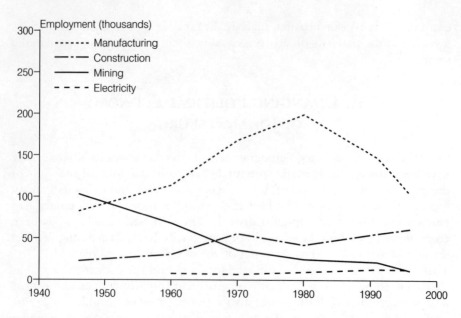

Figure 3.1 *Primary- and secondary-sector employment in Johannesburg, 1946–1996*

In contrast to employment trends in the manufacturing and mining sectors, employment in the tertiary sector continued to grow between 1980 and 1991 (see Figure 3.2).[4] Only after 1991 was there a sharp drop in employment in the community, personal and social-services sector and the commercial sector.[5] However, employment in the financial services, insurance, real estate and business services increased even more rapidly between 1991 and 1996 (see Figure 3.2). This deindustrialization of Johannesburg, with the simultaneous and strong growth of the service sector, was not caused by the relocation of factories to the suburbs or to nearby urban centres because similar trends have been found for all other urban centres within the Gauteng province (Crankshaw and Parnell, forthcoming). However, there is some doubt that the de-industrialization of Johannesburg is as severe as these population-census estimates suggest. Chris Rogerson (1995) has relied on the results of the industrial censuses to argue that, although employment in the manufacturing sector is declining, this decline is not nearly as precipitous as the population census would suggest.

These divergent sectoral-employment trends therefore indicate a major shift in the pattern of capitalist growth in Johannesburg since the mid-1970s. By contrast, the Fordist period was characterized by strong state intervention in the economy and a strong manufacturing sector, commensurate with the import-substitution industrialization policies that so often characterized Fordist growth patterns, especially in cities of the South. The post-Fordist period has been characterized by neo-liberal macro-economic policy and the emerging dominance of the service sector and 'flexible' forms of production and employment.

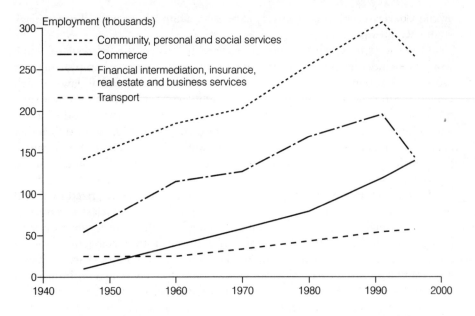

Figure 3.2 *Tertiary-sector employment in Johannesburg, 1946–1996*[6]

Racial Fordism, 1945–1975

The expansion of Johannesburg's manufacturing sector during the 1950s and 1960s was based upon a number of key features (Black, 1991). The first of these was the expanding mining sector, which provided the local demand for many kinds of manufacturing products. The second was the strong role played by the state when it created para-statal organizations to develop the country's capacity in the strategic industries of iron and steel, electricity and petroleum production. The third was that the expansion of the manufacturing sector took place in domestic market production, and for this it was dependent upon state protection in the form of tariff barriers on imported goods.

The strong role of the state in developing the manufacturing industries extended to labour market policies. During this period, the apartheid state was at its most interventionist, and it pursued a number of labour market policies that aimed to protect white workers from competition for wages and jobs from African workers. Whereas white, coloured and Indian workers were able to bargain with capitalists over their conditions of service through formal industrial-conciliation institutions, African workers were excluded. So, although African trade unions were not illegal, both capitalists and government refused to recognize them. Instead, they insisted that African workers be represented through management-dominated liaison committees, which, in any event, only had advisory powers (Webster, 1985, p134). Furthermore, the state acted harshly to stamp out militancy among African workers, frequently using the police to break up strikes and to harass unionists (Davies, O'Meara and Dlamini, 1984, p323). During this period, 'job reservation' legislation was introduced to prevent employers from replacing relatively expensive white labour with cheaper black labour (Crankshaw, 1997).

Other ways in which the state intervened to protect the interests of white workers included imposing restrictions on the movement and employment of Africans in urban areas. This took the form of 'influx-control' laws, which denied urban residential and employment rights to Africans who were not rural born, or who had not worked in an urban area for a specified period of time. The other measure took the form of an industrial decentralization policy that required employers whose workforce exceeded a certain ratio of African to white workers to relocate their factories to decentralized growth points near the reserves (Posel, 1991, pp131–133).

In many countries, the post-war Fordist boom was characterized by a deal between the state, capitalists and labour in which the working class received an increasingly higher standard of living in exchange for delivering higher levels of productivity (Harvey, 1989). In South Africa, however, this arrangement took a racially discriminatory form. White workers received the lion's share of rising wages and benefits, whereas African workers and, to a lesser extent, Indian and coloured workers received much lower wages and less benefits. For these reasons, this period of capitalist growth in South Africa has been described as 'racial Fordism', in which mass consumption was reserved for the white population and the bulk of mass production was carried out by the black population (Gelb, 1991, p13). However, apartheid policies also created inequalities within the African population (Hindson, 1987). Relative to their rural counterparts, Africans with full urban rights benefited from better jobs, housing and services. Unlike rural migrants who were not permitted to bring their families to live in town, Africans with urban rights were provided with family housing and services. From the mid-1970s, reforms to the schooling system also meant that many urban Africans were able to complete secondary school and experienced upward occupational mobility into white-collar and professional jobs in the service sector. These opportunities were denied rural migrants whose families lived in rural areas that received very little in the way of educational and other services.

Post-Fordism, 1976–1996[7]

Towards the end of the 1970s and closely in line with international trends towards neo-liberal macro-economic change, the government began to pursue an export-led growth strategy through the incremental removal of trade protection for South African manufacturers. The government also sought to encourage the operation of the free market by reducing government expenditure and controlling inflation. Inflation was controlled by restricting the supply of money, causing interest rates to rise to unprecedented levels. Consequently, manufacturing and commercial companies saw contracting profits as a result of the increasing costs of credit. This led to a recession in the mid-1980s. At the same time, the government also relaxed controls over the movement of capital, both in and out of the country. Although the intention was to attract more foreign investment, in the light of the recession induced by high interest rates, existing foreign investors took their money out of the country in search of more profitable opportunities. Therefore, instead of encouraging export-led production and foreign investment, neo-liberal economic policies in the South African context had the unintended effect of choking domestic manufacturing output and caused the dis-investment of foreign capital. The consequent devaluation of the Rand had the effect of making low tariff barriers irrelevant, since imported goods became too expensive for local consumers and producers alike. Anti-apartheid trade sanctions probably worsened this situation.

When apartheid rule ended with the country's first democratic election in 1994, the situation did not improve. The post-apartheid state continued to pursue a policy of high interest rates in order to control inflation and a policy framework that was meant to attract investment by creating a more stable macro-economic environment through reducing public debt. In this context of wanting to demonstrate economic prudence alongside political transformation, the negative effects of high interest rates were seen to be outweighed by the advantages of low inflation and low public debt. Nevertheless, high interest rates not only suppressed domestic demand for manufactured goods, but also for imported goods; this, in turn, led to an overvalued exchange rate that made manufactured goods too expensive for the world market. The impact on South Africa of the global recession of the early 1990s was exacerbated by these conditions. Thus, the export-led growth strategy of the 1980s and 1990s failed to bring about any recovery in manufacturing industry. In the case of Johannesburg and the province of Gauteng, of which it forms a significant part, it also prompted a shift in thinking regarding the economic future of this region.

SOCIAL POLARIZATION IN JOHANNESBURG: DEINDUSTRIALIZATION, URBANIZATION AND UNEMPLOYMENT

These changing state policies and their attendant changes in the labour market had important consequences for the racial and class character of inequality in Johannesburg. During the Fordist period, the expanding manufacturing sector provided job opportunities for mostly male unskilled manual workers, skilled artisans and semi-skilled machine operatives. Initially, about half of this demand for labour was met by urbanized white workers who were largely employed in the better paid, semi-skilled and skilled (artisan) occupations. However, as the rate of employment growth accelerated during the 1960s, the small labour force of white artisans soon proved to be insufficient for the needs of industry. This shortage of white artisans was due partly to the slow rate of growth of the white population and to the movement of young white men into tertiary-sector employment. Manufacturing capitalists responded to the skill shortage by calling for the fragmentation of the skilled trades and for the employment of African labour in these fragmented semi-skilled tasks. Since the skilled trades were the preserve of white artisans, this entailed confronting white trade unions and lobbying the government to reform its employment policy towards Africans.

After an initial attempt to resist these changes, the white trade unions capitulated and a set of compromises between business, white unions and the government was struck during the late 1960s and early 1970s. The essence of these agreements, across a variety of manufacturing industries, was that Africans could be advanced into semi-skilled and supervisory jobs on the condition that this did not adversely affect the employment conditions of white workers. In this way, the division of labour was restructured to allow capitalists to invest in more mechanized production lines that employed semi-skilled machine operatives. This period of accelerated growth in output therefore saw the expansion of semi-skilled machine-operative employment, which entailed precisely those jobs that had been opened up for African employment (Crankshaw, 1997).

The overall effect of this dynamic between employment growth and restructuring of the division of labour was that the manufacturing sector became one of the largest employers of unskilled and semi-skilled manual African workers in Johannesburg. This expanding sector was therefore an important source of employment for the relatively uneducated sections of the urbanized African population and for rural-born African migrants. As a result, the decline of the manufacturing sector from the late 1970s not only meant unemployment for many African workers in unskilled and semi-skilled jobs, it also meant that an important source of entry-level jobs for relatively uneducated workers was cut off. The long-term decline of the mining sector in Johannesburg only served to accentuate this trend.

In contrast to the manufacturing sector, employment in the service sector continued to grow steadily during the 1970s and the 1980s. Although employment growth in this sector during the 1960s was initially met with an adequate supply of educated white labour, by the early 1970s, shortages were evident, especially in routine white-collar and nursing jobs (Crankshaw, 1997). In order to meet the growing demand for better educated African workers, the government introduced important educational reforms from the early 1970s onward. In Soweto, 40 new secondary schools were built by 1974 (Hyslop, 1988, p471). These educational reforms were accompanied by the increased employment of blacks in private-sector businesses and government services. The growing African population of Johannesburg facilitated both of these trends. In the case of private-sector businesses, an increasing proportion of their clientele was black. This made it much easier for such businesses to employ blacks as receptionists, switchboard operators and cashiers, since they could increasingly do so without fear of complaints from white customers. In the case of government employment, it was the policy of providing racially segregated services that guaranteed the employment of blacks, rather than whites as clerks, nurses and school teachers in the expanding health and educational system for blacks in Johannesburg.

The expanding service sector has been, therefore, a source of employment for both educated urbanites and for poorly educated rural migrants. At the one extreme, the most skilled and best paid occupations are those of school teachers, nurses and technicians. At the other extreme, the worst paid occupations are domestic service and office cleaning. According to the 1996 Population Census, 59 per cent of unskilled workers in this sector are employed as domestic servants by private households.

The decline of manual jobs in the manufacturing sector has played a role in deepening the inequality among Africans in Johannesburg. Not only has it been a major cause of rising unemployment, but it has also shaped the pattern of unemployment. In the past, the manufacturing sector created a demand for workers who did not have the numeracy and literacy skills associated with a secondary-school education. With the decline in these unskilled and semi-skilled manual jobs, workers who have not completed their secondary-school education are more likely to be unemployed than those whose educational qualifications can secure them white-collar jobs in the service sector.

Unlike the manufacturing sector, the racial composition of employment in the tertiary sector has remained fairly stable over the period of 1946 to 1996. The percentage of Africans employed in this sector fluctuated, without any trend, from 58 to 66 per cent, as did the percentage of whites from 28 to 36 per cent. The occupational distribution of employment in these sectors is not racially equal, however. Unskilled occupations are almost entirely filled by poorly educated Africans. Nevertheless, there has been substantial African mobility into routine clerical and sales jobs, and the semi-professional occupations of school teaching and nursing (Crankshaw, 1997). So, the expansion of the service sector has meant, on the one hand, the inter-generational upward mobility of the urbanized and educated population, both Africans and whites, out of manual jobs in the manufacturing sector into white-collar, semi-professional and professional jobs in the service sector (see Table 3.1). On the other hand, the expansion of the service sector has also meant the growth of low-wage jobs, such as cleaning and domestic service, that are filled largely by poorly educated Africans, whether rural migrants or urbanites (see Table 3.1).

The dramatic shifts in the occupational division of labour that have resulted from deindustrialization have therefore had important consequences for the changing pattern of inequality in Johannesburg. During the period of 'racial Fordism', when unemployment was relatively low, the most important source of inequality was wage inequality. During this high point of the apartheid period, the gap between African and white wages was at its largest. The most important feature of inequality during this period was therefore the difference between African and white wages. In contrast to the 'racial Fordist' period, the post-Fordist period has increasingly been characterized by a rising rate of unemployment. As a result, inequality is no longer simply the consequence of differences in wages, it is also a result of income differences between the employed and the unemployed (Nattrass and Seekings, 1998). Although the vast majority of unemployed workers are African, this axis of inequality is not reinforced by a racial division between African and white workers. Instead, the division between unemployed and employed workers is largely a division between a multiracial middle class and an African working class, on the one hand, and unemployed Africans, on the other.

Table 3.1 *Racial composition of service-sector occupations in Johannesburg, 1996*
(percentage distributions)

	Legislators, senior officials and managers	Profess-ionals	Technicians and associate professionals	Clerks	Service workers, shop and market sales workers	Craft and related trades workers	Plant and machine operators and assemblers	Unskilled manual occupations
African	25	37	34	46	71	70	83	90
Coloured	4	5	6	11	4	6	5	3
Indian	8	6	6	6	5	3	2	2
White	62	51	54	37	20	21	10	5
Total	100	100	100	100	100	100	100	100

Source: authors' analysis of the 1996 Population Census

These changes in the national pattern of inequality are especially marked in Johannesburg because of the relatively large size of the city's African population. Johannesburg's middle class therefore comprises a large proportion of African managers and professionals. Correspondingly, the city also has a relatively large share of unemployed African workers. So, inequality in Johannesburg is increasingly shaped by the differences within the African population precisely because Africans form the majority of the city's population. The size of Johannesburg's white population has been stable during the 1980s and has probably been in absolute decline during the 1990s. By contrast, the growth rate of the African population has increased steadily since 1946 (see Figure 3.3). Consequently, between 1946 and 1996, the percentage of whites in Johannesburg halved, falling from 40 per cent to 20 per cent. The percentage of Africans rose, correspondingly, from just over half to almost 70 per cent.

Another way in which deindustrialization is changing the pattern of inequality in Johannesburg is that it has raised the participation of women in the formal workforce. Whereas, in 1946, women comprised only 22 per cent of the workforce, by 1996 this percentage had doubled to 43 per cent. The main reason for change in the gender composition of the workforce is falling employment in sectors that are dominated by male employment. Specifically, men are over-represented in the mining, manufacturing and, to a lesser extent, financial and commercial sectors. By contrast, women are over-represented in the community, social and personal-services sectors. Since employment in mining and manufacturing has declined and employment in the tertiary-sector increased, so the proportion of women in the workforce has risen. The other reason for the increase in female employment is that even in those sectors where they are in the minority, the proportion of women has risen steadily (see Figures 3.4 and 3.5).

It is unclear at this stage what these trends in the sexual composition of the workforce mean for gender inequality. On the one hand, it suggests that women are increasingly being drawn into employment while, simultaneously,

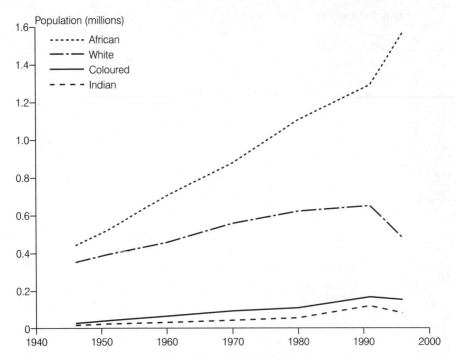

Figure 3.3 *The changing racial composition of Johannesburg's population, 1946–1996*

unemployment among men is rising. This development could have important implications for intra-household inequality. On the other hand, this trend also means that women are being drawn into the worst paid and least protected jobs in the service sector, thus creating a gender division of labour within this sector.

Deindustrialization is also shaping patterns of occupational inequality in Johannesburg. Sassen (1994) has argued that the expansion of service-sector employment has important implications for inequality because the income and skill distributions in this sector are more polarized than in the manufacturing sector. Our analysis of employment statistics for Johannesburg confirms this. Occupational profiles prepared from the results of the 1996 Population Census suggest that the service sector is more occupationally polarized than the manufacturing sector in Johannesburg (see Table 3.2). Compared with the manufacturing and mining sectors, the service sector in Johannesburg employs somewhat higher proportions of managers, professionals, technicians and semi-professionals. Similarly, the service sector employs a relatively higher proportion of unskilled manual workers than the manufacturing and mining sectors. Specifically, the managerial, professional and technical occupations account for 32 per cent of all employment in the service sector. This is significantly higher than the 21 per cent for the manufacturing sectors, although not for the 29 per cent in the relatively insignificant mining sector (see Table 3.2).

This unusually high percentage of managers, professionals and technicians in the mining sector is due to the fact that the head offices of all the mining

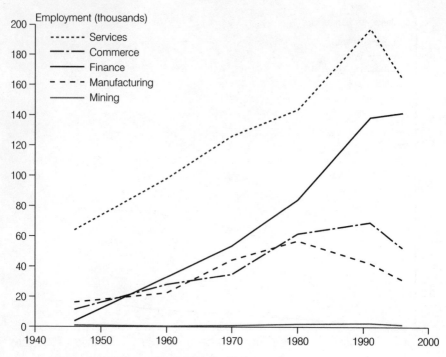

Figure 3.4 *Female employment by sector in Johannesburg, 1946–1996*

houses are based in Johannesburg. The estimate for Gauteng, as a whole, is somewhat lower, at 10 per cent (Crankshaw and Parnell, forthcoming). The same can be said for the category of 'elementary' or unskilled occupations. Unskilled employment accounts for 23 per cent of jobs in the tertiary sector and as much as 47 per cent in the community, social and personal-service sectors. This is double the percentage for the mining and manufacturing sectors (see Table 3.2). However, this relatively polarized occupational structure of the service sector does not express itself in a relatively polarized income distribution. Compared with the manufacturing and mining sectors, the service sector has a less polarized income distribution (see Table 3.3).

CONCLUSION

Instead of focusing exclusively on racial inequality, we have interpreted the changing patterns of inequality in Johannesburg in terms of recent debates in urban theory. In doing this, we have shown that Johannesburg exhibits many of the patterns of inequality that have been driven by the process of de-industrialization. Specifically, the decline of manufacturing employment is largely responsible for the rising levels of unemployment among poorly educated workers. Furthermore, the rise of the service sector is resulting in higher levels of occupational inequality. We argue that this new occupational

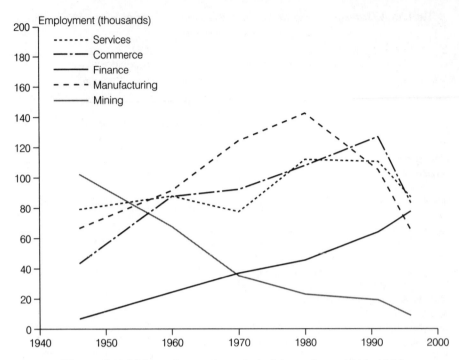

Figure 3.5 *Male employment by sector in Johannesburg, 1946–1996*

division of labour is also likely to lead to greater inequality between urbanized workers and less educated migrants from the countryside.

This new pattern of inequality has deepened the division between the educated middle class and the unskilled working class; insofar as this class division is associated with race, it will deepen racial divisions. However, we argue that Johannesburg's middle class is increasingly multiracial and the character of social inequality is increasingly intra-racial and not inter-racial. The same can be said of government policy. Although the Fordist period of capitalist growth was characterized by an interventionist state that, among other things, sought to ensure white privilege, the post-Fordist period has been characterized by the withdrawal of state involvement and intervention in the economy. Correspondingly, since the late 1970s, the state has been less and less willing to protect the interests of white workers. To the extent that racial inequality today is a result of state discrimination, it is therefore historical in character. Today, inequality is being driven largely by class dynamics.

These changing patterns of social inequality have been reflected in Johannesburg's geography and its built environment. The social changes associated with Johannesburg's Fordist and post-Fordist periods have taken the form of particular spatial orders that have their own consequences for class and racial inequality. In the following chapter, we turn our attention to the nature of these Fordist and post-Fordist spatial orders in Johannesburg.

Table 3.2 *Occupational distribution of employment by sector in Johannesburg, 1996*
(percentage distribution)

| Occupational Category | Mining | Manufacturing | Service Sector | | | |
			Commerce (wholesale and retail trade)	Financial, insurance, real estate and business services	Community, social and personal services	Total service sector
Managers, professionals, technicians and associate professionals	29	21	21	43	30	32
Clerks, service workers, shop and market sales workers	14	13	43	45	15	34
Craft and related trades workers	31	41	16	3	6	8
Plant and machine operators and assemblers	14	15	4	2	2	3
Unskilled manual workers	12	9	16	6	47	23
Total	100	100	100	100	100	100

Source: authors' analysis of the 1996 Population Census

Table 3.3 *Individual monthly income by sector in Johannesburg, 1996*
(percentage distribution)

| Occupational Category | Mining | Manufacturing | Service Sector | | | |
			Commerce (wholesale and retail trade)	Financial, insurance, real estate and business services	Community, social and personal services	Total service sector
R1–R1500	13	25	34	15	18	22
R1501–R2500	14	24	21	15	16	17
R2501–R3500	14	18	15	15	17	16
R3501–R4500	9	8	8	12	14	11
R4501–R6000	7	5	5	9	10	8
R6001–R8000	8	5	4	8	8	7
R8001–R11,000	7	3	3	6	4	4
R11,001–R16,000	7	3	2	5	3	3
Over R16,000	17	4	3	10	4	6
No answer	5	5	5	6	5	5
Total	100	100	100	100	100	100

Source: authors' analysis of the 1996 Population Census

Chapter 4

Post-Fordist Polarization: The Changing Spatial Order of the City

INTRODUCTION

Johannesburg's spatial order has usually been interpreted solely in terms of the changing pattern of racial residential segregation or desegregation. As such, the changing racial order of the city has been explained in terms of particular social and economic interests, and struggles over racial urban policies and practices. As we argued in Chapter 3, we believe that this approach is unnecessarily narrow and makes it difficult to understand urban social processes that are driving intra-racial rather than inter-racial inequality. This is particularly important if one is to identify and understand emerging patterns of urban inequality that are not specifically racial in character. In our account, we therefore attempt to explain Johannesburg's changing spatial order in somewhat broader terms than specifically racial ones. Instead of restricting our focus to the changing racial order of the city, we aim to describe and to begin to offer explanations of changes in the overall spatial order of the city. In doing so, we are particularly interested in the implications of the new spatial order for urban inequality – racial and otherwise.

Internationally, the urban studies literature that tries to understand the changing spatial order of cities usually does so by interpreting specific urban developments in terms of the capitalist mode of regulation of that city. In specific terms, scholars have been concerned to explain particular urban developments, such as inner-city decline or its opposite, gentrification and inner-city revitalization. Other urban phenomena include the development of suburbs, 'edge cities' and gated communities. Scholars have interpreted these phenomena in terms of their relationship with Fordist and post-Fordist regimes of capitalist regulation. Specifically, the rise of urban sprawl and suburban development is associated with the Fordist regime of accumulation, since it is a direct outcome of the combination of home and car ownership among increasingly affluent working and middle classes (Aglietta, 1979). Inner-city decline and the development of edge cities are both considered to be elements of the spatial order of post-Fordist regimes of accumulation. However, this does not mean that the post-Fordist spatial order is completely different from the Fordist social order. Clearly, there are continuities from the Fordist period to the post-Fordist period. Cities have, in different combinations and to a greater or lesser extent, exhibited changes in their spatial order that are associated with a post-Fordist mode of regulation. In the case of Johannesburg, we are specifically interested in the impact of deindustrialization on inner-city decline and the development of the 'edge cities' of Sandton and Midrand on patterns of inequality.

We argue that the spatial order of post-Fordist Johannesburg is more unequal than its 'racial Fordist' spatial order of the past. Moreover, we argue that this post-Fordist spatial inequality is increasingly intra-racial, rather than inter-racial, in character. Equally important are the social and economic forces driving this post-Fordist spatial order, which are the causes of this new, increasingly intra-racial inequality. To be sure, whites are the wealthiest race in Johannesburg but they are also a minority. This fact, coupled with the growth of the black middle class in the face of increasing unemployment among the African working class, means that intra-black inequality is an increasingly important feature of post-Fordist Johannesburg.

RACIAL FORDISM IN JOHANNESBURG

At the end of World War II, the geography and type of housing available to Johannesburg residents could be categorized roughly into a relatively high-density inner belt, which surrounded the central business district (CBD), and a lower-density belt on the urban periphery (see Figure 4.1). The inner residential belt that surrounded the CBD, which is now known as the inner city, was established roughly between 1885 and 1905. At this time, public transport took for the form of horse-drawn trams (Beavon, 2001); correspondingly, these inner-city neighbourhoods are relatively dense compared with those of the outer residential ring that were developed after the introduction of electric trams and motorized buses. By the end of World War II, these inner-city neighbourhoods comprised a mixture of houses and apartment buildings that were built from the late 19th century until the end of the 1930s. The houses were often semi-detached and were built on relatively small stands of 500sqm and 5000sqm (0.125 and 0.25 acres). The apartment buildings are quite distinct from those constructed in post-war developments insofar as they are relatively small low-rise buildings. Most comprise only four apartments and seldom exceed two stories. The only exception to this pattern can be found on the eastern and southern sides of the CBD, in Joubert Park and near Park Station, respectively. Here, the first generation of detached and semi-detached houses were replaced by multi-storey apartment buildings erected during the 1930s (Beavon, 2001). In the immediate post-war period, this expansion of apartment buildings continued northwards into Hillbrow. From the mid-1930s, the development of large apartment buildings was also started to the north, in Killarney (see Figure 4.1) (Musiker and Musiker, 2000, p52). Today the inner city of Johannesburg therefore comprises a range of high-density multi-storey residential buildings that sets it apart from the detached housing of the outer neighbourhoods.

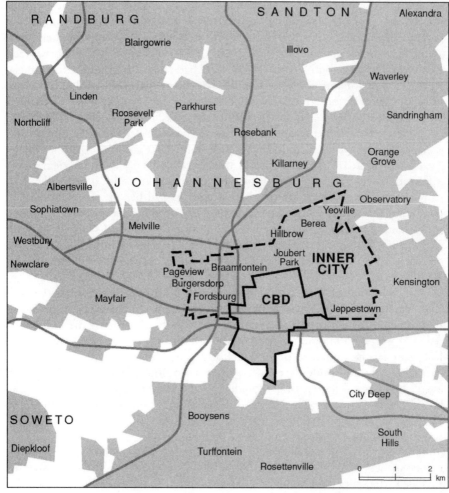

Figure 4.1 *The CBD, inner city and suburbs of Johannesburg*

In contrast to the inner-city districts, the outer residential belt was established after the introduction of an electric tram service. Early residents also relied upon a bus service and, increasingly, private motor vehicles in order to commute to the city centre (Beavon, 2001). Correspondingly, these houses were built for wealthier residents and were large, situated on stands of between 1000sqm and 4000sqm (0.25 and 1 acre). These elite residential areas were first built to the east of the CBD. From the turn of the century until the 1940s, there was still extensive development of affluent housing on relatively large stands in the eastern neighbourhoods of Kensington, Jeppe and Observatory (see Figure 4.1). However, following an early trend set by mine owners, the northern suburbs increasingly became the favoured residential area of Johannesburg's managerial and professional classes (Hart, 1976). The suburbs in the south, east and west tended to house working-class families employed in the industries and mines that developed on an east–west axis to the south of the CBD.

With the exception of a few small housing estates built by the state for poor whites, the working-class neighbourhoods of Johannesburg were almost all developed privately, either for home ownership or for the rental market. Most of these homes and apartments were built for and occupied by the urbanized white working class. Before the war, the state had already begun to enforce racial segregation in Johannesburg by forcibly relocating blacks and coloureds from areas designated for whites to racially homogeneous and state-controlled residential areas that comprised both hostels and family housing (Parnell and Pirie, 1991). However, there were still some areas where blacks, coloureds and Indians lived in proximity, outside of state-controlled accommodation. One of these was Sophiatown, a freehold area occupied largely by Africans and coloureds (see Figure 4.1). Originally a neighbourhood of middle-class homeowners, by the 1950s much of Sophiatown had become an overcrowded slum, largely because of the extensive practice of sub-tenancy both in formal houses and through the construction and renting of backyard shacks (Hart and Pirie, 1984). The only other freehold area of African and coloured residence was Alexandra, which was located in the peri-urban area north of Johannesburg (see Figure 4.1).

Other sources of formal accommodation for Africans were provided by the state, which also applied strict controls over the residents. State accommodation included six hostels for rural migrants and family housing in the suburb of Orlando, some 15 kilometres (km) to the south-west of the CBD (see Figure 4.1). Due to the shortage of housing and the subsequent overcrowding of Orlando, African residents invaded open land adjacent to the suburb and established large squatter camps (Stadler, 1979). Other residential areas of this period that were occupied by blacks were Fordsburg, Burgersdorp and Pageview, which were occupied mostly by Indians, and Albertsville, which was occupied by a racial mix of coloureds and whites (see Figure 4.1).

The pattern of residential development described above roughly corresponded to the geographical location of capitalist and state activity in the CBD. Manufacturing and mining establishments were not to be found at the heart of the CBD, but mostly extended along a strip on the south side of the CBD that stretched to the east and west. This strip of industrial development followed the rail and road networks that linked them to the mines and industrial developments in towns to the east and west, such as Germiston and Randfontein. By contrast, most service-sector companies had their offices and shops in the centre and on the northern flank of the CBD. Government offices were also located at the city centre.

This description summarizes the most important features of Johannesburg's spatial order at the end of World War II. Although deep racial and class divisions were already present in this spatial order, these divisions were deepened even further by the next 30 years of Fordist expansion. Compared with the Johannesburg of the mid-1970s, the spatial and social structure of post-war Johannesburg was quite mixed in racial and class terms. Relatively large numbers of Africans, Indians and coloureds lived in the north and western residential districts: areas that were otherwise populated by whites. Although there was an emerging class division between middle-class northern suburbs and working-class southern suburbs, this was not yet of the same scale and depth that would emerge over the next quarter of a century. During the growth decades of the 1950s and 1960s, the spatial pattern of a middle-class northern half of Johannesburg and a working-class southern half of the city was reinforced by state-imposed racial segregation and suburban expansion for the white middle class in the north.

The development of the affluent northern suburbs was made possible by the expansion of car ownership and state investment in roads and highways. The replacement of the existing tramway system with buses since 1948 had the effect of widening existing roads by an extra lane. The creation of these 'dual carriageways' almost overnight greatly improved access to the city centre by motor vehicle (Beavon, 2001). Until the 1950s, the limited number of bridges spanning the railway system impeded motor vehicle access to the city centre from the north. Access to the CBD by private motor vehicles was therefore greatly enhanced by the construction of five new bridges during the early 1950s (Beavon, 2001). Given the ease of access by motor vehicle to the CBD, traffic volumes increased during the subsequent decades. Between 1954 and 1964, car ownership in Johannesburg rose from 110,000 to 179,800 (Beavon, 2001).

The relatively uncontrolled release of land for greenfield development meant that suburban land was moderately priced and stands were large, never smaller than 1000sqm (0.25 acres) and usually 2000sqm (0.5 acres) in size. Elite suburbs were developed with even larger stands of 4000–8000sqm (1–2 acres) in size. This suburban development was driven by private investment, fuelled, in turn, by the upward occupational mobility of whites and by a state policy of subsidizing white home ownership. During the early 1950s, the state gave low-interest home loans for new residential developments in the northern suburbs, such as Parkhurst, Roosevelt Park and Sandringham, to returning soldiers who had served in World War II (see Figure 4.1). The state also had a policy of allocating large chunks of the salaries of state employees for housing expenditure only (Parnell, 1991a). A significant proportion of the white middle class, in the form of police officers, school teachers, nurses and civil servants, was therefore obliged to own a house in order to maximize their employment benefits. Since their salaries were high enough to allow car ownership, as well, the suburbs that were developed mostly to the north of Johannesburg were settled by an expanding professional and managerial white middle class.

The expansion of this class was driven by the growing service sector, and the state subsidization of white education ensured that whites were upwardly mobile from working-class occupations in the mining and manufacturing sectors into middle-class occupations in the service sector (Crankshaw, 1997). The level of services, in the form of roads, kerbsides, street lighting, refuse removal and public transport, was high, only in part because of the residential rates and service charges paid. Impressive service standards also derived, in part, from the fact that these white neighbourhoods received the lion's share of revenue from rates and taxes paid by businesses, as well. In contrast, black suburbs in the south received rudimentary services.

In contrast to this northward suburban development, the multi-storey apartment district of Hillbrow continued to grow throughout the 1950s and 1960s, and expanded eastwards through the residential district of Berea and into the western fringe of Yeoville (see Figure 4.1). Most apartments were bedsits/studios or one-bedroom dwellings and were built for the rental market (Crankshaw and White, 1995). These perimeter areas of the inner city, such as Yeoville, were therefore characterized by middle-class white households at particular stages of the life cycle. They invariably comprised one or two members, usually young single people, young couples, divorced people and pensioners. Correspondingly, by the 1960s, Hillbrow was a 'Bohemian area with an extensive bright light district with numerous restaurants, coffee bars, hotels, clubs, cinemas and shopping malls' (Hart, 1996, p198). By the end of the 1960s, however, the construction of apartment buildings in Hillbrow and Berea came to an end. Hart (1996) blames this on the state's introduction of the Rent Control Act in 1949, which was intended to protect the interests of working-class white tenants, but served to limit the size of the private rental market.

By the end of World War II, the rapidly urbanizing African population became the majority race in Johannesburg. This demographic trend was reflected in the growing importance of African residential areas in the expansion of the city. During the 1950s and 1960s, the apartheid state intervened strongly in the settlement patterns of urban African, coloured and Indian residents. From the late 1940s, through to the mid-1960s, new suburbs were developed in what became Soweto, expanding the suburb of Orlando into a vast sprawl of low-cost standardized houses and single-sex hostels (see Figure 4.1). Over this period, the Johannesburg Council built about 53,000 houses and enough hostels to house an additional 20,000 residents (Lewis, 1966).[1] These semi-detached and detached family houses were built and managed by the state, with the aim of controlling the urbanization of the African population. Home ownership was limited to only a small proportion of households; even then, these wealthier Africans could own their property only in terms of 30-year leasehold title (Parnell, 1991b). Only those Africans who met certain requirements qualified for rental family accommodation in Soweto. Others were granted temporary urban status and forced to live in the new single-sex hostels that were built in Soweto. Those without any urban rights were forced to return to their rural homes in distant labour reserves.

During the 1950s, the inner-city neighbourhood of Sophiatown was demolished and African homeowners and slum dwellers alike were forced to relocate to the standardized houses of Soweto (Lodge, 1981; Pirie and Hart, 1985). Many residents of Alexandra were also forcibly relocated to Soweto, although state attempts to demolish the entire neighbourhood failed (Sarakinsky, 1984). So, unlike Sophiatown, Alexandra survived throughout the apartheid period as an overcrowded slum and hostel neighbourhood for migrants. The squatter camps in the south of Johannesburg and in Alexandra were slowly cleared of residents, who were then re-housed, first in emergency camps, and then in the formal houses of the new Soweto (Parnell and Hart, 1999). The Indian neighbourhood of Pageview was declared a white Group Area in 1956, and Indian tenants began moving to the new Indian suburb of Lenasia soon after (see Figure 4.2) (Parnell and Beavon, 1996; Parnell and Pirie, 1991). However, due to resistance from Indian landowners and shopkeepers, forced removals dragged on throughout the 1960s and 1970s (Carrim, 1990). Similarly, the largely coloured neighbourhood of Albertsville was proclaimed a white area and coloureds were forced out into Riverlea (adjacent to Soweto), Westbury and Newclare (Parnell and Pirie, 1991).

Further south, the suburb of Eldorado Park was developed for the settlement of the coloured population from the mid-1960s (see Figure 4.2). Later, from 1980, nearby Ennerdale was developed in a similar fashion (Lupton, 1993). Unlike the middle-class suburbs of white homeowners, the suburbs of Soweto, Lenasia and Eldorado Park were linked to the CBD and industrial areas with a public train service and a government subsidized bus service (Beavon, 2001). These apartheid policies of racial residential segregation therefore shaped suburbanization in such a way that black and working-class suburbs were concentrated in the south of the city.

Throughout the 1950s and 1960s, the CBD remained the main location for businesses in the manufacturing and service sectors. The spatial structure of employment in the city centre also remained the same. The much expanded manufacturing sector was still found on the southern flank of the CBD. The location of the much reduced mining sector was also unchanged. Service-sector businesses were also still concentrated in the middle of the city centre and were, by this stage, expanding further northwards. Beyond Park Station, the detached and semi-detached houses of the northern inner-city neighbourhood of Braamfontein had been replaced by high-rise office buildings and, to a lesser extent, apartment buildings. Thus, the residential geography that was associated with this spatial employment pattern during the 1940s was broadly reinforced during the 1950s and 1960s. African, coloured and Indian working-class populations in the north had been forcibly removed to state-owned suburbs in the south-western quadrant of the city. Subsequently, the expansion of the African, coloured and Indian population, who comprised the majority of the working class, was increasingly concentrated in these south-western suburbs. By contrast, the expansion of the white population, increasingly upwardly mobile and middle class, was concentrated in the northern suburbs. The expansion of Johannesburg during this period therefore developed along typical Fordist lines. The only deviation from the international pattern was state-enforced racial residential zoning.

By 1970, Johannesburg's population was divided between a working class in the south and a middle (or service) class in the north. This class geography was not only a function of the division between black and white residents. Even by 1960, the white population was divided between a working-class south and a middle-class north (Davies, 1964; Hart, 1968; 1975). This pattern among white residents was unchanged ten years later (Hart and Browett, 1976) and had been reinforced by the relocation of working-class black residents from the inner city to the southern suburbs.

THE POST-FORDIST SPATIAL ORDER

At the onset of the post-Fordist period, Johannesburg was therefore a city whose population was increasingly divided into a black working class in the south and a white middle class in the north (Beavon, 1998a, p372). Although this spatial and class division was intensified from the late 1970s onward, the correspondence between racial and class divisions began to erode. As we have discussed in Chapter 3, the central feature of post-Fordist capitalism in Johannesburg has been the decline in manufacturing employment in the face of continued service-sector growth. Manufacturing decline in the city centre has translated into a rising unemployment rate, mostly in the southern suburbs of Soweto, where the least skilled workers are located. By contrast, the steady growth of service-sector employment meant increasing prosperity for most of the northern suburbs. Although the white population has taken the lion's share of middle-class employment in the service sector, it is also true that the increase in service-sector employment has led to the rise of a substantial black middle class, a particular feature of the last quarter of the 20th century. As apartheid restrictions broke down, first informally and then formally with the first democratic elections in 1994, this black middle class has tended to move out of Soweto into the northern inner-city neighbourhoods and, to a lesser extent, into the northern suburbs. Post-Fordist capitalism in Johannesburg has therefore begun to erode the entrenched correspondence between racial and class divisions that characterized racial Fordism.

Although Johannesburg has experienced an overall decline in manufacturing employment during the post-Fordist period, some areas have been more severely affected than others, with certain areas even experiencing an upturn in manufacturing employment. Those areas that have experienced the greatest downturns in employment are the central and western parts of the city. Areas that experienced employment growth were located in the northern suburbs. Examining trends in the numbers of manufacturing establishments from 1989 to 1999, Rogerson argues that the decline in employment was caused by the closure of almost half of the factories in the CBD (Rogerson, 2000, p8). In contrast, over the same period, manufacturing employment in the northern suburbs of Johannesburg, in areas such as Randburg, Sandton and Midrand, actually doubled (see Figure 4.2). This dramatic increase in employment was due to the addition of 200 new manufacturing establishments. However, much of this expansion in the north was the result of the relocation of factories from the city centre (Rogerson and Rogerson, 1997a; Rogerson, 2000). These findings were confirmed by the analysis of rental values for industrial space. Whereas the new industrial parks in Midrand were fetching 20 Rand (R20) per square metre in 1996, workshops in Selby and Village Main in the CBD were being rented out at less than R5 per square metre (see Figure 4.2) (Rogerson, 2000, p9).

The inner-city manufacturing sector is dominated by the sub-sectors of clothing, printing and publishing, textiles, food, fabricated metal products and 'other manufacturing', which comprises mostly jewellery production and diamond cutting. Altogether, these six sub-sectors account for almost two-thirds

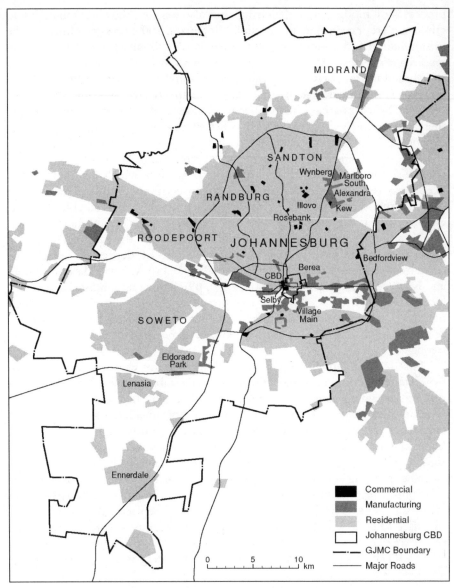

Figure 4.2 *Johannesburg's post-Fordist spatial order*

of all industrial employment in the inner city. The decline in inner-city manufacturing establishments affected these sectors more or less equally (Rogerson and Rogerson, 1997a).

Capitalists preferred the new industrial parks in the northern suburbs because they had easy access to the main highways, were more secure from crime and because the park-like quality of the new premises allowed the head office and factory to be located in one building. Thus the old premises in the city centre were rejected because they were 'unsuited to the production processes of modern manufacturing', but also because they are vulnerable to crime and are increasingly inaccessible (Rogerson, 2000, pp8–9). However, the unsuitability of the inner city to the needs of capitalists is relative. Recent research shows that African entrepreneurs who own small formal enterprises have found the inner city to be a much more suitable location for business than Soweto. They report that the inner city is relatively free of crime and is well serviced by comparison with Soweto. These small African capitalists are therefore renting low-grade C and D office space – precisely the offices that are experiencing the highest vacancy levels (Rogerson and Rogerson, 1997b).

The role of crime in pushing manufacturing establishments out of the city centre is closely related to its proximity to Soweto, which has increasingly become a refuge for criminals. The collapse of state control in African neighbourhoods, particularly the absence of a properly resourced police service, coupled with rising unemployment, resulted in spiralling crime rates in these neighbourhoods and in the areas surrounding them. In the case of Alexandra, rising crime rates have been an important cause of depressed demand by capitalists for factory space in the industrial parks in Wynberg, Marlboro South and Kew (see Figure 4.2) (Rogerson, 2000, p9). Since these industrial areas are located in the northern suburbs, they represent an exception to the geographical pattern of change in the manufacturing sector. However, because of their relatively small size, decline in these areas has not had an impact on overall trends.

Post-Fordist capitalism in Johannesburg was not characterized solely by manufacturing decline among old white-owned establishments. Rogerson argues that the remaining older firms, as well recently established ones, are beginning to adopt new, flexible forms of employment. Specifically, he argues that large employers are increasingly sub-contracting work to informal enterprises and home workers in order to circumvent labour regulations and trade unions with the aim of lowering labour costs. In particular, he suggests that capitalists in the clothing, printing and jewellery sub-sectors are making extensive use of such sub-contracting and home-working arrangements (Rogerson, 2000, p14). This informal type of manufacturing activity is therefore replacing the large factories that used to be based in the city centre. So, Johannesburg's working class is not only experiencing a high rate of unemployment due to factory closures; for those who continue to be employed in the sector, their working conditions are also being downgraded.

Accompanying the northward thrust of industry, commerce and the financial sectors, suburban residential development has also continued its northward expansion throughout the post-Fordist period. By contrast, there was almost no further development of multi-storey apartments in the inner city. Instead, a new form of relatively compact housing emerged during this period: the so-called 'townhouse complex'. These townhouse developments are essentially gated communities, and an important reason for their popularity lies in the security that they provide their residents against crime. They comprise fairly luxurious, if compact, homes with small gardens and a variety of shared facilities, such as a tennis court and swimming pool. Most importantly, access to such townhouse complexes is through a single gate that is guarded day and night. According to our analysis of the 1996 Population Census data, there were some 20,000 townhouses in Johannesburg, which made up 8 per cent of the total formal housing stock.

As in the 1960s, residential suburban growth has been fuelled by the expansion of middle-class employment for whites in the growing service sector. Unlike the 1960s, however, these suburban households have become less dependent upon employment in the city centre. In line with this trend, as we have argued, businesses, especially those in the expanding service sector, have favoured the option of low-rise, campus-style office developments in park-like surroundings (Beavon, 1998b) with plenty of cheap parking (J Rogerson, 1996). Businesses also stated a preference for occupying whole buildings, rather than sharing a building with other tenants. Where this was not possible, businesses favoured modern premises that featured a common foyer that allowed them access to their own premises without traversing other tenants' space (J Rogerson, 1996). Some employers also preferred open-plan offices. As a managing director of an information technology (IT) company, located in the edge city of Midrand, told Beall and Lawson (1999):

> *Our location selection is pretty sensible because most of our business is done through local IT companies and most of them have built their offices and situated their new buildings out this way. So that is why we are out here. I think if you look at the buildings in central Johannesburg, they are high rise, they don't lend themselves to open plan and they were built in the 1950s and 1960s when businesses were run very differently. I think for IT businesses, particularly when you are trying to do skills transfer, you need low-level buildings, you need open-plan buildings. I think that it was the requirement for a new type of environment rather than that people were scared to go downtown or didn't want to go downtown, because you can do a very good deal downtown today. But you can't find yourself an open-plan building down the centre of Johannesburg.*

A study of the top industrial companies in Johannesburg showed that there was a significant relocation of their head offices from the CBD to the northern suburbs. Between 1982 and 1994, 17 of the top 65 corporations relocated their head office from the CBD to one of the business nodes in the northern suburbs (C Rogerson, 1996; Tomlinson, 1996). During the early 1980s, the total office space in the northern suburbs amounted to only 9 per cent of all the office space in Johannesburg. By the late 1990s, this proportion had increased to two-thirds (Beavon, 2000, p5). The preference by businesses for office space in the northern suburbs during the 1990s is also revealed by an analysis of trends in office rentals from 1993 to 1999. Whereas real office rentals remained more or less constant in the CBD, they increased in real terms in the decentralized commercial nodes of Rosebank, Sandton and Illovo in the north (see Figure 4.2) (Viruly Consulting, 2000, p32).

One of the main reasons why service-sector businesses – both shops and offices – favoured these suburban locations was because of the increasing shortage of car-parking facilities in the city centre. This was at least partly due to the municipal policy of limiting the provision of off-street parking in new office blocks in the city centre (Beavon, 2001). This shortage of parking was exacerbated by the relatively large size of the CBD, which made it impossible for office workers to walk to meetings at the other side of the CBD (Tomlinson, 1999). In the absence of adequate public transport, office workers are therefore required to use motor vehicles to travel around the CBD itself, an extremely difficult task given the shortage of parking. Under these conditions, as Tomlinson puts it, 'one might as well be at a suburban node' (Tomlinson, 1999).

Not all office businesses were equally affected by the shortage and high cost of parking for employees. Small head offices, with highly paid professional and managerial staff who commuted to work by car, were severely affected by a shortage of parking. In contrast, large retail banks, which employed largely clerical staff who commuted by public transport, found the CBD quite suitable (Tomlinson, 1996). Another important reason why the northern suburbs were able to compete for businesses with Johannesburg's city centre is that they did not, at the time, fall under the authority of the Johannesburg municipality. Instead, they were granted independent municipal status during the 1960s and, in order to secure their own tax base, competed aggressively to attract business from Johannesburg's city centre (Beavon, 2000).

Similarly, for the retail sector, corner stores and inner-city shopping have been largely replaced by vast shopping malls, which were also built in Bedford View, Rosebank, Randburg and Sandton during the 1970s (see Figure 4.2). These new shopping malls were increasingly attractive to a motorized middle class. Not only were they closer to their suburban homes than central city shops, but they also provided extensive parking facilities, air-conditioned comfort and relative safety and protection from crime. By 1999, the retail and service premises in these suburban nodes occupied one and a half times the space of retail space in the city centre (Beavon, 2000). To quote Beavon (2000, p4):

> ... by the end of the 1980s the basic pattern of retail decentralization, with a focus on large malls, was already well established. What followed in the 1990s was a virtual shopping explosion that substantially reinforced the earlier pattern.

While a similar pattern of office development took place in the northern suburbs, with a dramatic increase in offices being built in the suburban nodes of Rosebank, Randburg and Sandton from the 1980s onwards, this was not similarly replicated in the south of the city. The only exception was the single, relatively small shopping mall of Southgate, which drew shoppers from the under-serviced area of Soweto.

As in the case with manufacturing enterprises, many service-sector businesses left the CBD because of rising crime levels. Business owners and staff in the CBD not only risk loss of property, but also risk being robbed at gunpoint. Their staff are also vulnerable to crime during their commute to and from the office (Tomlinson, 1996). According to a young African professional working in a northern suburbs office in Midrand (Beall and Lawson, 1999):

It feels much better because you are in the centre of Gauteng – half way to Pretoria, half way to Johannesburg – and it is safe. It is mainly office parks; whereas where I used to work at ABSA [Bank], it was in the centre of Johannesburg. In town, I can promise you, every hour you would hear the sirens, the cars outside – and that keeps on reminding you that there is crime in this country; there is crime. So that you end up feeling like emigrating, going to America, or going to the UK.

The northward migration of many service-sector businesses has led to a general decline in demand for inner-city offices and shops. Although this has led to relatively higher vacancy levels, the more important change is that businesses and shops that catered for a multiracial middle class have increasingly given way to enterprises that cater for the needs of the African working class (J Rogerson, 1995). By the mid-1990s, the CBD accounted for 64 per cent of the total retail expenditure of African consumers in Johannesburg (Beare and Taylor, 1996). Responding to this change in demand for consumer goods, specialist retail outlets, such as women's clothing boutiques, jewellery stores, specialist medical outlets, hobby and toy shops, relocated to the northern suburbs. Some general retailers, such as department stores, also closed down and were replaced by small general dealers. However, the majority of general retailers have remained in the CBD by stocking goods to suit the needs of lower-income consumers. Retailers that have seen increasing or stable demand are men's clothing stores and furniture stores (J Rogerson, 1995).

Another new feature of inner-city retailing has been the emergence of informal street vendors. At the last estimate, there were between 3000 and 4000 street vendors in the CBD, compared with 855 formal retail outlets (J Rogerson, 1995). The rise of this informal sector is largely due to changing local government policy, which became increasingly tolerant of informal-sector activity (Rogerson and Hart, 1989). The vast majority of these street vendors are African and most sell prepared food, fruit and vegetables or clothes and accessories (J Rogerson, 1995). Another emerging feature of the retail sector is what Tomlinson calls 'tourist shoppers' from other Southern African countries. Most of these foreign shoppers are traders who travel by train or taxi, bringing goods that they sell in Johannesburg. They then use the proceeds to buy goods to sell back in their home country (Tomlinson, 1999).

Although the deindustrialization of the CBD has been at the forefront of public consciousness, the impact of these job losses has been felt most acutely by the residents of the southern suburbs of Johannesburg. The closure and downsizing of factories in the city centre resulted in rising poverty in Soweto that was driven largely by unemployment (Keenan, 1984; 1988). Our analysis of the 1996 household survey of Soweto revealed an unemployment rate as high as 45 per cent. By contrast, unemployment in the northern suburbs was almost non-existent. So, the deindustrialization of the city centre has not only deepened the poverty of the African working class in Soweto, but it has begun to turn Soweto into a ghetto from which it will be increasingly difficult to escape. Apart from the fact that racial Fordism made it impossible for inner-city workers to live in downtown Johannesburg, the following statement by Wilson (1996, pxiii) on North American cities could equally apply to Soweto:

> *For the first time in the 20th century, most adults in many inner-city ghetto neighborhoods are not working in a typical week. The disappearance of work has adversely affected not only individuals, families, and neighborhoods, but the social life of the city at large, as well. Inner-city joblessness is a severe problem that is overlooked or obscured when the focus is placed mainly on poverty and its consequences. Despite increases in the concentration of poverty since 1970, inner cities have always featured high levels of poverty, but the current levels of joblessness in some neighborhoods are unprecedented.*

Wilson's perspective also makes clear, as do other writers on 'American apartheid' (Massey and Denton, 1993), that post-Fordism is also characterized by spatial segregation and that this, in turn, is associated with social exclusion. This makes understanding social polarization in post-Fordist Johannesburg all the more challenging, given the dual impact of current trends alongside the past legacies of 'racial Fordism'.

Whatever the causes of their present condition, the consequences are dire. Moreover, the solutions are unequivocally linked to significant investment in human development. Without an education that could secure them jobs in the expanding service sector in the north, Johannesburg's manual workers are reliant on the declining and increasingly informalized manufacturing sector for employment. Leaving Sowetans to follow unskilled jobs in the north is not an easy option because of the lack of public transport and the shortage of low-cost and informal housing in the north. Soweto is attractive to the working class precisely because it offers them access to cheap housing, both formal and informal, as well as a reasonable level of services. While the African middle class are able to make the move out of Soweto in order to take advantage of job opportunities in the expanding service sector, the working poor of Soweto are fast becoming the jobless poor and are swelling the ranks of the informal economy in all its multiple guises.

This increasing poverty among working class Africans was reinforced by state housing policy from the end of the 1960s. Until then, the state had provided standardized low-cost housing to rich and poor Africans alike. From the late 1960s, the state cut back on low-cost housing provision in Soweto in order to limit African urbanization. Soon thereafter, the creation of the Black Local Authorities (BLAs) meant that there was no longer any revenue to spend on housing. In effect, the state withdrew from the provision of low-cost housing for blacks (Hendler, 1989). Instead, it now turned to the private sector to fulfil this role. In effect, this meant that African households became differentiated according to the kind of housing that they could afford. As far as government policy was concerned, poor families who could not afford formal housing would be catered for by state-initiated site-and-service schemes. As for wealthy households, the government introduced a variety of reforms that allowed the private sector to build houses for home ownership within African townships.

In practice, however, the state's withdrawal from the provision of housing at the end of the 1960s produced a chronic shortage of low-cost housing by the mid-1970s. During the late 1970s, when the state still had firm control over Soweto, this resulted in severe overcrowding of formal council houses and the construction of shacks in the backyards of council stands (Crankshaw, 1993). Later, from the mid-1980s onward, the creation of a puppet black-controlled local government (the BLA), and popular political resistance to this form of government, meant that the government was no longer able to prevent homeless Africans from occupying open land and building illegal shack settlements. It is unclear whether the proliferation of land invasions was simply a result of the weakness of the state in the face of popular opposition, or if land invasions were partly encouraged by politicians in a populist attempt to gain legitimacy. Whatever the case, during the 1980s and 1990s, squatter settlements were established on vacant land within, and on the boundaries of, African townships, as well as in peri-urban areas throughout Johannesburg (Sapire, 1992). These backyard shacks and squatter settlements were not simply marginal forms of accommodation for the few households who could not secure formal housing. By 1996, 37 per cent of all dwellings in Soweto were backyard shacks or rooms and 10 per cent were shacks in squatter settlements and site-and-service schemes (Crankshaw, Gilbert and Morris, 2000). As far as hostel accommodation is concerned, these institutions continued to house rural migrants who maintained links with their rural homesteads. As such, hostel residents throughout this period continued to be relatively uneducated and were employed in unskilled and semi-skilled manual jobs.

From the mid-1970s, the government introduced reforms that allowed various types of home ownership for the emerging African middle class. In the absence of any reforms to allow for black home ownership in white townships, this led to the rise of residential differentiation within Soweto and Alexandra as wealthier Africans purchased their own homes. These home-ownership developments were built on greenfield sites, usually on the boundaries of existing state townships. This home-owning middle class, therefore, lived in their own homogeneous neighbourhoods, apart from the rest of the African township residents. However, even by 1996, this home-owning middle class accounted for only 9 per cent of Soweto's population. At least part of the reason for the small size of this middle class in Soweto is that, by this time, a sizeable proportion had left Soweto to live in the northern townships of the inner city and in the northern suburbs themselves.

The emergence of these differentiated forms of housing in Soweto and Alexandra reinforced class differences in the African population. The residents of backyard shacks, squatter settlements and site-and-service schemes tended to be those second-generation urbanites who were not upwardly mobile or new rural in-migrants. Unlike their counterparts of an earlier generation, they were not the beneficiaries of sub-economic council housing, and had no alternative but to build their own shack housing in backyards, squatter camps or site-and-service schemes. These shack residents therefore tended to be poorly educated and, correspondingly, were more likely to be unskilled and semi-skilled manual workers. With the decline of manufacturing employment from the late 1970s, they were also more likely to be unemployed. By contrast, the residents of the new privately developed housing schemes were relatively well educated and were more likely to be employed in managerial, professional and routine white-collar jobs (Crankshaw and Parnell, 1999).

There were, however, new opportunities for wealthier blacks to live in townships zoned for white residential use. Although blacks, coloureds and Indians were legally prohibited by the Group Areas Act from owning or renting accommodation in white residential areas, racial residential segregation began to break down in the inner city from the late 1970s. The structural reason for racial desegregation in the inner city was the housing shortage in black townships, coupled with a shortage of white tenants in the inner city. The shortage of white tenants in the inner city was probably due, at least in part, to the state's housing policy that encouraged young married couples to buy houses, instead of renting apartments. Whatever the reason, landlords were eager to fill vacant apartments and, for the first time, began to take in black tenants. By the mid-1980s, almost one quarter of all apartments in the high-rise inner-city area was occupied by blacks, coloureds and Indians (Crankshaw and White, 1995). This racial desegregation was not restricted to apartments in Hillbrow, Joubert Park and Berea. Increasingly, Africans, coloureds and Indians moved into the detached and semi-detached houses in the inner-city ring of pre-war housing stock (Fick et al, 1988; Rule, 1988; 1989). By 1991, when the government finally repealed the Group Areas Act, whites occupied only 43 per cent of all apartments and houses in the inner city. Five years later, this percentage had dropped to only 19 per cent (Crankshaw, 1996).

Although the racial desegregation of the inner city was associated with a certain level of neighbourhood decline, the occupational profile of black residents in the inner city was very similar to that of the white residents whom they replaced. The only change in the social structure that was associated with racial desegregation was the influx of a relatively small percentage of working-class Africans who occupied deteriorating apartment buildings in Joubert Park (Crankshaw and White, 1995). So, for the most part, the northern townships of the inner city continued to house middle-class residents, even though the population was increasingly African.

CONCLUSION

This chapter has advanced the following interpretation of Johannesburg's changing spatial order. Fordist economic growth in Johannesburg took the form of expansion in manufacturing and service-sector employment in the CBD. At the beginning the Fordist period, Johannesburg was characterized by a residential division that broadly followed the division of the CBD into a southern manufacturing district and a northern service-sector district. Southern residential areas were populated by a blue-collar working class and the northern areas by a white-collar middle class. This basic pattern was reinforced during the Fordist period in both racial and class terms. The apartheid government forcibly relocated most black residents from inner-city areas in the north and west to suburbs in the south. Since most black residents were working class during this period, this reinforced the class and racial division between the northern inner city and suburbs, and residential areas in the south. The Fordist period also saw the expansion of the northern suburbs of Johannesburg, which were characterized by home ownership and commuting by motor car. By contrast, the southern suburbs were distinguished by low-cost state housing, rental tenure and commuting by bus and rail. This division between the north and south of Johannesburg was reinforced by the post-Fordist decline in manufacturing employment in the inner city and the withdrawal of the state from housing provision for the poor. Residents in southern suburbs such as Soweto, Eldorado Park and Lenasia became poorer as unemployment rose and increasing numbers of people were forced to live in shacks. The breakdown of the Group Areas Act from the late 1970s also reinforced this growing inequality between north and south as many middle-class blacks left the southern suburbs of Soweto, Eldorado Park and Lenasia to live in the northern and western belt of the inner city, and even further north. This pattern of residential polarization was associated with the relocation of many service-sector and even manufacturing businesses from the inner city to the northern suburbs. As a result, Johannesburg at the end of the 20th century is even more divided today than it was at the height of apartheid.

The post-Fordist period also saw increasing social divisions within the African residential neighbourhoods of Soweto. Whereas the Fordist period was characterized by standardized state-owned housing and hostel accommodation for most Africans, the post-Fordist period was characterized by a highly differentiated housing market. Increasingly, poorer residents have resorted to squatting in shantytowns on vacant land within, and on, the periphery of Soweto. There is also a large population of backyard tenants, at least half of whom live in shacks. In contrast to these informal kinds of accommodation, many wealthier residents have renovated their homes or even built their own in the new housing estates developed by the private sector.

Post-Fordist Johannesburg therefore exhibits a fairly complex spatial order of inequality. As with many other cities, this spatial order has been shaped in important ways by deindustrialization in the inner city. In this respect, Johannesburg follows the general pattern of US cities, such as Detroit. However, the peculiar character of apartheid housing policy during the 1950s and 1960s, which established working-class dormitory suburbs for blacks, means that the poorest residents of Johannesburg do not live in the inner city. Instead, they have been cast out into the poorly serviced southern suburbs. In this respect, Johannesburg shares the social geography of many Australian cities, which are characterized by suburban rather than inner-city poverty (Badcock, 2000). However, unlike Australian cities, Johannesburg is not characterized by a revitalized inner city. Nonetheless, the basic problem that is posed by this post-Fordist spatial order is similar to that of most US cities that have undergone deindustrialization. A large proportion of Johannesburg's working-class population, mostly African, is located in a suburban location that is increasingly unable to offer them employment. This scenario has all the ingredients for the making of a new ghetto underclass in Johannesburg.

While the legacy of racial Fordism and the structural conditions of post-Fordism suggest persistent and even increasing urban social polarization, the new political dispensation in South Africa provides Johannesburg with some scope to mediate inequality through restructured local government. The creation of a new democratic and non-racial government in South Africa has opened up fresh political, legal and institutional mechanisms for overcoming segregation and reducing inequality. It is to the prospects offered by alternative city governance in Johannesburg that our attention now shifts.

Part 3

Institutional Responses to Urban Change

Decentralization by Stealth: Democratization or Disempowerment through Developmental Local Government?

INTRODUCTION

Since the late 1980s, there has been growing interest in local government and the process of decentralization. For some, this has been heralded as part of the 'good governance' agenda (World Bank, 1997; McCarney, 1996a) and indicative of enhanced democratization in countries of the South (Manor, 1999). For others, there is scepticism over a 'decentralization euphoria' that leads not to democratization but to the disempowerment of local authorities and local societies alike (Harvey, 1989; Schuurman, 1997; Tendler, 1997). In South Africa the debate on decentralization has been muted. This is hardly surprising given the centralizing tendencies of the ruling national party, the ANC – understandable in a context where the apartheid legacy rewarded political mobilization on the basis of ethnic and regional identity and where local and regional power blocs sought to undermine ANC presence and influence. Notwithstanding the national emphasis of the negotiated settlement, the end of apartheid changed the face of South African local government irrevocably, as democratic municipal authorities were formed across the country for the first time in a process we call 'decentralization by stealth'.

Reconstructing South African cities and towns that were fractured, first by decades of racial Fordism and then by the polarizing trends of post-Fordist development demanded massive economic, political and spatial intervention. The ending of apartheid offered such an opportunity. While the liberation movement geared itself for the reintegration of South Africa into the global economy and prepared to reorientate state expenditure to effect greater equity, the question of effecting spatial integration of cities was left as the responsibility of the, as yet unconstituted, local authorities. In order to maximize the window of opportunity ushered in by democracy, local government faced four distinct challenges:

- leading the spatial integration of urban settlement;
- forging a non-discriminatory ethos into the work of the existing municipal authorities;
- developing efficient bureaucratic structures within the newly amalgamated municipal structures; and
- adapting to the expanded responsibilities of local government.

Over and above these changes, there was (and still is) an overarching (if untested) expectation that local government is the agency best placed to implement change and achieve development through redistribution and meaningful delivery to the poor. The onerous character of these demands, typically made of local government in poor and middle-income countries, are brought into stark relief through an understanding of the challenges and dilemmas accompanying Johannesburg's transition to democratic local governance.

This chapter seeks to explain the paradox of 'decentralization by stealth' in South Africa by exploring the politics of local government in the context of the wider transition from apartheid to a liberal democracy. We pursue two aspects of the transition. First, we reflect on the political imperatives of establishing non-racial democracy in local governance for the first time in South Africa's history. Second, we trace the philosophical and technical assumptions that informed the design of the new local government system in South Africa. These related trajectories help to explain the rationale behind the post-apartheid development framework and the decentralizing forces that emerged amid the otherwise centralist discourse of the political transformation.

Of most obvious international interest is the extent to which South Africa's local government system, tasked as it is with delivering the aspirations of reconstruction and development to ordinary people, is able to meet popular expectations by providing, managing, coordinating and financing democratic urban development. Pointing to the international fascination with the South African experience, Mabin (1998, p1) notes:

> *If restructured and empowered local government can deliver spatial restructuring with progressive social results in South Africa, it can surely accomplish similar wonders elsewhere in the world.*

Although Johannesburg's route down the decentralization path will be shown as somewhat ambiguous, we argue that the city's recent governance experience parallels that of other urban centres. Like many cities in fragile states, Johannesburg's pattern of governance is associated with increasing democratization and devolution of government responsibilities, on the one hand, and the centralizing of state powers, on the other. These tensions are being played out in a context where national economic reforms have unleashed a shift from exclusive state provision of public goods and services to multi-sectoral partnerships. As such, there are interesting and general lessons to share from what, on the surface, looks like an exceptional experience: that of the deracialization of city government in Johannesburg.

A useful starting point to question the possibilities of a successful transformation of government in Johannesburg is the work of Manor (1999), who suggests that there are three conditions for stable and successful decentralization. First, there should be a deconcentration or decentralization of administrative responsibilities. Second, there must be fiscal decentralization; and, finally, there must be devolution of democracy. While this last factor is seen as a critical ingredient of sustainable local government, Manor (1999, p7) warns that on its own, it will be insufficient:

> *Democratic authorities at lower levels in political systems will founder if they lack powers and resources – meaning both financial resources and the administrative resources to implement development projects.*

Central to the concern of this and the subsequent chapter is the extent to which the balance between financial and administrative powers, and between centralized control and local autonomy, has been adequately addressed through the de facto decentralization process in Johannesburg, and the relationship this bears to democratic local governance.

THE DERACIALIZATION AND DECOLONIZATION OF LOCAL GOVERNMENT

Democratic decentralization, while commonly culminating in the devolution of powers and functions (though not necessarily resources) to local levels of government, takes many different forms (Manor, 1999). In African countries, where colonialism left only embryonic inter-governmental structures and little by way of operational local democratic government, the move to 'decentralization' is something of a misnomer. In practice, a number of countries (for example, Lesotho and Uganda) are, in some areas, installing effective local government for the first time (Leduka, 2000; Villadsen and Lubanga, 1996). Thus, the issue is not so much about state decentralization, through a removal of powers from national structures, as about expanding state power through the creation of additional layers of government (Simon, 1992). For example, one of the most complex aspects of instituting comprehensive systems of local government in the post-colonial context is negotiating the interface between traditional authorities and the system of elected politicians (Mamdani, 1996).

While apartheid represented the most extreme tradition of excluding Africans from structures of urban government, many other African nations also inherited poorly defined and badly structured municipal authorities from their colonial masters (Stren and White, 1989). Shocking as it may seem, even a city as 'modern' as Johannesburg did not abandon its quasi-colonial model of local government until almost the end of the 20th century. As many cities across Africa are discovering, empowering local government to meet the needs of the urban poor requires complex reconfiguration, in order to ensure the institutional capacity to effect and operationalize a political commitment to equity and democracy. In this respect, the South African experience of building a tier of decentralized local government that encompasses all citizens is in step with trends across much of the continent.

Until the end of apartheid in 1994, South African cities were run by whites for whites in much the same way as colonial cities elsewhere had been run for colonial settlers or expatriates (King, 1990; Simon, 1992). From its beginnings as a mining town in 1886, Africans were not formally recognized as citizens of Johannesburg. In other words, even in the declining years of apartheid, the name 'Johannesburg' referred only to that portion of the urban area that was occupied by whites, coloureds and Indians and run by the Johannesburg City Council (JCC). And, even though they lived within the Johannesburg boundary, coloureds and Indians had no vote in municipal elections.[1] Within the JCC there were racially separate departments that were managed by white officials and white politicians who oversaw the municipal affairs of coloureds and Indians. A similar position pertained for Africans until 1971, when African residential areas such as Soweto and Meadowlands, now included in the jurisdiction of the GJMC, were placed under the Bantu Affairs Administration Boards (BAABs). In 1983, BAABs gave way to the ill-fated Black Local Authorities (BLAs) that became the object of violent political mobilization during the twilight years of apartheid (Bekker and Humphries, 1985; Mabin, 1999).

It is important to realize that, in Johannesburg, racial residential segregation was not just about physical partition, but also about administrative division (see Figure 5.1). In both the quality of urban space and in resources for city government there were vast inequalities. The worst examples were the segregationist administrative structures set up as part of the apartheid machinery of separate development (Swilling and Boya, 1997). In addition to their political illegitimacy, the BAABs and BLAs had no revenue base, and so they were the focus of persistent protest from urban African residents (Swilling and Shubane, 1991). An attempt to redress the absence of funding in black areas was introduced as part of the apartheid reforms through the Regional Service Councils in 1985; but this was too little, too late and was either rejected or ignored (Bekker and Humphries, 1985). Slogans such as 'one city, one tax base' were the clarion calls for urban reform that emanated from anti-apartheid organizations that opposed the rule of the BLAs in greater Johannesburg, and wanted blacks to share in the wealth of a city to which they belonged and contributed.

Thus it was, and remains, that money lies at the heart of the unequal structure of city government in Johannesburg. The colonial or segregation model of urban finance rested on racially separate municipal accounts, and this is something that was maintained by the apartheid regime. The infamous 'Durban System', adopted throughout South Africa under the 1923 (Natives Urban Areas) Act, ensured that African urban areas had to be self-financing. Following the Durban model closely, since 1928 when the law was applied in Johannesburg, revenue for African township development was generated by a municipal monopoly on the brewing and sale of beer in the townships. For six

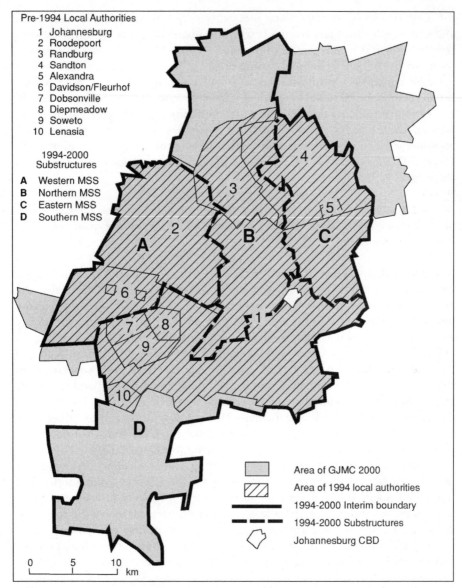

Figure 5.1 *Shifting boundaries of municipal administration in expanding Johannesburg*

decades, Africans who worked, travelled and shopped in Johannesburg did not receive any benefits from the revenue paid through commercial rates and taxes on city properties. Nor did they receive any cross-subsidy from affluent white residential areas. On the contrary, white areas were developed on the proceeds of black investment in the city. It is little wonder, therefore, that residents of white suburbs enjoyed among the highest living standards in the world, while black areas of the city experienced extreme poverty and neglect (Beavon, 1997). It was both the scale and proximity of these injustices that mobilized the opposition to apartheid at local government level.

The battle against racism and inequality in South Africa took many years and was fought on many fronts. It was the urban youth taking to the Soweto streets in protest against racial oppression in June 1976 that marked a critical moment in the anti-apartheid struggle. Apart from the immediate issue of inferior education, problems such as overcrowded houses, poor urban infrastructure and the absence of democratic city government were also driving forces that mobilized the black urban population against apartheid control. Central to the mass organization that ensued was the rise of 'the civic movement'. The significance and impact of the movement is evident from Heymans's remark, made on the eve of the liberal democratic transition (Heymans, 1993, p1):

> *It has become well-nigh impossible to discuss, plan or implement development in South Africa without engaging with, or at least having to take account of, civic associations.*

The origins of civics can be traced to the days when the exiled ANC was banned in South Africa and alternative structures for opposing apartheid inside the country had to be found. Civic associations, or 'the civics' as they became known, were community-based organizations (CBOs) that were ostensibly apolitical structures that mobilized around quality-of-life or development issues (Mayekiso, 1996). The civics were organized into the South African National Civic Organization (SANCO), and its leadership remained fairly separate from that of the United Democratic Front (UDF), the internally-based umbrella body that embraced a vast number of different anti-apartheid organizations within South Africa during the 1980s and early 1990s. The UDF largely identified with the ANC. However, on the ground it was often the UDF that coordinated or dovetailed with the work of the local-level civics (Seekings, 2000).

The civics were important in representing 'the community' in township-based politics, and they worked together with the UDF in linking individual communities into the mass democratic movement. However, it has been argued that, in the post-apartheid era at least, many civics organize only the township elite, thus incurring some alienation on the part of poorer residents (Everatt, 1999). Nevertheless, it was the civics who gave voice to slogans such as 'people's power' and subsequently provided an initial organizational constituency for Developmental Local Government (DLG). This unleashed a political culture of urban development that persisted into the post-apartheid period and remains in evidence today. The history of grassroots democracy stood as a necessary counterweight to the vanguardist tendencies of the national liberation movement. Indeed, it might be argued that some of the tensions between the centralizing and decentralizing trajectories of government in South Africa today have their origins in the contradictions of the national liberation struggle. Particularly in the final stages of the anti-apartheid struggle, the ANC sought to establish and maintain central control, a strategy that sometimes conflicted with the activities and objectives of ordinary township residents who also participated in issue-based politics street-level organization and urban protests.

THE DECENTRALIZATION PARADOX OF THE SOUTH AFRICAN LOCAL GOVERNMENT TRANSITION

To demonstrate their discontent and achieve local democracy, the civics hit the apartheid state where it hurt most – in the purse. Community-organized rate and rent boycotts were successfully applied as a means of making segregated municipal regimes ungovernable, thereby forcing a transition of power (Chaskalson et al, 1987). The Soweto Civic Association was particularly successful in using boycott politics to highlight both bad living conditions in the townships and the discriminatory role of apartheid local-government structures (Swilling and Shubane, 1991). From as early as 1988, there was dialogue between the Soweto People's Delegation and the Soweto Council on how to resolve the rent crisis. In April 1991, the Central Witwatersrand Metropolitan Chamber was set up as a forum in order that the province, local councils and the Soweto Civic could consider the future of urban management in greater Johannesburg (Turok, 1994). Indeed, it was the resulting negotiations that Mabin (1999, p160) argues gave way to a 'national discourse of unifying fragmented local government'. Seekings (2000) also argues that it was the imperative of negotiating an end to the Soweto rent boycott that raised the more general question of the financial and administrative relations of different tiers of government, and highlighted the imperative of local government reform. In turn, it was the creation of non-racial municipal structures (with one tax base for the whole city) that was a precursor for building non-racial democratic local government in post-apartheid South Africa.

Despite their impact on the streets and their influence in city halls, the civic associations emerged as less important in national politics than once had been anticipated. This can be seen most clearly in the ANC's ongoing opposition to the civics' demands for increased power at local level. What the civics were fighting for was visible, funded and democratic urban government – exactly what they had been denied under apartheid. However, their demands for any substantial devolution of power in the post-apartheid period fell on deaf ears. There are any number of explanations for the victory of a centralized over a decentralized model of government in the post-apartheid period. One is the ANC's understandable resistance to calls for federalism by conservative opposition parties. Another is the dominance of ANC exiles in national politics, many of whom did not have a local power base or constituency. Also important among the factors involved was the relative marginalization of the civics in the context of the Alliance formed by the ANC, the Congress of South African Trade Unions (COSATU) and the South African Communist Party (SACP) prior to entering the negotiation process leading up to political transition.

The marginalization of the civic movement by the ANC during the negotiations has been widely discussed (Everatt, 1999; Seekings, 1996). Among the reasons given are that SANCO was dominated by personalities from the Southern Transvaal (the greater Johannesburg area) and the Eastern Cape, and so was not as representative of grassroots structures across the country as it might have been. More importantly, SANCO's national leadership had an uneasy relationship with both the UDF and the recently unbanned ANC (Seekings, 2000). Finally, in 1990 SANCO made a decision to split the 'political' role of the organization from its 'developmental' role, which effectively meant concentrating on grassroots mobilization and local-level issues, thereby marginalizing itself from national processes by ceding its 'political' function to the ANC through an election pact (Everatt, 1999).

Because of their relatively weak position within the national liberation movement, the civics, and SANCO more specifically, were unable to place the issue of devolved powers and functions for local government onto the main 1994 transition agenda. Instead, the National Local Government Negotiating Forum ran with this agenda, meeting in parallel sessions during the period of the negotiated settlement that ultimately brought apartheid rule to an end (Wooldridge, 2001a). The compromise on devolution, reached in 1994, was that the ANC agreed to local government becoming an autonomous sphere of government under the new constitution of 1996 (Cameron, 1999). However, the design and execution of the local government framework, including the definition of powers and functions and agreements on proposed legislation and financial flows, had to wait until well after 1994. In fact, the Demarcation Board only agreed upon final local government boundaries in 2001. This was just in time for the first full local government elections. To some extent, therefore, we must see the interim phase of local government (1995–2001) as an extension of the anti-apartheid fight for deracialized local democracy, rather than a battle over the nature of decentralization.

Curiously, although democratic local government lay at the heart of the post-apartheid vision of a more equal society, little was done during the transition to a liberal democracy in South Africa to pave the way for the reconstruction of this tier of government. Despite this lacuna, municipal government could not be left simply to function unchanged along the racially defined criteria inherited from apartheid. An interim local-government framework was therefore adopted (Cameron, 1999). Particularly in the metropolitan areas, this transitional phase was marked by acute political competition, excessive posturing and dramatic and fundamental restructuring. The latter extended from the location of the office photocopier, to the realignment of planning priorities, and the distribution of budgets and organizational structures. Nowhere was the contest over the integration, reconfiguration and construction of non-racial local government more protracted or more vicious than in the nation's premier city. In Johannesburg, the struggle encompassed not only the official termination of racial administrations, but also personal battles for position, as well as principled debates over policy. The latter included discussion on, among other things, tariffs and taxation, outsourcing of services and maintenance of infrastructure, area-based versus city-wide interventions to address poverty reduction, project versus programme management, and the role of CBOs and community-development forums in decision-making processes. Fundamental to the nature of decentralization, these debates were not articulated in terms of decentralization, although the issues of democracy and non-racialism were always close to the surface.

THE DESIGN OF DEMOCRATIC LOCAL GOVERNMENT

Local-government transformation processes have not been quick, simple or painless anywhere in South Africa. In Johannesburg, change was made even more difficult by the council's inheritance of a considerable unpaid debt deriving from the rent and services boycotts in the African townships. Richard Tomlinson's periodization of the structural transition of the interim phase of local government, from 1994 to 2001, highlights the complexity and incremental nature of the process of change (see Table 5.1). Democratic local government did not emerge instantly in the wake of the abolition of racial discrimination. It had to be created. The debate over the form, structure and content of post-apartheid local government is critical. The success of apartheid rested, at least in part, on the fact that the system of racial privilege was embedded in every aspect of municipal practice – from zoning and housing provision, to staffing and the composition of the electoral roll. An entirely new structure and modus operandi had therefore to be put in its place. Designing a system of local government to overcome apartheid required a fundamental reconceptualization of municipal law, boundaries, finances, and institutional practices – everything, including the politicians, had to be changed.[2]

The technical process of reforming local government from its authoritarian and discriminatory past into something completely different was driven by a number of factors. The most pressing and direct was the imperative of reconfiguring state institutions to enable them to deliver their constitutional mandate. Under the constitution, the purpose of local government was specified as to:

- provide democratic and accountable government for local communities;
- ensure the provision of services to communities in a sustainable manner;
- promote social and economic development;
- promote a safe and healthy environment; and
- encourage the involvement of communities and community organizations in the matters of local government.

Given that local government did not exist in most rural areas and was dysfunctional in almost all urban areas, the scale of the challenge of upholding the constitution cannot be overstated. In the context of the constitutional mandate, it was clear that local government was bound to assume a developmental role, but one that was still undefined. Chipkin (2001) has argued that the form of the developmental role of municipalities that was envisaged by the ANC shifted. The initial statist conception of local government's task (one of *leading* development) was downgraded to one of *facilitating* development. This occurred as the ANC reoriented its focus from the original redistributive goals of the RDP to the more neo-liberal objectives of the GEAR policy (Marais, 1998; Nattrass, 2001).

The new system of local government, at least as envisaged by the 'White Paper on Local Government' (South Africa, 1998) and the legislation it

Table 5.1 *Phases in the restructuring of metropolitan local government*

Period	Local government structure	Dynamics in Johannesburg
Apartheid phase:		
Pre-1994	13 racially demarcated local government bodies	Rather than merely a period of decentralization, this was essentially a period of disintegration from a metropolitan perspective. The different racial groupings operated under different legal and planning systems and had vastly different resources bases, different service levels and different opportunities.
Negotiation phases:		
1991–1993	Central Witwatersrand Metropolitan Chamber	1990 Soweto Accord led to the formation of the chamber in order to resolve outstanding problems that would lead to the resumption of rent and services payments, and essentially would work out how to unite metropolitan Johannesburg – to end the apartheid city.
1993–1994	Greater Johannesburg Local Negotiation Forum	The chamber was restructured into the forum in terms of the Local Government Transition Act of 1993. The forum was charged with negotiating the appointment of a 'pre-interim' council to govern until local government elections in 1995. The forum proposed a strong metro with seven sub-structures, which was proclaimed in November 1994.
Pre-interim phase:		
December 1994– November 1995	Strong metropolitan council with seven sub-structures	Strong GJMC established to manage the process of transition. This arrangement never came about as disputes about the boundaries of the sub-structures led to a reassessment of the earlier agreement and a revised proclamation.
Interim phase:		
November 1995– October 1997	Weaker metropolitan structure with four metropolitan local councils	Greater powers and functions were assigned to metropolitan local councils.
October 1997 onwards	Strengthening of metropolitan council	Financial difficulties encountered by the GJMC, problems with redistribution and management difficulties throughout the system all prompted increasing re-centralization.
Final phase:		
Post-2001	Dominant metropolitan council	The 'White Paper on Local Government' prescribed a dominant metropolitan government. Local government elections were held for the Greater Johannesburg Metropolitan Council in May 2001.

Source: adapted from Tomlinson et al (1998)

unleashed, revealed a tension within local government to serve the objectives of the RDP and of GEAR (USN, 1998). Bond (2000a) quite accurately points out that the White Paper represents the depoliticized analysis typical of much neo-liberal policy formulation. In fact, the accompanying policy documents included a well-conceived, pro-poor framework of municipal government, complete with tools designed to implement the policy drive for municipal reconstruction. But the White Paper also made clear that the imperatives of financial viability and job creation would be the central tenets of all municipal action (Pieterse, Parnell and Wooldridge, 1998). In the words of a booklet prepared by the Urban Sector Network to explain developmental local government to councillors (USN, 1998, p4):

> *The tension between poverty alleviation and economic growth in our DLG system is a reflection of a national tension between policies of the RDP focusing on basic needs and the GEAR macro-economic framework that focuses on the international health of our national economy. In essence, our system of DLG has become the Reconstruction and Development Program at the local level. At the same time, however, DLG must work within the frameworks established by GEAR. The GEAR strategy, launched by government in 1996, is aimed at job creation and economic growth through control of the supply of money (fiscal control) and a reduction in the amount of money South Africa must pay back each year on loans (deficit reduction). There is also a national commitment to the modernization of industry, the enhancement of competitiveness of exports and technological innovation. GEAR has major implications for urban areas. Crucially, GEAR places higher priority on debt reduction and reducing social spending. In the urban context this means privatization, the rationalization of the civil service. It is unlikely that GEAR will address the needs of the poorest and most vulnerable in our major cities or in our medium and small towns. The tension between GEAR and the RDP will be fought out at the local level within the context of DLG.*

It was within this nationally conceived and undoubtedly contradictory schema for DLG that officials and politicians interpreted their brief for uniting the divided city of Johannesburg, and that residents framed their expectations of the new council. It is to a more specific understanding of the components of DLG that we now turn, with an eye to the centrality of the Johannesburg experience in forging the national systems of non-racial local government and in shaping the possibilities for democratic decentralization.

Developmental Local Government

Officially, DLG is described as 'the dynamic way in which local councils work together with local communities to find sustainable ways to meet their needs and improve their lives' (South Africa, 1998, p17). The developmental vision of the post-apartheid dispensation is underpinned by six central principles. First, local governments must decrease the vast problems of poverty found in every city, town and rural area by delivering services and building infrastructure. Second, municipalities must facilitate economic growth in their areas. The third principle concerns coordinated and integrated governance and the relationship between the national, provincial and local structures. However, this principle also addresses the relationship between local government officials and councillors, as well as organized groups and individuals in the municipality's area. Fourth, DLG must be democratic and participatory. The fifth principle focuses on vulnerable groups in communities, identified as women, the disabled and youth who, under the constitution, have the right of equal treatment and a freedom from discrimination. Finally, DLG is founded on the commitment to sustainable environmental development. These principles differ very little from those one might find in any United Nations document on local government or treatise on best practice.

To achieve this ambitious (and contradictory) vision of DLG, there had to be radical institutional transformation. The core systems that shape the operation of local government are municipal powers and functions, organizational structures, planning processes and procedures, and financial management and accounting. The assumption is generally made that reforms in these areas are a necessary, although not sufficient, condition for local government to effectively act against inequality, given the architecture of the overall intergovernmental system.

Municipal Powers and Functions and the Institutional Structure of Local Government

The powers and functions of new municipal structures in South Africa differ very little from those of the old white local authorities. In practice, this means that the core social welfare responsibilities of health housing, education and welfare continue to lie with national and provincial departments. The scale of the budgets that are available to the new local councils is not significantly greater than those that were controlled by the old white municipalities, even though the population to be served is substantially larger. In the case of the new GJMC boundaries, the population is almost three times the size that it was under the apartheid era. The capacity of local government to effect poverty reduction is thus restricted to effectively implementing or managing higher-level directives, delivering on traditional local-government competencies, such as waste management and emergency services, improving the environment, promoting local economic development, and coordinating land development.

The extent to which the local authority is able to direct spending under the complex inter-governmental spending framework is also limited. It hinges upon its ability to get other tiers of government to accept the priorities of the local authority, in its role as facilitator of development. The sole advantage of this lack of administrative power is that the budget for much expensive line-item expenditure is drawn from provincial and national budgets, minimizing the problem of unfunded mandates. In large, complex urban areas, such as metropolitan Johannesburg, the organizational allocation of resources, powers and functions across wards, sub-structures and centralized metropolitan bodies is as important as funding drawn from higher tiers of government. The potential of urban areas to fund their own redistribution and development is widely recognized in the politically charged debates about metropolitan government that occurred during the late 1990s (Wooldridge, 1999a; 1999b; Tomlinson, 1999). In post-apartheid Johannesburg, the metropolitan debate centred upon the redistribution of rights and responsibilities and whether this would take place across circumscribed municipal boundaries or the entire metropolitan region. The fact that patterns of racial and class inequality underpinned these questions of distributive justice meant that debates about municipal form assumed a sharp political edge.

In the interests of maximizing the limited powers and functions of local government and optimizing what are ultimately restricted and largely self-generated budgets (South African municipalities typically raise about 90 per cent of their own revenue), the institutional model of municipal government came under substantial national scrutiny. There were two core aspects to the debate about the appropriate institutional form of urban municipalities. Both were played out in Johannesburg under intense national gaze (Bond, 2000a; Friedman, 2001). First there was the question of how directly the municipality should provide basic services, such as water and electricity. The general questions of cost-sharing and the privatization of services in Johannesburg are taken up in Chapter 6. Then there was the debate about municipal versus metropolitan government.

In the interim phase from 1995 to 2001, when the future of local government in Johannesburg was being negotiated, the government of Johannesburg was divided between Greater Johannesburg Transitional Metropolitan Council (GJTMC) and four municipal sub-structures (see Figure 5.1). A vicious party-political contest ensued over which of the functions allocated to local government would most appropriately be carried out by the GJTMC, and which should lie with the municipal sub-structures. In essence, this debate was about resources and redistribution, although it was played out as being about the process of unifying and deracializing old apartheid structures. As such, it foreshadowed what would ultimately occur though law in introducing a single-tier uni-city model of metropolitan government. In the Metropolitan Negotiating Forum that was a forerunner to this decision and which had overseen the ending of the Soweto rates and rent boycotts, the more progressive political parties came to a united position and agreed to a two-tier structure for governing Johannesburg (Turok, 1994; Mabin, 1999). However, in the light of subsequent power struggles, the ANC changed its stance towards the two-tier structure and agreed to enforce a dominant metropolitan council. The inability to resolve the distribution of powers and functions between the metropolitan council and its sub-structures in Johannesburg was a key element that drove the obligatory introduction of a 'uni-city' model into the national framework for local government (Schmidt, 1999).

Particular areas of debate that arose during the interim phase of local government included the setting of tariffs and the collection of revenue for services. Municipal sub-structures were empowered to provide services, such as water supply and electricity, and were responsible for collecting revenue for these. However, the GJTMC provided the bulk connections. The first contest was over who could use the surplus generated by income from service consumption. Although Johannesburg is a city characterized by great poverty, it is also a wealthy urban centre, capable of generating substantial revenue for redistribution. The rate base within the area of Greater Johannesburg was very uneven. For example, while the Eastern Municipal Sub-Structure (EMSS), which was home to rich commercial and residential areas such as Sandton, had less than one quarter of the population, it generated almost half of the commercial rates and more than half of the residential rates for the metropolitan area (see Tables 5.2 and 5.3). By contrast, the Southern Municipal Sub-Structure (SMSS), home to the vast and sprawling townships of Soweto, Eldorado Park and Orange Farm, and the Western Municipal Sub-Structure (WMSS) were net spenders rather than contributors to rates (see Tables 5.2 and 5.3). Thus, one of the most critical questions posed in post-apartheid Johannesburg, a city still characterized by vast spatial inequalities in wealth, was who was to decide on the distribution of revenue and expenditure across the metropolitan region. In addition to conflict between the metropolitan council and the sub-structures over finances generated from services, there was also frustration over the varied expenditure across the sub-structures. Conflicts arose because of the relative sums available for capital expenditure (compare the EMSS, which spent only 20 per cent of its budget on salaries, to that of the SMSS, which spent 40 per cent).

Table 5.2 *Projected rateable income by type of source, 1996–1997*

Type of source	Rateable income	
	Rands (millions)	Percentage distribution
Contribution by business	825	57
Contribution by advantaged residential areas	379	26
Contribution by disadvantaged residential areas	75	5
Other contributions	162	11
Total rates income	1441	100

Source: GJMC (1998a; 1998b)

Resolution of the problem of redistribution across the sub-structures in Johannesburg was pre-empted by a series of dramatic events that effectively forced the city into a metropolitan structure by default rather than design. In the latter half of 1997, in response to the unstable financial position of the metropolitan government, national and provincial government intervened by taking over the running of the GJTMC and its four sub-structures (Abrahams, 1998; Emdon, 1994; Tomlinson et al, 1998). Prompted by a deficit of 130 million Rand (R130 million) per month – at the time, around UK£13 million per month – substantial bulk electricity arrears and impending insolvency in each of the sub-structures (*The Star*, 12 March 1998), a provincial proclamation was passed that established an interim management committee known as the Committee of 10. The Committee of 10 (later expanded to 15 representatives)

Table 5.3 *Percentage distributions of projected rateable income by sub-structure,*
1996–1997

	Municipal sub-structures				
	Eastern	*Southern*	*Northern*	*Western*	*Total*
Contribution by business as a percentage of total rates	45	35	17	3	100
Contribution by advantaged residential areas as a percentage of total rates	44	14	32	10	100
Contribution by disadvantaged residential areas as a percentage of total rates	63	7	24	6	100
Estimated proportion of the population	23	42	19	16	100

Source: GJMC (1998c)

was made up of councillors drawn from each of the sub-structures and the GJTMC, and was assisted by a technical team of urban professionals, including financial managers and organizational development consultants. They effectively ran Johannesburg from October 1997 until the local government elections in 2001. Despite considerable protest, both opposition and ruling party representatives served on the emergency committees, lending legitimacy to the nomenclature 'metro in drag', as it was dubbed by waggish local journalists. During this phase, therefore, management of the city was located neither in the sub-structures nor in the GJTMC as such, but was unified under a single-appointed structure that fell under the direct control of the province and national government.

Given this history, a major dimension of the tasks that beset the Committee of 15 was to address the financial viability of metropolitan government in Johannesburg; as a result, there was a very strong focus on credit control. Significantly, the technical task team was headed by an independent charted accountant (*The Star*, 5 May 1998). The committee, in addition to looking after the fiscal base of the city, also gave its attention to proposals to streamline the powers and functions of municipal and metropolitan government. The opposition parties opposed the structure, which they described as 'bringing in the mega-city through the back door' (*Business Day*, 5 March 1998; *The Star*, 9 November 1998). However, they nevertheless agreed to participate in the process in order to free metropolitan government from the control of the province and the National Department of Finance.

Before disbanding itself, the Committee of 15 agreed that its successor committee, the Transformation *Lekgotla*, would have extended metropolitan powers (*Citizen*, 11 May 1998). Effectively, therefore, what the Committee of 15 decided, with respect to the powers and functions of government in Johannesburg, foreshadowed the requirements set out in the subsequent National Municipal Structures Act of 1998 that was passed soon afterwards.

Thus, the impact of the Johannesburg experience was crucial in establishing a model for metropolitan government nationally. Despite the victory of the ANC and others promoting the uni-city model as one which was the most democratic and redistributive, the adoption of a metropolitan model was not uncontroversial and was lamented as much within progressive circles as among more conservative forces (Kihato, 1997). However, what was lost in the flurry of debate about the form of city government was that, for the first time, there was a comprehensive tier of government at the metropolitan level that represented all residents of South African cities. Whereas the fight for municipal non-racialism was the most public of struggles, its outcome in the form of decentralization, ironically, was achieved by stealth.

Reconfiguring Municipal Planning Law and Practice: Lessons from Johannesburg

Accompanying the change in organizational forms and functions of local government, there have also been efforts to transform the practice of planning in South Africa. Apartheid planning and land-use legislation was aimed at reinforcing the segregated city, and it was clear that they, too, had to be fundamentally altered. Thus, legislation was passed that put in place an alternative framework for municipal planning aimed at encouraging spatial integration and compaction, as well as more equitable urban change (Emdon, 1994). In practice, it is local government that implements and applies the planning regulations, even when these laws are set nationally. This is true of the Development Facilitation Act (DFA) that was passed in 1995, one of the first pieces of legislation aimed at moulding alternative, more equal, settlement patterns. The DFA aimed at facilitating the development of low-cost housing schemes to urgently meet the settlement and shelter needs of Africans who were increasingly squatting on the urban periphery of Johannesburg and other large cities. The DFA provided a national legislative framework for rapid land development for poor people and stipulated that municipalities should prepare policy guidelines, known as Land Development Objectives (LDOs), that corresponded to the principles laid out in the DFA.

The DFA was the first evidence of an alternative vision of settlement planning from the historically dominant values that had underpinned land development – namely, the private market or racial segregation. Further planning legislation soon followed; but now the local authorities themselves were the object of the legislation, and not just its implementers. Legislation (including the Municipal Systems and Structures Act and the Local Government Transition Act, Second Amendment) required that the LDO policy prioritization process had to be followed by the municipalities' preparation of an Integrated Development Plan (IDP). In practice, the LDO and IDP processes now occur simultaneously and are known as the IDP (Mabin, 2001), although in Johannesburg the LDO and IDP processes were, at first, initiated separately.

The new urban planning framework thus required local authorities to develop IDPs as strategic plans that linked, to the budget, the different legal requirements of municipal business. These requirements included responsibilities such as environmental protection and economic development, which were to be connected, in turn, to the priorities identified by communities. The most innovative aspect of the law was that it dealt with development planning, understood in its broadest sense to include land-use, transport, infrastructure, environmental, economic and social planning, with efforts to link these to municipal institutional and financial planning. This cross-sectoral approach put local government in a much more favourable structural position to achieve its objectives of poverty reduction. In theory, it overturned the legacy of sectoral planning inherited from the apartheid period, where the efforts of one department to combat poverty were contradicted or undermined by the activities of another.

Despite the potential benefits of this move towards integrated planning, the actual application of the IDP framework has, in many ways, been uncomfortable. The old structure plans were abolished; but all that replaced them were the principles in the DFA, which did not provide adequate guidance for spatial-planning decisions. The link between IDPs and municipal budgets was weak, and did not provide an adequate framework for linking municipal organizational planning to real development 'outputs'. The links between planning for a discrete spatial area and municipal corporate or strategic planning for the city as a whole, based upon the activities of line departments, were unclear. Moreover, developing effective municipal IDPs relied upon the inputs of numerous provincial and national departments. In the case of Johannesburg, this was not generally a major problem; but it has been a critical issue in other parts of the country where provincial government lacks the capacity to implement planning. Ineffective inter-governmental and inter-departmental coordination means that the viability of municipal IDPs is undermined. Even the fact that Johannesburg is the capital of the province of Gauteng has not ensured seamless liaison between the metropolitan council and the provincial government. In short, although there are a number of new planning policy instruments in place, inter-governmental cooperation cannot be assured. The planning innovations of local government depend upon substantial organizational restructuring and institutional reorientation in order to align values, policy and practice, particularly when linking planning processes to the vexed issue of budgets. As elsewhere, this utopian state of integration has yet to be achieved in Johannesburg.

One of the requirements of the LDO/IDP process was that residents were to participate in developing priorities for their areas. A major difficulty turned out to be incorporating the multiple, and often contradictory, views that citizens expressed. The GJMC's IDP process, like that of the LDO process that came before it, included extensive, well-intentioned and conscientious consultations with key stakeholders (GJMC, 1997). Through the LDO process, virtually every department in the GJMC, as well as the sub-structures, realigned their activities towards more poverty-sensitive action. Chapter 7 examines one positive example of how citizens' participation in the LDO process was a determining factor in shaping development in their area; it also demonstrates that residents' engagement is not guaranteed by the formal processes and procedures themselves. Moreover, the general experience of the city in incorporating residents' contributions to policy, programmes and projects is far from satisfactory, as evidence from the first IDP produced in Johannesburg reveals.

The first IDP for Metropolitan Johannesburg (GJMC, 1998d) is an impressive volume, replete with rich base-line information that details different aspects of the city's profile. There are, for example, geographic information system (GIS) maps on topics as diverse as rainfall, the incidence of serious crime, the distribution of bulk sewer capacity, and the value of land. The volume indicates both the strengths and weaknesses of metropolitan government, as well as defining strategic objectives and setting out policy goals. For example, the IDP document is clear about committing the Greater Johannesburg Integrated Development Plan to the broader economic development goals of the Gauteng Province, of which Johannesburg forms an important part and whose vision states: 'Gauteng is South Africa's "smart province", dedicated to building a globally competitive economy and developing our cities and our people' (GJMC, 1998d, p64).

However, the IDP document is vague about detail and fails to specify how any of its objectives will be met. Friedman (2001) makes a similar point about the subsequent Strategic Metropolitan Development Framework (SMDF), a document drawn up to give overall direction to reconfiguring the apartheid spatial legacies of Johannesburg, and which, in practice, held more sway in policy debates than the first IDP. The issue for us is not about which strategic planning document is the most authoritative; rather, the fact that there is more than one version is indicative of the chaotic state of Johannesburg during the interim phase of local government transition. In Johannesburg, as is so often the case elsewhere, the problem was not simply about policy but also about implementation. Within the metropolitan council itself, there was open recognition that the first IDP and the SMDF failed to provide a sufficient strategic framework for action (either in relation to growth or to poverty alleviation). This recognition prompted a further series of metropolitan-wide consultations in 1998 on how to define the implementation plan for the city in order to meet its goals of becoming a 'world class African city'. Since then, the Johannesburg medium-term planning process has been subsumed within what became known as the *iGoli 2010* process (see Chapter 6).

Even more interesting than the duplication of medium-term strategic-planning documents was the fact that the goals of the IDP and the SMDF bore only marginal resemblance to those expressed by the residents who participated in their tens of thousands in the LDO consultation process in Johannesburg. In fairness, the scales with which the IDP and SMDF documents engaged differed. They addressed metropolitan goals and, as such, were more concerned with economic issues, while the LDO documents drew together residents' aspirations for local-level or neighbourhood development (GJMC, 1998d). Nevertheless, the variation may also be due to the fact that officials and consultants drew up the IDP and the SMDF, with scant reference to the LDOs that were the rather chaotic product of hundreds of neighbourhood consultations across Johannesburg.

The fact that there was such widespread and extensive participation of residents in the LDO/IDP process in Johannesburg was not all due to local government efforts to initiate participatory planning, but arose also from the existence of local-level democratic traditions that were built largely by the civics. For example, Maganya (1996) argues that the Community Development Forum (CDF) structures, as they exist today, were a deliberate recreation of the old community-based civic structures. After 1994, ANC alliance-linked politicians pushed local communities into building CDFs as umbrella forums that brought together all the interest groups of a particular neighbourhood into a single organizational formation. For the ANC alliance, it was therefore the CDFs that were seen to continue the tradition of engaged civil society in the era of reconstruction and development implementation. CDFs are sometimes called RDP forums (after the Reconstruction and Development Programme in whose vision they were formed); they were perceived to take on the mantle of strengthening the hands of largely poor black community interests when engaging with the still largely white local-authority officials. Township-based CDFs had the additional advantage of bolstering the political clout of the, as yet inexperienced, black councillors with whom they were often closely allied. With very little effort, therefore, it was possible to mobilize communities to participate in these forums that the municipal sub-structures established as part of the LDO process.

In the case of Johannesburg, the city had a plethora of CBOs, ranging from the officially recognized CDFs, to street committees and various interest- and issue-based groups. Most could trace their style of local organization to patterns and imperatives laid down by the civics during the anti-apartheid struggle. As evidence of the richness of civil society in Johannesburg, Everatt (1999) has reported that three-quarters of residents in unserviced informal areas in Gauteng had street committees in their areas. Furthermore, just over one third of residents had block committees, although less than one third knew the name of the civic association operating in their area. While the political muscle of the national civic body, SANCO, and other organizations of civil society may have waned during the process of local government restructuring, particularly at the national level, the entrenchment of democratic urban planning and development practice nevertheless owed much to the challenges posed by the civics to the norms of apartheid planning (Bollens, 1999).

As the profile of local civic structures grew and the imperative of demonstrating responsive government became more intense in the post-apartheid era, it became more common for municipalities to employ someone who was specifically charged with the task of community liaison. Typically, such individuals were black, spoke an African language and had been schooled in civic politics rather than formal town and regional planning. At the same time, the programmes of professional planning institutions attempted to expand their intake of disadvantaged students and to make the curricula more relevant to the South African situation. The outcome was a dramatic shift away from conventional town planning with its focus on physical planning, structure plans and legalistic regulations, a classic situation of the academy catching up with the practice. In its place, development planning flourished, with an emphasis on socio-economic needs, dialogue with citizens and planning as a political process (Bollens, 1998). Ironically, the basis for a new framework of planning theory and action was built on the back of traditions of advocacy and assertive citizenship, set up by the civics at precisely the time when their power in national politics atrophied, when their resources were depleted at a local level, and when many of their leaders left to take up political posts in the new government. In a strange twist of fate, the local-level resources and autonomy for which the civics fought so hard came increasingly under threat. This is because the nature of decentralization in South Africa remains uncertain and the depth of local democracy persists as an issue of ongoing political contest.

Abrahams (1998), Chipkin (1997) and others (Bollens, 1998; Swilling and Boya, 1997) have argued that it was this tradition of advocacy politics and community protest that gave rise to democratic governance and culminated in the holistic attitude to city planning in South Africa, now known as integrated development planning. What the civics lacked by way of national political legitimacy, especially in relation to the ANC, they made up for in terms of community knowledge and local political literacy. As a result, they managed to force municipal officials (and private-sector developers) to engage with locally constituted residents' structures. Black Johannesburg residents, because of apartheid, had no formal representation on council structures; but they participated in urban management debates and policy formulation procedures through the civics. After 1995, when the first non-racial elections were held at local level for the interim local-government structures, the practice of having the civics represent the formerly disenfranchised groups could have fallen away. Elected councillors were now there to provide the legitimate voice of black citizens. However, there was a general reluctance to abandon the tradition of direct resident engagement with the authorities, and so processes and structures for civic participation have been streamlined into the series of formally constituted Community-Development Forums, or CDFs, described above.

One reason for the longevity of the CDF or RDP forums has been that, for officials, it eases the imperative of engaging in multiple forms of participatory planning by providing an obvious and accessible conduit into the community (Oldfield, 2000). For example, when each Johannesburg municipal sub-structure formulated its developmental vision through the LDO/IDP processes during the late 1990s, there were extensive consultations with representatives of civil society through various workshops and report back meetings (GJMC, 1997). In some cases, SANCO's pre-eminence was challenged early on. In other areas, such as in the hostels, the Inkatha Freedom Party (IFP) maintained its grip, representing the predominantly Zulu hostel residents who were loyal to the party, which has its main base in the province of KwaZulu–Natal (KZN). In other examples, civics never featured at all, and narrow interest groups held sway. In the longer term, civics may, indeed, become less significant as the organizational landscape of urban governance becomes more varied. Already, middle-class neighbourhoods and affluent ratepayers' associations have bought into the forum structure and process, utilising and even capturing the format to achieve their own interests.

CONCLUSION

Planning and implementing urban development has long been accepted as the purview of local authorities. But in South Africa, as in other post-colonial societies, the institutional architecture of local government that was inherited from the past was incomplete. The ending of apartheid, and the imperative of establishing local non-racial democracy in response to the demands of black urban protesters, facilitated the construction of a more robust system of democratic municipal government. Thus, despite the liberation movement's reticence to devolve power from the national scale, a de-facto process of decentralization has occurred since the famous 1994 elections. In Johannesburg, this has entailed the tedious integration of disparate administrative regimes into a single metropolitan authority.

The CDFs have now been institutionalized as an integral part of the city management process. The intensity that marked their formation, and their early involvement in consultative processes with local government, have led to something of a participation fatigue, particularly on the part of the city, which is unfortunate. There is an onus on SANCO, among others, to ensure maintained commitment. When SANCO decided to focus on local development rather than national politics, it may not have realized that the organization and its branches could be establishing a legacy against which to judge future democratic governance. What remains to be seen is whether SANCO branches will remain operative, representative and widely consultative, and whether they will be able to lead or, indeed, share the arena of urban governance with new and possibly competing organizations. Whether or not SANCO emerges to represent the collective interests of civil society, or whether its place is taken by alternative local-level structures, it is likely that local government will continue to seek out community-based consultation, through CDF representatives. The imperative of participatory planning is now legally inscribed in the legislative code of land development in South Africa. It is thus technically impossible for development to occur without community input and engagement with the local authorities, even if the political imperative is absent. In other words, a devolved, participatory model of urban development now exists in South Africa.

In the wake of the integration of local government in Johannesburg and the entrenchment of processes of local democracy, it is possible to reflect on Manor's (1999) conditions for stable decentralization. Manor argued that democracy at the local scale was an essential precondition of success. The South African decentralization experience was shaped primarily by the powerful struggle to end oppression. The particular impact of the Johannesburg people's call to install a unitary, non-racial city government where there was one tax base for all citizens positively marked this aspect of the South African decentralization experience. However, Manor's warning that devolution of democracy alone is insufficient to secure successful decentralization is pertinent. Manor stated that, in order to succeed, local democracy must be accompanied by administrative devolution and financial resources.

While decentralization was never the expressed objective of the South African transition, it was clear that the success of the goals of the ANC's reconstruction and development programme hinged upon the developmental performance of local government. In this regard, it is imperative to assess the extent of administrative devolution and the scale of the funding for the mandate of local government. Because of the nature of the centralist transition in South Africa, local government was not allocated any of the traditional developmental or welfare functions of housing, health or education. Instead, in line with international planning practice and the global trend towards neo-liberalism, local government was mandated simply to coordinate social, economic, environmental and spatial planning, albeit in the context of a new participatory and integrated planning framework. The track record of the IDP process suggests that local government lacks adequate powers to achieve its coordinating functions, especially in driving spatial integration. On the question of municipal finance, the relative affluence of Johannesburg sets it apart from other local councils where there are obvious problems of implementing the unfunded mandates associated with the ambitious goals of development. In Johannesburg, however, the financial difficulties of local government are of a rather different nature, and it is to an evaluation of the 'the bottom line' – the municipal budget – that we now turn.

Chapter 6

The Politics of Fiscal Austerity in Creating Equitable City Government

INTRODUCTION

The financial position of a city profoundly affects the absolute and relative power of its citizens to leverage local government resources. There is nothing like the spectre of municipal bankruptcy to focus the collective minds of residents, politicians and officials on defining 'core business', getting 'back to basics' or seeking 'external development partners'. This has been the recent experience of Johannesburg, which, despite being the richest city in sub-Saharan Africa, saw its reconstruction severely curtailed by real and perceived resource constraints. In Johannesburg, the discourse of budgetary crisis, of municipal bankruptcy and the imperatives of sound financial management came to dominate the post-apartheid local government agenda alongside (and, some argue, in conflict with) the pro-poor rhetoric of DLG (Bond, 2000b).

The centrality of the financial saga that underpinned the management of Johannesburg at the turn of the century makes it imperative that we clarify the budgetary and resource issues that were faced by the city at the time. To this end, we explore the origins of the fiscal crisis that brought the interim local government arrangements crashing down. Through an analysis of *iGoli 2002*, the name given to the policy and planning processes that were set in motion to respond to the threat of municipal bankruptcy, we trace the impact of the fiscal crisis on the configuration of power within the municipality. We also examine the implications of the institutional transformation that was initiated by the ethos of fiscal austerity for those in civil society who seek urban redistribution, renewal and revitalization.

Our basic argument in this chapter is that the extent of the fiscal crisis in Johannesburg was 'talked-up' in the accompanying policy and planning document, *iGoli 2002* (GJMC, 2001a), in order to allow metropolitan restructuring and the reconfiguration of some service-delivery arrangements. However, the *iGoli* document also represented a significant shift of power within the Johannesburg Council and heralded the declining fortunes of loosely configured anti-apartheid veterans engaged in local governance. It therefore symbolized the ascendancy of neo-liberal tendencies within the council. As such, there was more to the city development process as outlined in *iGoli 2002* than the debates on service delivery to which the document gave rise. Lost in the shadows of the battle over the pros and cons of privatization were other crucial avenues for uniting divided cities. We argue that the viability of participatory planning frameworks and of democratic governance structures within city politics, stand in danger of being erased from the urban-reconstruction agenda by virtue of the, albeit important but disproportionately dominant, debate on services. For it is within the spaces of formal and informal negotiation that residents' groups and other organizations will find the power to influence and transform city futures in the post-Fordist era.

While the structural legacy of inequality and social exclusion is almost overwhelming in South African cities, the new framework of DLG and the old tradition of civic politics offer promising institutional environments within which residents can mobilize to influence municipal and metropolitan agendas. As such, we suggest that there should be greater emphasis placed on other functions that are part of the municipal agenda, such as planning, environment and social development. However, we do not wish to detract from popular struggles over service provision. Nor do we wish to further fracture the fronts on which civil society must engage in order to achieve justice in the face of neo-liberal policy trajectories. Rather, using the Johannesburg case, we seek to highlight the fragile gains that have been made through the demand for participatory planning within the delivery of housing and services. We conclude by pointing to the danger of allowing hard-won concessions, achieved by sustained civic engagement, to become fossilized in progressive policy documents that never see the light of day, either because of an increasingly quiescent and docile public or because a more powerful discourse of financial efficiency has been allowed to usurp the commitment to consultative planning and democratic governance.

CRISIS? WHAT CRISIS?

Councillor Thusini Makhosonke, chairperson of the Budget and Finance Committee in the Northern Metropolitan Sub-Structure (NMSS), recalled that the news that a financial crisis was facing the GJTMC came as something of a shock to the newly elected councillors. The perception that the city was rich and could easily afford to redirect its expenditure to ensure the uplifting of disenfranchised black residents was one of the carrots that had lured activists into the local government arena as a site of opposition to apartheid (Swilling and Boya, 1997). In a flurry of expenditure, the post-1994, non-racial council had set about addressing the vast service backlogs, building new sporting facilities and generally investing in transforming the blighted apartheid landscape. But in 1997, all prospects of the freshly elected council spending its way out of inequality were dashed. In the face of a substantial deficit, the city's capital budget was slashed and pro-poor management in Johannesburg became more complex as the budget was reconfigured for a climate of fiscal austerity.

In fact, 1997 was not the first financial crisis, even for the interim local government of Johannesburg. Setting aside the issue of the unfunded nature of some of the new municipal functions, especially environment and economic development, local authorities were constitutionally responsible for providing basic service consumption. This was surely the most serious and enduring of all municipal funding crises (Wheelan, 2001). In this regard, Johannesburg suffered from the same fate as all other local councils in South Africa, albeit on a more limited scale due to the size of its own resources. But there have also been locally specific fights over money. We have already seen in Chapter 4 how the EMSS's reluctance to transfer surplus across the city prompted the ANC to introduce a metropolitan government so in order to ensure redistribution. This move to a compulsory metropolitan government was prompted not only by the negative experience of redistribution across sub-structures, but also by the Sandton rate boycott that started in mid-1996.

In a copycat of the Soweto rates boycott that had so weakened the rigid control of the apartheid municipalities, the affluent population of Sandton flexed their financial muscle and indicated their reluctance to contribute to urban reconstruction. For the council, this was a crucial lesson in the political and economic power of the urban elite in Johannesburg. Drawn from a very high-income neighbourhood in the EMSS, and formed in response to the dramatic hike in rates introduced to increase revenue in the historically white neighbourhood of a wealthy local authority, the Sandton Ratepayers' Association was, without question, the best-organized civic group in the interim phase of local government anywhere in the country (Wooldridge, 1999a).

From its inception during the early 1960s, the Sandton City Council intentionally kept rates low relative to neighbouring municipalities, such as Johannesburg and Randburg, in return for only providing basic municipal services, which excluded street lighting and paved sidewalks in residential areas. The continued low level of rates in Sandton was made possible into the 1980s and 1990s by escalating commercial investment in its popular decentralized office and commercial centre (Rogerson and Rogerson, 1997a), commensurate with the spatial restructuring of Johannesburg under the post-Fordism described in Chapter 4. In other words, the low rates of Sandton had been artificially maintained both by apartheid and by the decentralized growth of the service economy.

After 1994, with the newly elected local councillors in place, the council decided to impose a uniform rating system across the whole Greater Johannesburg area, which was 6.45 cents in the Rand.[1] Prior to this, rates levels had varied across the metropolitan area, with Sandton having the lowest rates and the old Indian area of Lenasia in the south of the city having the highest, at 6 cents in the Rand (R) (Abrahams, 1998). The standardization of rates implied an increase in GJMC revenue of some R400 million. For Sandton, this meant that rates jumped from 2.65 cents to 6.45, an increase of nearly 300 per cent. The proposed increase was met with public outrage, and for 18 months the rates boycott ensued. In addition to boycotting payment, many private and commercial owners were motivated by the Sandton boycott to appeal against existing rates. Led by the Sandton Federation of Ratepayers (SANFED), an estimated 10,000 ratepayers (out of 118,000) placed objections to their property valuations with the EMSS. Although less than one fifth of these were successful, the applications may have cost the city as much as R20 million in refunds (*The Star*, 13 April 1998; *Business Day*, 10 June 1998). By the end of the Sandton boycott, the EMSS was owed R220 million (Allen et al, 2001). The relative cost of the Sandton boycott is illustrated by comparison with other boycott-induced shortfalls in revenue in Johannesburg. In 1997, when the proportion of rates collected in Soweto was only 38 per cent, the loss of revenue amounted to a sum of R7 million. In the CBD, where 70 per cent of rates were paid, the lost revenue amounted to R15 million, more than twice that lost in Soweto, but only a fraction of the burden of the lost interest and revenue from the Sandton rates boycott (*Business Day*, 2 April 1998).

The 1997 financial crisis, unlike the earlier Sandton boycott or the EMSS/GJMC crisis, was not about redistribution or about the power to govern. It was about balancing the books. In October 1997, the central government, anticipating that Johannesburg was heading for a large budget deficit, imposed a new system of externally regulated financial administration on the city. Under the watchful eye of the national department of finance and under the direct stewardship of the provincial departments of local government and housing, the council imposed upon it a financial 'super executive' to run its financial affairs. Through a Committee of 10 (subsequently 15 and renamed the Transformation *Lekgotla*), the financial powers of the GJMC and the municipal sub-structures were abrogated and a financial restructuring plan was put in place. During this period, *iGoli 2002* (GJMC, 2001a) was formulated as a short-term planning mechanism for getting the city out of its financial crisis. Subsequently, *iGoli 2010*, a medium-term planning process, was initiated (Allen et al, 2001). In Johannesburg, *iGoli*, meaning 'city of gold', is the name given to the policy, planning and budgetary process that fulfils the national requirements for the city's IDP. It is also the process that has attracted international CDS funding. Understanding *iGoli* is not possible without the reference point of the financial crisis of 1997, from whence it arose.

The Financial Problems of South Africa's 'Richest' Urban Area[2]

Despite having huge monetary resources, Johannesburg's financial problems remain indisputable. The centrality of the financial saga that underpins the management of the city makes it imperative that we devote our attention to clarifying the budgetary and resource issues faced by the city. To this end, we must explore the origins of the fiscal crisis and review the extent of the available resources relative to expenditure and debt. The published Johannesburg budget for 1999–2000 shows total expenditures of R8.5 billion. However, the way in which the budget is presented gives a somewhat misleading picture, for two reasons. First, all revenues and expenditures are stated in gross terms. Since there are large trading undertakings (electricity, water, sewerage and buses), these inflate both revenues and expenditures enormously. Thus, more than half of the gross budget items comes from charges for electricity, water and sewerage connections. The published figures would be more meaningful if trading undertakings were separated out and only the net revenues or deficits were included in the budget. Second, the budget shows revenues and expenditures that are mere book transactions, such as the metropolitan levy that is a transfer between municipal local councils and the GJMC, as well as bus subsidies for pensioners and scholars. These tend to inflate the size of the budget.

Accordingly, Table 6.1 shows a simplified summary of 1999–2000 budgeted revenues and net expenditures for Johannesburg as a whole. Internal transactions have been excluded; only net revenues from trading undertakings have been included, and direct revenues from charges have been deducted from expenditures to show the net expenditure on services. Table 6.1 shows that on the revenue side:

- two-thirds of consolidated net revenue come from rates (property tax) – explaining the power of elite residents and business in city politics;
- one quarter comes from Regional Service Council (RSC) levies;[3]
- 5 per cent comes from the surplus on electricity;[4]
- small amounts of net revenue come from vehicle-licensing (GJMC issues licences on behalf of the province and earns a small amount from doing so) and from the surplus on the fresh produce market; and
- only 3 per cent of revenues (R90 million) comes from transfers from the province (of which about 40 per cent is a contribution to the ambulance service and 25 per cent for health services, the rest – a mere R27.6 million – comes from a general grant).

On the expenditure side:

- council and mayoral expenditures consume 5 per cent;
- general administration, including finance and planning, consumes 27 per cent;
- infrastructure and urban services (net of charges) consume 25 per cent;
- sports, recreation, parks, arts, culture, libraries consume 18 per cent; and
- health, welfare and housing services (net of rents) consume 12 per cent (this expenditure is largely set against provincial or national budgets, minimizing the unfunded mandate problem).

The Johannesburg budget shows a surplus of R159 million, about 2 per cent of the gross budget. Within the expenditure budget, R400 million is set aside for working capital reserve (to offset under collection of revenue) and R106 million for a capital development fund.[5]

There is, however, one major problem with both budgeted and actual figures for revenues. It arises because of the use of accrual accounting, which credits income at the point at which it becomes due, rather than when it is actually received. Where payments that are due are not actually received, they are recorded in the balance sheet as debtors. This is not a significant problem when revenue collection performance approaches 100 per cent. However, since the time of the Soweto rents and services boycott in Johannesburg, there has been

Table 6.1 *Johannesburg's 1999–2000 budget*[6]

Sources of revenue	Revenue (millions of Rand)	Percentage share of revenue
Rates	R1902	66
Regional Services Council (RSC) levies	R705	25
Electricity surplus	R145	5
Gas surplus	–	0
Vehicle-licensing	R11	0
Fresh produce market surplus	R18	1
Subsidies from Gauteng Province	R90	3
Total revenue	R2871	100

Expenditure allocations	Expenditure (net of revenue from charges) (millions of Rand)	Percentage share of expenditure
Council/mayor	R125	5
Chief executive office	R75	3
Administration	R202	7
Finance administration	R327	12
Planning/economic development/tourism	R135	5
Sports/recreation/parks/cemeteries/zoo	R384	14
Arts/culture/libraries/museums	R96	4
Health services: primary/environmental	R186	7
Social services/welfare/development	R28	1
Housing	R118	4
Emergency services	R146	5
Traffic management	R148	5
Roads and drainage	R396	15
Waste management	R110	4
Water and sewerage	R16	1
Infrastructure technical support	R92	3
Bus service	R129	5
Total net expenditure	R2712	100
Surplus/deficit	R159	

Source: GJMC, 1999a

a growing level of debtors for rates, electricity, water, sewerage and housing. The outstanding debt in September 1999 was R2.8 billion, which was equivalent to one third of Johannesburg's gross budget. Thus, when the accounts for 1998–1999 recorded that 99.2 per cent of budgeted revenues were being realized, this was not, in fact, the case, since around 8 to 10 per cent of the 'actual' revenue was represented by debtors. Real revenue collection was probably nearer to 90 per cent.

Accrual budgeting lay at the heart of the immediate problems faced by the GJMC in 1997. On the face of it, the GJMC had huge resources and appeared to be performing well. The recorded deficit for 1998–1999 was R291 million, or 3 per cent of the gross budget (GJMC, 1998b, p24). The real deficit, though, was probably nearer to 10 per cent because of under-collection of revenues

The city had, in effect, been running a substantial deficit for some years, while giving the impression that it was balancing its budget. As a result, the city was in a 'financial crisis' for several years; in fact, the 'crisis' had been brewing for a much longer period of time. A number of causes underlie the problems that manifested themselves, or were brought into the open in 1997. They include:

- a long-standing practice of high spending based upon high standards of provision for a minority of the population; the new responsibilities for vast areas with seriously inadequate infrastructure and services required a major change of culture and standards that has only partially been achieved;
- a tradition of an expenditure-led, incremental budgeting, without any rigorous review of expenditure needs, or of the benefit incidence of expenditure, and the assumption that resources will always be there to meet expenditure needs;
- simultaneously, a huge, pent-up demand from previously disadvantaged communities for improved (or even basic) levels of service, leading to unsustainable levels of capital spending in the initial post-apartheid period;
- high levels of borrowing, not just to fund capital expenditure but also, latterly at least, to cover short-term cash-flow shortfalls, using expensive call bonds;
- a high level of staffing, with relatively low productivity and with a powerful trade union opposed to fundamental change;
- a failure to address the problem of the very low levels of revenue collection in the former black areas inherited from the central government, together with declining collection rates in other areas in the immediate post-apartheid period;
- the failure to recognize the seriousness of the revenue situation because the accounting system gave a false sense of security about the level of revenues being collected; budgeting continued to be on the basis of 100 per cent revenue collection;
- problems of financial management and control resulting from the creation of the four Metropolitan Local Councils (MLCs) (Tomlinson, 1999);
- the reduction in grants from central government; although these were never very significant, the proportion of national funds paid to Johannesburg relative to other municipalities has declined.

In effect, then, there certainly were insufficient resources to meet all of the demands for reconstructing Johannesburg, and there were (and are) unquestionably serious financial management issues in the city, including those of overspending. However, it would be an overstatement to call October 1997 either an abrupt financial crisis or a sign of long-term financial ill health as the subsequently more healthy, if still vulnerable, financial performance of the council demonstrated. In response to the 1997 alarm, the GJMC adopted clear financial reforms (GJMC, 1998e; 1999a). These included a move away from accrual budgeting to a three-year budget cycle, and a shift from an expenditure-led budget to a resource-led budget, which is balanced in cash terms (on the basis of revenues actually received), as well as enhanced credit control (Allen et al, 2000). Expenditure programmes now have to be more clearly justified to a committee of elected representatives and finance officials. That these changes were sensible and in the interests of all concerned is not in dispute. What we take issue with is the accompanying hype over purported impending financial collapse that permeated thinking within the council, provincial and national government, and among the public at large, and which provided the political justification and momentum for a substantive realignment of post-apartheid local government. The crisis became the pretext for a shift away from the state-centred and equity-driven development envisaged in the RDP (ANC, 1994) and towards a partnership-based approach in which the state merely facilitated and integrated a more efficiency-driven process of development. The terms of this reorientation are set out in our discussion of *iGoli 2002* (GJMC, 1999b) below.

WHAT IS *IGOLI 2002*?

The task of defining a developmental path for local government in Johannesburg was always going to be contentious. The debate was conducted primarily within the ruling ANC, among their Alliance partners (SACP and COSATU) and, to a lessor extent, between opposing political parties. The policies and plans laid out in *iGoli 2002* lay at the heart of this debate, which saw vigorous public engagement. Few Johannesburg residents could remain unaware of the issues associated with the massive restructuring of the metropolitan council and its services, although there were widely divergent views on the benefits of the *iGoli* proposals, and more than a little confusion over its parameters.

For Johannesburg's leaders, *iGoli 2002* (GJMC, 1999b) was a clear policy initiative with far-reaching implications. Mayor Isaac Mogase (1999:3) described it thus:

> iGoli 2002 *is an innovative transformation and development plan with the primary goal of effective, efficient and sustainable democratic governance ensuring stimulation of socio-economic investment opportunities which have local, provincial, national and international significance.*

A senior ANC councillor in the GJMC, Kenny Fihla (1999a, p3), had no problem defining the scope of *iGoli 2002*. He said that:

> iGoli 2002 *is a three-year plan, developed to address the challenges of finance, institutional arrangements and service delivery which faces Greater Johannesburg at the dawn of the new millennium. It is a plan that ushers in the birth of the uni-city by transforming local government in Greater Johannesburg through changed governance, financial viability, institutional transformation, sustainable development and enhanced service delivery.*

But *iGoli 2002* meant different things to different constituencies. It became the platform of the left-wing opposition to perceived neo-liberal tendencies within the ANC. It was depicted by business interests as the only sensible policy statement of the post-apartheid dispensation (*Business Day*, 9 March 2000). It was projected as the only viable alternative by those who held sway within the party structures of the ANC (ANC, undated). Within the city, the financial and organizational conditions to which *iGoli 2002* was a response meant that few contested the need to address the structural problems of the council. Debate centred rather on whether *iGoli 2002* was the most appropriate response to the crisis of local government.

As a background to our discussion on the *iGoli 2002* debate, it is helpful to review some of the changes in municipal business that were being proposed. Under *iGoli 2002*, a uni-city structure took over from the four sub-structures (North, South, East and West) and the GJTMC. At the same time, a number of internal organizational changes were introduced (see Figure 6.1) (Allen et al, 2001, p51). Under this scheme, about half of the council's business was placed under utilities or agencies, approximately 10 per cent was privatized or corporatized, and the remaining 40 per cent remained under the old arrangements of the core administration (see Table 6.2). In addition, a financial plan, a labour relations plan and special projects, such as the Johannesburg Development Agency, were introduced (GJMC, 1999b).

Table 6.2 *The relative weights of the proposed components of the* iGoli 2002 *restructuring*

	Institutional structure	Percentage of council activity
Programmes A and B	Utilities and agencies	50
Programme C	Privatization	3
Programme D	Corporatization	7
Programme E	Core administration	40

The Origins of the *iGoli 2002* Policy

The origins of *iGoli 2002* are widely asserted to lie in the financial crisis of 1997. Indeed, the fact that the city owed ESKOM (the Electricity Supply Commission) three months' payment and had a negative cash flow precipitated the intervention of national and provincial government. It was undoubtedly the prospect of the bankruptcy of the largest and most important city in the country that led to the appointment, by provincial government, of a committee of nominated representatives who were tasked with extraordinary powers to govern Johannesburg. However, Schmidt (1999) and others (Wooldridge, 1999b) have suggested that the state's response to the Johannesburg financial crisis also facilitated a radical transformation of the organization of local government across the country. In other words, the budgetary crisis laid the foundations for the adoption of a metropolitan model of government for the whole country. In short, the fiscal problems of Johannesburg provided an opportunity for national government to simultaneously address its concerns with the institutional and operational structures of all of the large municipalities, under the guise of remedying the problems of Johannesburg.

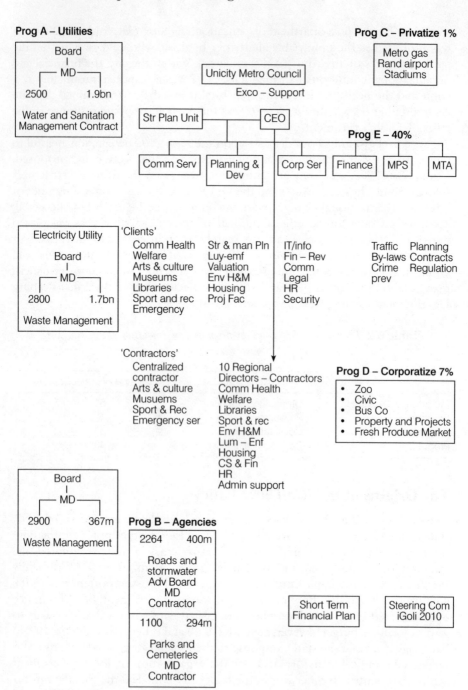

Figure 6.1 *The* iGoli 2002 *organizational structure proposal*

From the point of view of Johannesburg's voters, the principle of accountable and democratically elected local government was significantly challenged by the institutional transition induced by the financial crisis. Appointees to the Committee of 10, later expanded to the Committee of 15, were representative of, rather than accountable to, the five councils (the GJTMC and the four municipal sub-structures). In practice, this meant that ordinary residents could not lobby the committee, nor was the committee obliged to seek out the opinions of the public. Given the importance of the decisions that were made or set in motion by the committee, this was a serious shortcoming in the practice of local-government democracy.

iGoli 2002 was a legacy of the various emergency committees of the Committee of 15, which at the end of its term of office proposed the appointment of a Section 60 Committee of the council, to be known as the Transformation *Lekgotla*. The work allocated by the Committee of 15 to the Transformation *Lekgotla* (as a body no longer controlled by the higher tiers of government) is significant in that it foreshadowed the issues that would dominate *iGoli 2002*. The *Lekgotla*, meaning 'council' or 'committee', was established in terms of an agreement between the five councils in which they empowered the *Lekgotla* to perform certain of their key functions. This involved, in other words, the creation of a de-facto uni-city to prepare for the formal establishment of a uni-city after the local government elections of December 2000.

Emphasis, in the Transformation *Lekgotla*'s brief, was placed on finance, service delivery, human resources, organizational transformation and design, communication, and the development of external partnerships. This was in line with consultants' critiques of performance efficiency (Price Waterhouse, 1998). Social, economic and environmental development (the new powerful pro-poor functions constitutionally ascribed to local government) were excluded from the original remit of the *Lekgotla* (GJMC, 1999c). Under the planning and urbanization functions ascribed to the *Lekgotla*, provision was made for the review of LDOs; however, this only occurred because this was a legal obligation under the DFA. No other provision to consult with the public was enforced. In retrospect, it is easy to trace the 'technocist' concerns of *iGoli 2002* to the brief that the Committee of 15 handed over to the Transformation *Lekgotla* (Schmidt, 1999). Equally, the fact that mandatory public participation was maintained within the operating remit of *iGoli 2002* must be attributed to the constitution and national legislation.

As a body with 'emergency powers', the Transformation *Lekgotla* was able to act swiftly and decisively. It did, albeit with political approval of the five councils, if not the citizenry. For example, Petrus Mashishi of the South African Municipal Workers Union (SAMWU) made much of the fact that the council's posting of thousands of posters on township walls amounted to propaganda, not consultation (*Business Day*, 10 October 1999). One of the Transformation *Lekgotla*'s most significant moves involved the appointment of a high-powered team that was quickly dubbed the 'three knights' by the press (*Mail* and *Guardian*, 22 March 1999). Joining Kenny Fihla as chairperson of the Transformation *Lekgotla* were Khetso Gordhan, chief executive officer (CEO) of the council and ex-director general of the national Department of Transport, as well as Roland Hunter (ex-Planact and Gauteng provincial government), who took up the position of chief finance officer. Gordhan, in particular, had a reputation as a 'fix-it' man who was willing to implement massive changes and to streamline government bureaucracies. Under his helm in Pretoria, the Department of Transport was radically trimmed and dramatically privatized. With that reputation, alongside the 'dream team's'[7] impeccable anti-apartheid political credentials, (Gordhan was detained, Hunter imprisoned and Fihla spent time in exile), the three were given the responsibility of restructuring the way Johannesburg did business, a task made easier only by the latitude induced by the exaggerated financial crisis.

Welcoming the appointment of Gordhan in Johannesburg, the *Financial Mail* announced (*Financial Mail*, 8 January 1999, p22):

> *This week the restructuring – some might call it the rescue – of Johannesburg has begun, involving probably the most radical change in style of government since the ANC came to power in 1994… there are at least three reasons for optimism that the recovery programme now underway in Johannesburg could improve the city's fortunes. The first is to be found in the impressive capabilities and track record of the new manager. The second is that the metro council's ANC leadership seems finally to have found a coherent strategy for metropolitan government that embraces the private sector. Thirdly, government negotiators recently signed a framework of agreement with COSATU that will enable local governments to outsource service provision without a labour backlash.*

On 19 January 1999, less than a month after the appointment of Khetso Gordhan, a Bite the Bullet Workshop was called. The stated purpose of the meeting involving senior management and other 'key stakeholders' was 'to present ideas of reorganization to increase income or reduce expenditure while enhancing performance' (GJMC, 1999d). The intensive strategy exercise in early 1999 led to the preparation of a comprehensive and far-reaching three-year plan to address the institutional and financial challenges. What emerged was *iGoli 2002*, a policy that was loosely based on the design principles of the Committee of 15 and their consultants' organizational review. Despite these strong roots in the committee, admittedly a much narrowed and less representative committee procedure than usual in the council, the *iGoli* plan has increasingly become associated with one man, Khetso Gordhan, the new city manager. Setting out his vision for the city, Gordhan stressed the importance of focusing on organizational arrangements and finance practice in order to enable the council to be 'run as a business' (GJMC, 1999a). For this particular remark, as well as for the substance of *iGoli 2002* more generally, Gordhan has been heavily criticized (McKinley, undated). Opponents of the *iGoli* plan were clear: despite what the new leadership of the city suggested, *iGoli* was a policy that was not good for labour and not good for the urban poor.

IS *IGOLI* 2002 A POLICY THAT CAN UNITE A DIVIDED CITY?

The plan prioritizes the unserviced and the poor. It focuses on lifeline services, cross-subsidies within and between services, addresses backlogs, as well as the economic growth and financial constraints that will make available more resources to improve the city's operating and capital expenditure. (Fihla, 1999a, p6)

iGoli 2002's objectives were clearly premised on achieving both efficiency and equity. The subsequent debate that emerged within the ANC Alliance related to the strategies for achieving greater efficiency and the question of whether improved performance necessarily enhanced equity. Whereas the ANC-led Johannesburg officials and senior councillors associated with the Transformation *Lekgotla* backed the national Department of Finance's position on GEAR, this generally neo-liberal macro-economic policy framework was not shared by all. No sooner had business welcomed the *iGoli 2002* initiative than the Johannesburg authorities began to draw criticism from organized labour for its anti-poor, socially polarizing implications. According to those individuals opposing *iGoli*, who were made up largely of SAMWU, COSATU and the SACP, the views of the Johannesburg authorities were indistinguishable from the discredited approaches to poverty reduction that relied on the trickle down of growth (Bond, 2000b).

Disagreements over *iGoli 2002* amount to more than an internecine fight that spilled beyond civic chambers or the meeting rooms of the ANC caucus. The conflict became the basis of the most organized campaign by labour against the ANC government since the Alliance in support of the 1994 electoral victory. The underlying positions that were adopted reflect diametrically opposed approaches to the entire project of post-apartheid reconstruction and development; these were larger disputes that came to be played out on the Johannesburg stage. Despite the memorandum of understanding between government and trade unions over privatization in 1998, SAMWU declared a dispute with the GJMC in October 1999 (*Business Day*, 5 November 1999). Under that 'framework agreement', the GJMC, as part of the South African Local Government Association (SALGA), agreed to prioritize the public sector as the preferred deliverer of services, while SAMWU agreed not to oppose the privatization of state assets (Wooldridge, 1999a; *Business Day*, 16 September 1999). Both parties felt that the framework agreement was violated, either by the design of or the response to *iGoli 2002* respectively. The dispute was referred to the National Economic, Development and Labour Council (NEDLAC); but, in the meantime, municipal workers took the matter to the streets in protest. About 12,000 protesters handed Fihla, the anti-apartheid veteran-turned Transformation *Lekgotla* chairperson, a memorandum just before he had to be 'whisked away from angry workers who were baying for his blood'.

Yet, *iGoli 2002* was also promoted as a tool for reducing inequality, promoting poverty reduction and ensuring a better city for all (Allen et al, 2001).

Analysis of the council's press releases, the city's documents and the memoranda of the ANC on *iGoli 2002* suggests that the promoters of *iGoli* saw it as contributing to DLG and poverty reduction in specified, if diverse, ways (see Table 6.3, left-hand column). Three main justifications for the pro-poor rationale of *iGoli 2002* were provided. First, it was hoped that the plan would release more money for new investment through greater efficiency. Second, the response to the existing municipal crisis was seen as a politically strategic intervention that would enlist the support of most stakeholders. Third, *iGoli* was seen as remaining rooted in the longer-term planning principles that were explicitly in the interests of the poor. Overall, the approach embedded in the policy statements, and discussions by *iGoli*'s promoters, suggested that equity and poverty reduction could not occur without enhanced municipal efficiency or 'sustainable growth' (Allen et al, 2001, p43). The reorganized and improved delivery of basic services across the city was projected as the key to stimulating economic growth, reducing unemployment and facilitating social development.

Within Johannesburg, the primary objection to *iGoli* was expressed in ideological terms (see Table 6.3, right-hand column). Central to the argument of the left was that the retreat of the state, especially in the face of such obvious imperatives for social and economic redistribution, made no sense. Concerns claimed as secondary, although clearly weighty, related to the longer-term loss and outsourcing of municipal workers' jobs. More general issues about the impact of *iGoli* on the poor were to be found within the SAMWU/SACP attack on *iGoli*; although fears such as those relating to unaffordable tariff increases and poor infrastructural maintenance by privatized utilities were not as prominent as one might have expected. Indeed, there was much more focus on the undemocratic process of formulating *iGoli*, than on its potentially unequal outcomes. In one of its most strongly worded condemnations, SAMWU reported (SAMWU, 1999a, p1):

> *iGoli 2002 is a plan designed to make Johannesburg attractive to business. It was not an inclusive process – there were a handful of officials, high-ranking councillors and consultants who drew up the plan. What kind of democracy is being built when citizens are seen as nothing more than 'customers'? What kind of partnership is being built when unions are only informed about the plan once it has been adopted?*

The point about the lack of consultation over *iGoli* by the city with its Alliance partners is interesting, not least because this interpretation was contested. Whereas the chairperson of the Transformation *Lekgotla* claimed that 'the city had consulted widely over the past eight months on its *iGoli 2002* transformation plan' (Fihla, 1999a), Alliance partners had a very different view of the process. SAMWU noted that the council had failed to call it to meetings and suggested that there was a tendency for the council to ignore internal democratic procedures. The union went as far as to declare *iGoli* an undemocratic process in both the commercial and the alternative press (*Business Day*, 10 October 1999; *Homeless Talk*, 5 December 1999). On its website, the union declared (SAMWU, 1999b):

Table 6.3 *The* iGoli 2002 *debate*

	How iGoli 2002 *will promote poverty reduction* (GJMC, 1999b; 1999c; Fihla,1999a; Schmidt, 1999)	*How* iGoli 2002 *will negate poverty reduction* (McKinley, undated; Weeks, 1999; *Business Day*, 16 September 1999; 1 October 1999; 27 October 1999; SAMWU, 1999a)
Funding	1 It will overcome the previous position in the GJMC where there was no funding for infrastructure targeted at the poor. 2 Balancing the budget will enhance the funds available for capital expenditure. 3 It will remove the situation of top-heavy, expensive administration and release resources for the capital budget. 4 Improved efficiency will result in increased revenue for cross-subsidies.	1 It threatens existing cross-subsidization to the working class.
Political process	1 It will restore the confidence of ratepayers and residents in the ability of the council to perform its mandate and to ensure their ongoing participation in local government.	1 There has been insufficient consultation with major stakeholders within the tripartite alliance. 2 The process reveals the political arrogance of the GJMC executive who attack rather than consult Alliance partners. 3 The council violated agreements with the SACP, COSATU and the ANC. 4 GJMC is breaking its links and no longer bringing governance closer to the people.
Ideological basis of the policy	1 *iGoli 2002* is founded on pro-poor values including: • participation; • meeting basic needs; • ensuring affordability; • sustainability.	1 *iGoli* is a neo-liberal approach to service delivery based upon financial concerns, not social need. 2 Business objectives undermine political accountability. 3 *iGoli* supporters come from international finance. 4 No community group has expressed support for *iGoli*. 5 Privatization reduces the ability of the state to define an active social and economic agenda.
Efficiency	1 Improved water and sanitation supply will 'enhance quality of life and health for residents and	1 Officials' efficient performance is dependent upon expensive bonus payments to senior management.

increase attractiveness for investors'.

2 The new investment plan will channel resources to areas of greatest need (poverty focus is implicit, not explicit).

3 Services will be better maintained because loan finance can be raised by utilities.

4 Areas of special need known as Priority Interventions Zones (including, some but not all, of the poorest neighbourhoods) will be targeted.

2 Performance indicators remove the ability to negotiate need in the local context, making for inefficiency.

3 State-driven investment and service provision is the most efficient way to transform society. Privatization undermines this process.

4 The aim of zero deficits is misplaced, as the cause of the financial crisis is managerial incompetence.

Other

1 Privatization of council housing will allow long-term tenants to purchase houses at reduced rates.

1 The council has no plan B in place to address the needs of the poor when *iGoli 2002* fails them.

Jobs

1 There will be no job losses over the next three years.

1 Many SAMWU jobs are under threat.

2 It threatens labour standards and introduces sub-contracting.

3 *iGoli* is selling off assets that create jobs (eg fresh produce market).

Tariffs

1 Delegated powers (to utilities) will promote efficiency and, eventually, lower tariffs.

1 Under-privatized utilities that are run for profit tariffs will increase.

The employer is now informing and imposing iGoli 2002 *on the stakeholders at the same time. Unions, communities and democratically elected councillors have been actively excluded from the formulation of the plan. This undermines the spirit of the 'White Paper for Local Government' and the constitution.*

The relationship between the Johannesburg Council and the unions was not the only relationship that was strained by *iGoli*. Both the ANC and SACP suffered casualties. ANC Councillor Trevor Ngwane was removed from office after he criticized the *iGoli* business plan for its controversial commercialization and privatization plans that would lead to services becoming unaffordable. Ngwane was the chairperson of the ANC's northern sub-region, a Pimville councillor and chairperson of the town planning committee (*Mail and Guardian*, 27 October 1999). He later joined SAMWU as an organizer. Ngwane's suspension was formally criticized by the Freedom of Expression Institute, noting that the ANC in the GJMC, in stripping Ngwane of both party and council membership, had blurred the line between party and state. SACP provincial executive member Dale McKinley was likewise stripped of his position for publicly criticizing the terms of the ANC/SACP Alliance (*Mail and Guardian*, 1 September 2000).

Perhaps the most telling reflection of the relationship between the city and organized labour can be drawn from a Venn diagram (see Figure 6.2) that was completed by senior city officials in response to our request to identify the

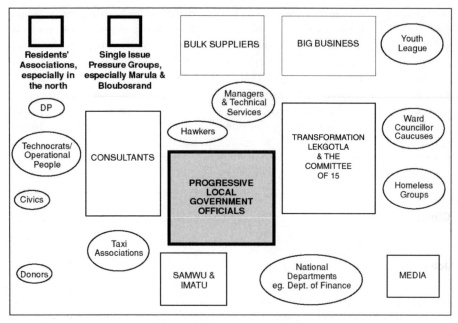

Figure 6.2 *Local government officials' view of the main players in city politics*

players who were the most influential in determining the council's direction. The unions were depicted as less important players than the ANC national and provincial executives, the Transformation *Lekgotla* and the role of private consultants. Interestingly, according to our analysis of the Venn diagram,[8] the unions nonetheless had significantly more status than the civic organizations, ratepayers and other civil-society groups. In other words, amidst the increasing levels of conflict over *iGoli*, labour emerged as the major player and, according to one official informant who participated in the focus group, was seen as having the power to 'make or break Johannesburg's ability to move on privatization'. What is most striking about this particular official's interpretation of the city's relations with civil society organizations is that it reflects the dominance of organized labour and the SACP over other community-based voices in the opposition to *iGoli*. The civics, for example, although clearly supportive of the SAMWU position, appeared in this conflict only in a supportive role in a single incident of mass street protest. There is, moreover, no record of any engagement by a civic organization, ratepayers' association or NGO with the city on *iGoli*, directly or indirectly, or on the major *iGoli* initiatives, such as creating service partnerships. Yet, as we show in Chapters 7–10, the battle for better service provision lies at the heart of community organization in most poor neighbourhoods. Clearly, the civics and CBOs more generally have been unable to take advantage of conditions of enhanced local democracy and to organize as effectively as they might at the city scale.

Nevertheless, the fact that the situation is more nuanced than polarized positions allow can be illustrated by reference to the fact that under *iGoli 2002* one of the first major projects was the creation of a water and sanitation utility.

A management contract was issued to a consortium led by Northumbrian Water and Suez Lyonnaise des Eaux at the end of 1999. An overview of the process to date suggests that, from the point of view of promoting inclusive governance, the practice of efficient and equitable service delivery to the poor is more complex than either the GJMC or SAMWU believed. The most obvious point in this regard is that a large proportion of the poor of Johannesburg currently receives a huge indirect subsidy on the cost of services; they are either not billed for water and sanitation services, or they do not pay their bills. In the case of water, a further 'subsidy' is drawn by about half of all informal residents through illegal connections (GJMC, 1999b). Thus, the formalization of any relationship of service delivery, privatized or not, is likely to impact negatively upon the poor, at least in the short term. This is true even for those consumers who are not billed directly, such as the tenants in inner-city apartments and in Soweto's backyard – they already pay privately for water supply and sanitation with landlords, having responded to the increased pressure to pay for services by raising rents (GJMC, 2001b).

Historically, the supply of water and sanitation failed basic environmental standards, had no free basic allowance of water and was not a service that extended to all citizens. There were also severe institutional problems within the line department arising from the creation of non-racial local government (Allen et al, 2001). Under the new dispensation, the utility is obliged to meet nationally defined standards or it will forfeit its licence to operate. As such, it may well improve water supply in Johannesburg. These delivery standards include supplying 6000 litres of water per month free of charge to every Johannesburg household. There is, however, already evidence that the poor are invisible stakeholders in the overall scheme of the Johannesburg Water and Sanitation Utility, and the long-term role of the utility in providing both efficient and affordable services remains untested. In the short term, the board of directors includes no community spokespeople and does not purport to be representative. Residents' representatives were advertised for in the local press (nonsensical, in a highly illiterate society). The corporate management strategy includes no brief to develop pro-poor tariffs, an 'indigence' policy or other strategies for targeting the poor. Working groups cover a range of topics, but not social or community development or education. Given that it is in the detail, as well as in the broad principle of how services are delivered, that poverty-sensitive frameworks of governance are established, there appears to be cause for concern. To date, there has been insufficient attention paid to the needs of the poor in designing service partnerships that will reduce the unacceptable inequalities that exist in Johannesburg's infrastructure and services, both in provision and maintenance.

What the *iGoli 2002* debate created was a stalemate at the level of policy formulation, between the city, on the one hand, and one section of civil society (the unions), on the other. Pitched exclusively at a broad level of political debate on the shortcomings of neo-liberal policy, discussion on democratic local governance in Johannesburg became overly simplistic, hinging entirely upon whether services should be delivered by the state or the private sector. This narrow focus meant that the service-delivery function of local government was prioritized above any other roles for the state or for public–private partnerships in urban poverty reduction. The particularities of the *iGoli* debate have also ignored the fact that the test of inclusive governance lies in the specifics of how services are provided to, and consumed by, the poor, how they are funded, managed, maintained and cross-subsidized, and, most importantly, how they are coordinated, monitored and controlled. In Johannesburg the discussion about how to make service delivery contribute to a CDS that aims to reduce inequality has barely got off the starting blocks.

Fuelling the polarized debate around *iGoli*, it would appear that SAMWU and the GJMC agreed on one thing – that basic service delivery lay at the heart of local government – even though they held profoundly different views on how basic needs should be secured. Of concern is the fact that the stalemate left little room (or trust) for a wider range of players to reflect on and revise service-delivery strategies. Moreover, the opportunities to advance other pro-poor strategies (such as participatory development approaches, social development, local economic development, environmental health) within the metropolitan area appear to have been minimized. In a city where it is not unreasonable to predict full housing and service provision in the medium term, this seems short-sighted. Moreover, given the high levels of social dysfunction and exclusion in Johannesburg, the narrow emphasis on infrastructure and meeting basic needs through housing and services as the sole platform for addressing urban poverty seems misplaced.

CONCLUSION

Over the past two chapters, our discussion has moved from the dissection of the design and architecture of the 'decentralized' local government system in South Africa to its functional operation in the reconstruction of Johannesburg's urban space. When the euphoria associated with local democracy gave way to fiscal austerity, there was an obvious shift in the regimes of power. What is clear is that the populist interests of those who gained political influence in the first phase of interim local government in Johannesburg were not coterminous with those of the ANC nationally, where the neo-liberal agenda of GEAR was ascendant. Because of the hyped interpretation of the financial position of Johannesburg during the late 1990s, the constellation of power within the city that coalesced around *iGoli 2002* was generally more concerned with efficiency than equity. However, political commitment to the equality clauses of the constitution remained; where it was absent, it was technically required as part of the developmental design of the local government system and the tradition of participatory planning. While the *iGoli 2002* process was widely associated with the closing down of opportunities for democracy, equity and participation, the metropolitan council, through its legal commitment to alternative city development, has maintained its policy of prioritizing the needs of citizens. It is thus in the institutional context of DLG, and the contradictory financial constraints imposed upon local government practice, that residents of Johannesburg had to negotiate their access to municipal resources. Our attention now shifts to examine how effective and flexible these institutional arrangements of the interim government were for residents in the highly divergent and polarized residential areas of post-Fordist Johannesburg.

Part 4

Living in a Divided City

Chapter 7

The Inner-city Challenge: Locating Partners for Urban Regeneration

INTRODUCTION

For quite some time, and certainly long before changes in Johannesburg's governance in the post-apartheid era, the inner city had been read as a space that was systematically slipping beyond the control of both national and local government. Moreover, these patterns were dramatically talked up in the local press at a time when government seemed unwilling or unable to respond. As the political transition unfolded, and while the metropolitan council got its political and administrative house in order, there was a very real sense that no one was minding the inner-city store. It was in this context that the state of the inner city became a symbolic test of the state's control over city development. As a result, and in line with the developmental vision of reconstructed local government, much effort is now being directed toward inner-city regeneration in Johannesburg.

The case for the regeneration of the Johannesburg inner city rests on both its commercial and residential problems. Metropolitan intervention in the inner city, once it finally occurred, was biased in favour of getting the commercial landscape right. However, the regeneration vision did involve tackling the problem neighbourhoods and buildings that lead to the inner city being perceived as a frightening or difficult place in which to be. We argue that this bias towards improving the economic viability of central Johannesburg, while quite understandable and indeed worthy, has worked against the interests of ordinary inner-city residents and has precipitated the view that 'community' in the inner city is dead. While the city was fairly successful in identifying partners for commercial regeneration, at least in the formal sector, its record has been less impressive with respect to engaging with informal and illicit economies and in the residential sphere. We make the point that the overwhelming complexity of inner-city problems, and the adoption of an ambitious commercial regeneration strategy, has tended towards a discourse of public–private partnerships, to the exclusion of other sectors, despite a discourse of community participation.

Johannesburg's inner-city regeneration has, moreover, hinged upon a 'precinct-and-project' approach to planning. Following the precinct-and-project logic, city officials identify particular interest groups and engage with their representatives over specific space or time-bound issues. This occurs at the expense of extended engagement with residents as citizens in the context of a protracted process of urban governance. In this way, the consultation exercises and partnerships established by the council in the inner city differ from the neighbourhood-scale engagement embarked upon by CDFs elsewhere in the city. In this chapter we trace the council's search for partners in the regeneration of the inner city, exploring both its relatively successful links with business and the shortcomings of its ongoing association with residents. Our attention focuses on the work of the Inner-City Office (ICO) and on the work of Yeoville, one of the lesser-studied inner-city suburbs. Through an assessment of the partnerships sought, wrought and missed in the various regeneration projects that were taken up, we seek to understand the prospects for state–society relations at the suburban or neighbourhood scale.[1]

THE CASE FOR INNER-CITY REGENERATION IN JOHANNESBURG

Internationally, inner-city decay is one of the most pervasive of urban problems. Correspondingly, the formation of public–private partnerships to drive massive urban renewal projects dominates city management, particularly in the north. Johannesburg's inner-city problem is depicted by local academics, the press and politicians as bigger and more serious than anywhere else in the world. In fact, the built environment of the Johannesburg CBD and its surrounds is in remarkably good condition. True, vacancy rates in the office buildings are high and the infrastructure of some apartment buildings has begun to show severe signs of wear and tear. The more sophisticated shops have moved to the suburbs and the streets and theatres are quiet at night for fear of crime. But the critical factor that served to put and keep the inner city at the top of the metropolitan agenda was not characterized by these problems alone. Underpinning the ubiquitous focus on 'crime and grime', and the degree of hysteria about the public health risks of informal street trade and densely occupied buildings, was 'the race question'. For over a decade, the desegregation of the inner city, from a once white-dominated space to one now almost entirely peopled by blacks, has been at the forefront of Johannesburg's elite public consciousness. In this radicalized conception of the city, desegregation and ghettoization are inextricably linked.

The democratization of local government, instead of assuaging widespread fears of CBD downturn and inner-city decline, compounded public anxieties about the maintenance of 'standards' by seizing on the issue of urban regeneration of the inner city. This was especially the case during the interim phase of local government and included the active encouragement of formal business. Because of the latent potency of 'the race question' in South Africa, inner-city regeneration has gained rather than lost its political prominence on the post-apartheid metropolitan agenda. This is despite the fact that, by any measure, the population of the inner city is not the poorest in Johannesburg, and there are more dire problems of poverty and blight elsewhere in the metropolitan area. The inner-city planning focus of the old Johannesburg City Council has survived multiple rounds of post-apartheid local government restructuring, to become the ICO of the GJTMC. The future of the regeneration agency is, moreover, assured. Under the *iGoli 2002* recommendations, the ICO's successor, the Johannesburg Development Authority (JDA), is charged with the ongoing revitalization of the inner city. Against this clear prioritization of the inner city and the seeming endorsement of a 'project-and-precinct' approach to solving its problems, we ask how inner-city regeneration can assist in uniting the divided city of Johannesburg.

The territory referred to as the inner city of Johannesburg is both large and diverse, with a commercial core surrounded by a high-density residential zone that houses some 700,000 people. This is almost one quarter of the city's 2.8 million population (see Figure 4.1).[2] Generally lost in both official and popular discourse on the inner city is a sense of how the functional diversity of the area has affected its development. While appearing an obvious point – all inner-city areas are characterized by a combination of commercial, retail and residential uses – in Johannesburg, the complexity of mixed land use was compounded by apartheid planning and its differential treatment of land according to its racial occupation, as well as by functional zoning. Because of the legacy of apartheid's land-use regulations, commercial, retail and residential changes in the inner city did not unfold sequentially or harmoniously, a fact that helps to explain the timing and the slow decline of the urban core.

From as early as the 1970s, while the legislation associated with the segregationist Group Areas Act was still firmly entrenched, the movement of corporate premises to the city's periphery had already begun. The skyline of downtown Johannesburg is still dominated by the building that once housed the Johannesburg Stock Exchange (JSE) in Diagonal Street, a grand blue-glass structure designed to resemble a multifaceted diamond. The city's streets are wide and paved and are host to some really splendid examples of colonial and modernist architecture (Chipkin, 1993). However, a closer look shows the JSE and many of its greatest beneficiaries to have relocated to Sandton. The once-proud Carlton Centre, with its 50,000 square metres of office space, suffered an occupancy rate of only 30 per cent until it was taken over by the transport para-statal Transnet. As Tomlinson (1999) has pointed out, the parallels with urban decay in many American cities are striking. However, as he also makes clear, one needs to be careful not to extend the analogies too far. Unlike many other parts of the world, the decamping of corporate capital to the 'edge cities' (Beauregard, 1995; Garreau, 1991) of Rosebank, Sandton and Midrand did not instantly spell the end of the vibrancy of the CBD, although office vacancy rates did rise steadily (Beavon, 1998). Today, downtown Johannesburg resembles other African cities as closely as it does Detroit, Pittsburgh or Philadelphia. Street vendors, hawkers, pavement hairdressers, street children and muggers all jostle for space and place on streets lamented as sites of 'crime and grime'.

Throughout the 1970s and early 1980s, inner-city residential areas continued to enjoy a bohemian reputation, providing a flourishing urbanism unknown anywhere else in South Africa (Mabin, 1998). In residential terms, it was not until the end of the 1980s that any significant changes in the inner city manifested themselves. It was only when state housing subsidies for whites induced them to move out of the inner city into home ownership in the suburbs that pent-up black housing demand found some respite in the desegregation of city rental accommodation (Crankshaw and White, 1995; Morris, 1994). Coloured, Indian and African professionals were first to venture illegally into the 'whites only' city. When they subsequently moved on to the desegregated suburbs, the class profile of inner-city residency shifted to lower-paid service workers. As rental to black people became legal, so the rents dropped. This, in turn, saw demand rise on the part of the local African population who were forced out of the townships by the housing shortage. This was accompanied by the immigration of large numbers of foreign-born Africans who headed for inner-city residential areas, leading to further increased demand and, ultimately, overcrowding (Morris, 1999).

The first parts of the inner city to change their racial composition were the high-rise areas of Hillbrow, Joubert Park and Berea (Crankshaw and White, 1995; Morris, 1994). In 1985, 70 per cent of apartments were occupied by whites, 25 per cent by coloureds and Indians, and 5 per cent by Africans (de Coning, Fick and Olivier, 1987). By 1991, the proportion of apartments occupied by whites had dropped to 54 per cent, while by 1996 it was a mere 5 per cent. Correspondingly, the proportion of apartments occupied by Africans increased from 41 per cent in 1991 to 85 per cent in 1996. The residential areas of the inner city may legitimately continue their long-held claim to be the most cosmopolitan part of the city, although representation of nationals from other parts of Africa now dramatically outstrips that of the once-dominant European migrants. During the 1960s and 1970s, about one third of all residents in the high-rise areas were foreign born (Jubber, 1973), most coming from Europe. Today, however, most foreigners are from other African countries.

There is general agreement that inner-city decline has been hastened by racial desegregation. The reasons have more to do with the dynamics of landlord–tenant relationships than with changing occupational and educational profiles associated with race (Crankshaw and White, 1995; Morris, 1994). Landlords, or their appointed lessors, neglected the most decayed buildings and allowed services to deteriorate. Research suggests that the resources and managerial style of landlords were crucial in determining whether or not racial desegregation was accompanied by the physical decline of apartment buildings (Crankshaw and White, 1995). Those who were committed to developing good relationships with their tenants and had the resources to maintain their buildings were able to make long-term profits without going into a cycle of physical decline. By contrast, landlords who lacked the financial resources to maintain buildings and who were not committed to working through difficulties with their tenants soon entered a vicious cycle of conflict and physical decline. Local government also contributed by failing to address the problem because legislation that aimed to prevent neglect by landlords was both inadequate and was seldom applied by officials.

In spite of all these changes – office decentralization, the changing racial composition of tenants and the associated decline in the built environment in the inner-city residential rim – the day-time vitality of the CBD persisted. In the first instance, the retail function was maintained by the presence of relatively affluent black people who were the first in-movers to the city centre. Furthermore, throughout the 1980s and 1990s the lack of retail facilities in African residential neighbourhoods forced Sowetans to shop in downtown Johannesburg. Nevertheless, the stability and scale of formal retail activity have gradually declined with the extension of mall culture and the growth of shopping centres within former African townships. However, retail activity has never collapsed and has been significantly buoyed by the growth of Johannesburg as a regional shopping centre for Southern Africa.

DOWNTOWN DECLINE AND THE PARTNERSHIP BUSINESS

The cries of 'downtown downturn' (Beavon, 1997; 2001) accompanying Johannesburg's transformation into an African city have been fuelled by the much vaunted 'capital flight' out of the CBD. Alexander and Oldert (2000) cited in Beavon (2001) show that during the beginning of 1991, of the 759 firms listed on the JSE, 197 had their registered offices in the CBD of Johannesburg. By 1998, the Johannesburg CBD was still home to 129 listed companies; but by 2000, only 38 of them remained, while 7 were companies that had not been listed before. Fear and, indeed, racism on the part of many whites who decline to venture out into streets so uncompromisingly occupied by black shoppers, visitors, workers and traders, alongside crime, have also fuelled the northward drift. Nevertheless, flight has not been absolute. The face of retail has changed dramatically, with banks, shops, markets and stalls all catering for a predominantly African trade. Indeed, the bulk of the private banking sector remains located in the CBD, a pattern that defies the stereotype of capital flight (Monitor 2000a). Former CEO of the metropolitan council Ketso Gordhan described the transition thus (Beall and Lawson, 1999):

> *Johannesburg used to be an old, established white commercial-retail and financial centre. It is going to become, over the next five to ten years, a multifaceted African city. It is going to have different types of retail activities addressing the needs of the current consumers who have come to the city. We have over 300,000 visitors a month from the countries to the north of us who come to Johannesburg exclusively to shop. So, there is a thriving retail business, but it's not what it used to be. We have a thriving manufacturing sector in the inner city, which was never part of the old Johannesburg... So, it is a different type of city, and I think that our job as a local government is to read the writing on the wall and go with the flow.*

In the declining days of apartheid, it was capital that took a lead in initiating the partnership for regeneration aimed at bringing the CBD under control (Mandy, 1984). The branch of capital involved in commercial property development was particularly concerned because it stood to lose profoundly as rents declined and property values went into free fall. Through the Central Johannesburg Partnership (CJP), and the various forums, associations, coalitions and partnerships that have followed in its wake, our research suggests that capital has continued to have an influence both on the regeneration of the inner city and on the metropolitan council's approach to this process. A key moment was the setting up of the CJP in 1992, a partnership that was essentially one between the formal business community and the local authority. Although it had a limited life span, not least of all because, as a structure, it excluded other stakeholders, it was extremely influential in determining subsequent institutional arrangements and visions for the inner city.

Capital's stake in the early efforts to revitalize the inner city was aptly summed up by a representative of Anglo-American Property Services (Beall and Lawson, 1999), an offshoot of one of South Africa's giant multinational conglomerates:

> *Anglo-American Property Services has put a lot of effort over the last five to ten years into trying to generate some interest in the inner city, because that's where a lot of the stock that they manage is located... Anglo-American Property Services also put a lot of funding into the CJP, and I suppose the work that the CJP did has all been preparatory work, in a sense, creating the right sort of rhetoric and bringing international experience here. And rhetoric starts changing attitudes, and then people can think in terms of new paradigms; and that's certainly been there, in the pot, even through the wrong structures... So, you can never wipe out the value, really. I mean the value's been there and I think that Anglo-American Property Services has been significant in contributing to the creation of it.*

In order to establish the rhetoric and shift the paradigm, the CJP was intent on learning from the American experience. This they did through a series of events such as study tours to the US and commissioning the head of the American Downtown Association to act as a consultant to the CJP. The CJP also contributed to community workshops and public-visioning exercises, involving a wide range of people who reached an uncanny degree of consensus on the importance of ridding the city of 'crime and grime' (Tomlinson, 1999).

What particularly captured the imagination of business and proved to be a tangible legacy of the CJP was the concept of business improvement districts (BIDs). BIDs were seen as vital for regaining control of the streets, which, in turn, was seen as a prerequisite for reversing inner-city decay. The main aim of BIDs was to consolidate the vision of the municipality and the business sector in the inner city. Four BIDS were established within the inner city. The largest comprised 24 city blocks, the next biggest comprised about 14 blocks, and the two smaller BIDs consisted of between 4 and 5 blocks each (see Figure 4.1). Through the collection of a voluntary levy, property owners and businesses also paid for a host of visible services that operated exclusively within the boundaries of each BID. BIDs provided services for their districts over and above those provided by the council, but ran in cooperation and coordination with the council. Typically, they included paying for private security officers, who were in radio contact with a privately financed central control room and with backup from an armed response unit, and supervisors who patrolled the district on motorcycles. A second level of service offered was street-cleaning and basic maintenance, such as repainting traffic poles. Interviews held with representatives of the CJP, participating businesses and staff employed by the BIDs confirmed that the latter have been very successful in their impact.

The Johannesburg vision of commercial revitalization took its cue from international, as well as local, capitalists. The external influence can be seen in the promotion of major urban projects such as the Newtown Cultural Precinct, which the chief executive officer justified as 'a strategy that has worked in many parts of the world and major cities in the US'. The American approach to crime and grime through a 'zero-tolerance' stance, in respect of informal street traders and law-breakers, was also endorsed by the CJP and the city government. In the case of Johannesburg, where the city had no policing, function zero-tolerance policy could not be mimicked. The council, however, cooperated with business and endorsed an initiative to get the by-laws changed in order to prevent unregulated street-vending and to ensure the removal of street vendors to formalized markets. Much later, in 2001, a metropolitan police force would be established. Getting the informal traders off the streets became one of the two principal initiatives of the metropolitan council's ICO, which was formed in 1998. Among the markets it constructed for informal street traders was the Yeoville Rocky Street Market, completed in late 1999.

Capital has also had a role to play in terms of the CBD as a place of residence. For example, the onslaught against 'crime and grime' by business improvement districts has been supplemented by social initiatives aimed at tackling rough sleepers – for instance, the introduction of *Homeless Talk*, a newspaper sold by homeless people that is now almost self-sustaining and independent, and the establishment of a night shelter. The initiatives were also instrumental in promoting a 'car-guard scheme' where homeless people are encouraged to protect parked vehicles from petty thieves and hijackers in exchange for a gratuity from car owners. On a grander scale, Anglo-American Property Services has been considering turning vacant CBD offices into targeted residential accommodation. As one of the company's representatives explained (Beall and Lawson, 1999):

> *Our research is telling us, on the residential side, that the people who are locating in the inner city, who like it here, are not your families. They're the singles or the couples without children who tend to see this as a place to live for five years. It's almost like a reception area – you leave home, you want to put your foot in the urban economy and this is the place to do it because there's a bit of activity goes on at night... and people can rent for a fairly small percentage of their disposable income.*

An obstacle in the way of these ambitions, however, was the presence of privately owned apartment blocks that were neglected or even abandoned by absentee landlords who had left them to fall into shocking disrepair.

Addressing the problem of blighted buildings was the second major platform of the ICO; it did this through its Better Buildings Programme. The programme kicked into operation when the debt owed to the metropolitan council by the building owner exceeded its market value, enabling the council to facilitate its sale to a willing developer who could engage in upgrading. The council was then able to recover its debts through 'structured repayment schedules linked to the profitability of the new housing units' (Allen et al, 2001, p107). Tackling the issue from the other end were organizations such as the Inner-City Housing Upgrading Trust (ICHUT) that were supported by commercial property interests and largely funded by the US Agency for International Development (USAID). The ICHUT provided short-term housing finance to groups of tenants or small private developers who wanted to buy and upgrade abandoned buildings. In addition, ICHUT helped tenants to apply for government housing subsidies and longer-term loans from the National Housing Finance Corporation, with the aim of creating additional housing stock of a reasonable quality and standard in the inner city.

What we can conclude from the above is that the role of the formal business community in the inner city has been indispensable to its reinvigoration. However, capital is invariably self-interested, and the investment of time, energy and resources in improving residential accommodation is as much about keeping general property values up as about providing homes and shelter. Even the altruism of schemes for the homeless is thinly veiled, as was suggested by the city improvement districts manager of the CJP when he said: 'We believe that homelessness is a major problem that detracts from people reinvesting back into the city.' Nevertheless, the impact of the partnership with business has been positive, and here the interests of capital converge completely with those of the metropolitan council, which continues to be concerned about plummeting rateable values and non-payment of services on the part of entire buildings.

While the boundaries between the local authority and formal business are fairly porous, those between formal business and those in the informal economy are not. In this respect, capital is an exclusive rather than an inclusive group, with financial, retail and property interests seeking not to embrace or even benignly tolerate competition from informal traders, but rather to keep it out or contain it in circumscribed markets. In this, the ICO has been complicit.

Commercial Regeneration: the Project-and-Precinct Approach

In other contexts, the ICO might be described as an urban development corporation (UDC). The ICO, like UDCs elsewhere, has addressed the complex social and economic fabric of the inner city chiefly through the execution of time-bound projects. The ICO took some of these projects over from other departments; some projects, it conceived itself (Allen et al, 2001, p107). High-profile examples include its two premier initiatives, the Metropolitan Trading Company (MTC), set up to execute the construction and management of markets, and the Better Buildings Programme, designed to tackle so-called 'bad buildings'. ICO projects also included the redevelopment of the area around the Supreme Court, a local economic-development project involving the garment industry, and the construction of a multimillion Rand taxi rank, designed to contain the pandemonium created by a largely unregulated, competitive and violent taxi industry (Khosa, 1991; 1992) (see Figure 4.1).

Remarkable though some of its achievements are, the ICO has not been without its critics. While its project approach to city revitalization in many ways has made pragmatic sense for investors, residents and the city authorities alike, the ICO has suffered from tunnel vision, which has affected its dealings with residents in the inner city. The genuine commitment of the ICO to community consultation and participation can be seen in the nature of its projects, its involvement in multi-sectoral consultative visioning exercises, and a number of 'good-practice' outcomes. By virtue of its structure and functions, however, the ICO has not engaged in real participatory processes of 'good governance' with all stakeholders, or with the residents of the inner city at the neighbourhood scale.

One area where there are accusations that the ICO has failed Johannesburg's citizens is in relation to the controversial market construction projects implemented by the MTC, and the uncompromising approach to informal street traders by the ICO and the city. The MTC loosely classifies informal traders either as 'entrepreneurs' – those who have some capital to set up and run a business – and 'survivalists', those who trade low-cost goods simply to get by on a day-to-day basis. Foreign, particularly West African traders, have flocked to South Africa in recent years (City of Johannesburg, 2001). They tend to be more experienced and organized and have dominated among the 'entrepreneurs', while the South African street traders and hawkers are more likely to be trading as a survival strategy (Gotz and Wooldridge, 2000). In the Rockey Street Market in Yeoville, for example, foreign traders were granted prime places, leaving South African street traders feeling that an inadequate consultation process had served to exclude them (see Figure 4.1). Even those who received places in the Yeoville Market complained that they suffered the loss of passing trade and argued that the market had actually reduced their income rather than enhanced it. Competition between local and foreign African traders has helped fuel feelings of xenophobia across the inner city more generally, with instances of public outrage being dubbed by the press the 'pavement wars' (Wooldridge, 2001b, p16). These battles have included both spontaneous clashes and organized gatherings. Examples include over 500 local hawkers calling for a boycott of their goods in November 1997, and a march, in September 1998, of around 2000 local hawkers through the streets of Johannesburg who protested against their competition.

In terms of residential neighbourhoods, the ICO with the support of the metropolitan council has sought to upgrade failing apartment blocks and to contain dysfunctional areas, a policy supported by formal capital operating in the city, keen to limit the spatial spread of drugs trade, prostitution and the seamier side of inner-city life. In combination with the introduction of individual metering and billing systems, the council uses local by-laws as a way of addressing problem buildings, such as hotels or night clubs known as venues for sex workers or where drug dealers operate. Unable to deal with the people inside, the buildings are closed down for contravening health, food or fire regulations, or where there are absentee landlords and squatters take over. In this case, as a last resort, buildings might be earmarked for demolition. Projects for individual buildings or groups of buildings are accompanied by a precinct approach to social development. For example, the Monitor report for *iGoli* 2010 (Monitor, 2000b) recommends that the safety and security strategy for notorious areas such as Hillbrow should be based on interventions that are designed at the level of a police station area or a small group of similar suburbs. The Monitor report draws on the experience of initiatives implemented in other cities, such as New York's 'broken window' strategy; these initiatives recognize the relationship between urban decay and crime. However, as Wooldridge (2001b, p24) points out, 'the development of a local safety and security strategy in Hillbrow is critical to the revitalization of the neighbourhood', but this strategy needs also to 'restore community trust', which requires tackling police corruption, as well as negotiation with 'local cartels and gangs'. It is, however, problematic to assume that these difficulties can be overcome simply through a precinct approach and a policy of containment, without adequately addressing the wider community.

RESIDENTIAL REGENERATION IN THE INNER CITY: THE CASE OF YEOVILLE

To date, much of the attention on the inner city of Johannesburg has focused either on the CBD or on the infamous high-density area of Hillbrow. The reason for this is that the acutely problematic area of Hillbrow was the first site of desegregation, and its high-rise rental accommodation has housed the poorest and most transient sections of the inner-city population. Yeoville has, hitherto, received rather less attention, a fact that reflects its relative respectability and also its slightly less central location (see Figure 4.1). However, because it has deracialized, densified and seen capital flight of its own, Yeoville has increasingly begun to attract attention from the press and has come into the purview of the council. The fact that several projects, including the Yeoville Market, have been located in the area has meant that both the redevelopment and partnership spotlights are now being firmly trained on the community. As a transient area of internal complexity, Yeoville poses particular challenges for the city. Thus far, the ICO's search for the endorsement of, and participation in, its regeneration vision has found few willing partners in Yeoville, a fact that requires explanation. We offer three general pointers. First, we suggest that the case for regeneration of Yeoville is weak, and is thus unlikely to have invoked strong resident interest. Second, the city holds a preconceived notion of 'the community' and has thus misread the passive reaction to its overtures as a sign of apathy. Finally, the city tends to dictate the redevelopment vision in terms of its own powers and functions, and so it has not allowed the real needs and interests of residents to come to the fore.

The Case for the Regeneration of Yeoville

Yeoville is a fairly typical Johannesburg inner-city area, although the district has always had its own character. During the late apartheid era, there arose a mixed-race avant-garde who challenged segregation laws, mixing freely around music, clubs, restaurants and other magnets of an alternative lifestyle. As one long-time resident of Yeoville put it, 'It seemed a good place to be. Rockey Street was vibey and there was a lot to do socially'. Lured by reasonable rents and transport costs, students, artists and, from the 1980s onwards, anti-apartheid political activists were attracted to living in Yeoville, which was already populated by a cosmopolitan population comprising immigrants from Southern Europe and a large but declining Jewish community.

The original houses, built from the early 1900s to the early 1940s, were usually erected on their own stands of about 400 square metres, although a small proportion were semi-detached, constructed on the same size of stand. These houses were built in the colonial fashion of a square, symmetrical house with a small front porch, a living room, a dining room, a kitchen and two or three bedrooms. Between the 1920s and 1950s, many low-rise apartment blocks were also built, and according to the 1996 Population Census, two-thirds of all residential units in contemporary Yeoville are apartments and only 14 per cent are houses. Other common forms of accommodation in Yeoville are the quarters that were originally built for domestic workers. Some are the small outbuildings located at the back of houses, many of which have now been renovated into 'cottages' or 'granny flats', as they are popularly known. 'Servants' quarters' were also built on the top of apartment blocks, a series of rooms designed to house single domestic workers employed by apartment owners or tenants. Today they are dubbed 'houses in the sky' and are often home to whole families. The 1996 census estimates that servants' rooms and backyard accommodation make up 18 per cent of all residential units in Yeoville, in a context where almost half of all houses and about three-quarters of all apartments and backyard rooms are rented.

During the apartheid era, Africans, Indians and coloureds were excluded from inner-city areas, and in Yeoville racial desegregation came somewhat later than for other places such as Hillbrow. However, by 1996 Africans made up 57 per cent of Yeoville households and whites only 35 per cent. The remaining 8 per cent of households comprised coloured and Indian households in more or less equal proportions. There was, of course, also a growing, un-enumerated, illegal foreign population. An important consequence of the racial transition in Yeoville is that it has probably led to a higher turnover of residents than there would otherwise have been. According to the 1996 Population Census, only 9 per cent of today's Yeoville residents were born in Yeoville and the majority (71 per cent) moved to live there between 1991 and 1996. Of these, only about 7 per cent were foreign born: 4 per cent in neighbouring African states, 1 per cent in African countries further north, and 2 per cent in Europe. More recently, the extent of foreign in-migration to the Yeoville area has become much more marked (GJMC, 2001b).

A variety of survey and census reports confirm that for Yeoville, as for other parts of the inner city, racial desegregation was not accompanied by dramatic changes in the social class and educational profile of its residents (Crankshaw, 1996). However, although a high proportion of residents continued to be employed in professional, semi-professional and routine white-collar occupations, a substantial and growing proportion is employed in unskilled manual jobs, so that the occupational profile is fairly polarized. There is an impoverished minority living among relatively well-resourced inner-city residents. What emerges from the accounts of many older residents about changes in Yeoville is a sense of increasing dislocation and unease, resulting from the flight of better-off (usually white) homeowners from the area and the influx of new tenants, usually black and often foreign. Many former residents who could move, did so, as Yeoville increasingly changed in character; but leaving became more and more difficult by virtue of the fact that the banks 'redlined' Yeoville as a risk area, refusing to extend mortgages on properties there. Those who could afford it simply rented out their properties or left them in the charge of caretakers. Those most likely to stay were pensioners who could not afford to buy alternative homes elsewhere and became trapped by the falling values of their properties. Their anxiety and fear often expresses itself in the form of escalating racism, and their indignant paralysis has encouraged the sense that Yeoville is a place where 'community is dead'.

There is no doubt that crime, and particularly violent crime, are key factors in eroding a sense of well-being for everyone living in Yeoville today, with most informants identifying 1995 as the year it began to escalate. Two high-profile robberies certainly contributed to the decision by the commercial banks and chain stores to move out of the area. As one informant put it, 'Yeoville has changed in the sense that people no longer walk freely and are scared of being on the streets.' There are also problems associated with the living environment, emerging from poor maintenance of buildings and increased evidence of homelessness and survivalist economic activities. However, Yeoville is not a ghetto and, like many inner-city residential areas in South Africa, offers sound infrastructure, a good location and established (if fragile) economic opportunities.

Yeoville's economic life has seen a transformation. The once bohemian Rockey Street no longer comprises book shops and health food shops, but rather *shebeens* and brothels, cash-loan and one-price shops. The Greek and Italian restaurants have given way to West African eating establishments. The dingy night clubs that have always been a trademark of the area remain, although it is now easier than before to buy drugs on the streets outside. As the number of homeowners declined, so the local hardware stores announced their closures and were replaced by stores selling padlocks, cheap suitcases and blankets and lotto tickets. The Italian delicatessens and Jewish bakeries have closed or relocated to the more affluent nodes of Rosebank and Illovo, while informal businesses are springing up all over Yeoville, ranging from barbers and car repairers, to food vendors of various kinds. Some argue that shifts in retailing are due to an escalation of crime, while others emphasize the changing face of Yeoville's custom, with the truth probably lying somewhere in between. It is against this context of transition that the city is being called upon to play a higher-profile role in the management of the area.

COMMUNITY DYNAMICS IN YEOVILLE

Public perceptions, at times reinforced by our research, see Yeoville as an area deprived of 'community'. Indicators given to support this view are the impression that the place is dirty and that people do not venture out and mix for fear of crime. The picture we present rests on a more textured view of community life that dwells less on the demise of old forms of community and more on the changing nature of social interaction. Unlike earlier accounts that emphasize a lack of social capital in Yeoville (Harrison, 2001), we argue that Yeoville's future is not inevitably one of urban decline, anomie and apathy. However, ensuring a positive future for Yeoville and all its residents does hinge upon harnessing the potential for community engagement among diverse and largely exclusive groups that are often intensely suspicious of one another, sometimes for good reason.

For the local authority to play an appropriate developmental role in such an area requires it to develop an unprejudiced and holistic view of the place and to sustain a dialogue with representatives of civil society in all its multiple forms. To assist in this process, we have identified a number of community groupings that are part of the new social fabric. These we describe variously as 'community deserters', 'community stalwarts', 'community invaders' and 'community builders', all with different roles to play and levels of impact in terms of sewing the seeds of civic engagement and a revitalised urban government.

Dancing in the Old-fashioned Way: Community Deserters and Stalwarts

The strong feeling that there is no real sense of community in Yeoville is largely associated with the exodus from the area of a number of different groups, those we dub the 'community deserters'. This is not meant to be judgmental or pejorative, but to reflect the real sense of loss experienced as a result of their departure. Important among them were the Jewish, Greek and Italian communities who, in the past, provided Yeoville with much of its cosmopolitan atmosphere. The closing down of synagogues, churches and shops associated with these communities served to underscore, in a very dramatic way, the impact of their withdrawal. Another group that might be hailed as 'community deserters' are those erstwhile anti-apartheid activists who, for a long time, lived in Yeoville and formed the core of the local ANC branch after the organization was dis-banned and prior to the 1994 elections. Many of the leadership have now taken up key roles in national and provincial politics, causing them to move away from the area. The gap left by these high-profile community activists is sorely felt by those who stayed and probably lies at the heart of the perception that there is no longer a political community in Yeoville.

The constituency that considers itself their political heirs in Yeoville, we call the 'community stalwarts'. These individuals are among those who find organizational change in Yeoville most difficult to come to terms with and community politics enervating. Many of them are closely associated with the

Yeoville Community Development Forum (YCDF) and the Yeoville Community Policing Forum (YCPF), both of which are recognized as key CBOs in Yeoville. However, these organizations have been largely inactive, other than in creating an impressive website, and are not well known to those without an activist background or an Internet connection.[3] One of the older community leaders who is still involved explained that not enough people want to be involved and, given the history of Yeoville as a former white area, that there is not enough black leadership in the organization. He felt that, personally, he had legitimacy because of his historical involvement in anti-apartheid politics, but recognized that his playing a leadership role could and should not be sustained in a post-apartheid Yeoville.

There is also a good deal of fear associated with community activism, exacerbated by the nature of the issues that have to be taken up and by how difficult it is to campaign around them. Ongoing work on landlord–tenant relations has now become quite limited, not least of all because of the pervading sense of insecurity and the fact that some of the buildings have become very problematic, due to high levels of crime. One of the activists interviewed reported 'stories of people stocking AK47s in the building' and said: 'I don't do door-to-door work anymore.' One effect of this is a tendency to look back with nostalgia on the political struggle of the mass democratic movement:

> *Putting up posters every weekend, going door to door and canvassing, sort of having mass meetings – that sort of stuff. We had a large office, an administrator, good membership, the [ANC]branch was able to sustain itself through stop orders, so it had a regular income. And it was active in community issues. It was broader than national politics stuff, it was local issues – working with, and taking up, domestic workers' issues, landlord–tenant relations… Post elections … the ANC overwhelmingly wins and people feel: 'well, we have got into government, let's get on with our lives' – a lot of the active people – so we found a lot of demobilization, almost. As a result, the branch suffered, we closed down our office.*

The local branch of SANCO, an important community stalwart organization dating back to the anti-apartheid struggle, has been more successful in sustaining itself than the ANC. Although many tend to be dismissive of SANCO these days, it continues to operate a branch in Yeoville and appears to have a base among ordinary people, doing systematic work around housing and urban services issues. In due course it could be among the 'community builders'. It is also the SANCO branch rather than the ANC that provides the local councillor with a support base in Yeoville. Although, like SANCO, they are politically active and are potentially 'community builders', we categorize the councillors as 'community stalwarts' because they are a phenomenon of the pre- and post-apartheid eras and have changed little in the way they do business. The most common forms of engagement with their constituency remain personal connections and formal public meetings, neither of which serves to connect with Yeoville's changing population. A councillor we interviewed said that those who come to public meetings are either the old regular political activists or the old property owners 'who have had it with the council'. While SANCO does its job with the broader community of South African residents, immigrant communities are not yet integrated: 'In ward meetings, for instance, if there are 50 people, 5 would be from other African countries.' From the point of view of the various residents we interviewed, most had little or no contact with the councillor and some did not know who their present ward councillor was.

Although this lack of engagement constitutes a very real problem and is one that would be recognizable to many local authorities elsewhere, it is still true to say that many of those who argue that there is no real community organization in Yeoville anymore come from an historical position, common in South Africa. This historical position only recognizes community organization as such when it is party politically engaged and motivated. From the perspective of the 'community stalwarts' – who are all local-level activists with an ongoing commitment to grassroots democracy – the disparate networks and loose organizations that characterize what one of them described as the 'lumpen proletariat' are not, somehow, seen as valid. Among the many immigrants from other African countries, there are numerous social networks; but these are also seen as beyond the political pale. As one veteran activist said in response to being asked about the forms of organization that are found among the immigrant communities: 'These African networks are very separate from local networks and they don't see themselves as part of the community.'

Strangers in the Night: Community Invaders

For most residents, the breakdown of community in Yeoville is associated with what we might label 'community invaders'. These are people who are perceived of as incomers without any real commitment to the area – the so-called 'strangers in the night'. In truth, there are very few groups who are genuine 'community invaders'; many of those perceived as strangers or outsiders, such as foreign migrants and refugees, are already an important part of Yeoville's social fabric. Moreover, many of those who do come into Yeoville and then leave are important contributors to the local economy. On the one hand, there are the Soweto youth who see Yeoville as a place to '*jorl*' or revel for a while, temporary sojourners attracted to the night life. In this sense, they do not differ significantly in profile from the in-comers who sought their entertainment in the trendy Yeoville of the past. As a worker for *Homeless Talk* put it: 'Yeoville is a place to meet people and make money. Rockey Street is the centre of Yeoville, and when people get tired of it they move on.' Such groups may be transient and difficult to organize politically, but they are beneficial to the community in that they bring life and custom to its heart. It is hoped by those involved in local economic development that Yeoville will be able to attract many more 'community invaders' of this sort, restoring to the area its reputation as a centre of jazz music and alternative culture, albeit in different forms than in the past.

However, there are those for whom the appellation 'community invaders' is apt. They are the criminal gangs, the drug lords and corrupt elements of the police force who make Yeoville their base or a significant part of their tramping ground. The argument has been made in respect of Hillbrow (Wooldridge,

2001b) that criminal gangs can protect communities, serve to keep the peace and free the area of other sources of crime. This may or may not be the case for Yeoville; but when we looked for the things that divided people in Yeoville and the source of greatest apathy and 'exit' (Hirschman, 1970), the prevalence of crime and violence was an issue of deep concern. As such, the construction of new forms of civil society in Yeoville is genuinely at risk from these 'community invaders'. Their impact on the community has been to engender insecurity and mistrust, as described by one of our informants:

> *When I come back from work, I close the door and do not go out, because of the fear. There is no trust – nobody trust nobody. I work – I go home – stay there – sleep – work – go home – I just stay there. You can't go out!*

Crime also fuels existing social fears and prejudices such as racism, which is not confined to whites, as was confirmed by one of the rooftop tenants we interviewed:

> *Racism is not only white–black, but even between our tribes… Even between ourselves, as far as our tribes are concerned, maybe I go to Shoprite and someone will rob me and maybe the guy speaks Zulu – then I will be saying 'the Zulus' – not one Zulu – 'all of them are thieves'… When I walk in the street behind a white person, he is going to be afraid, he can't trust a black person. Even though I am not going to rob him, he is still afraid because they say 'blacks will rob you' – never mind who you are; there is that suspicion.*

Similar fears have been projected onto foreign immigrants who, among the numerous residents of Yeoville, are seen by many South African residents as high-order 'community invaders'. Refugees and immigrants are associated with the escalation of grime, crime, violence, rising rents and every other social ill in Yeoville. From the perspective of immigrants it works in this way:

> *… rumours … are continuously spread by everyone that foreigners are responsible for whatever is wrong. It is like 'thank you, foreigners, that you are here, now we can blame you for everything!' South Africans do not look at their own – they just ignore their own problems and pretend that the foreigners cause all their problems. People fear foreigners at the same time – I heard there is a word even for that now: xenophobia!*

As much as South Africans might blame foreigners for escalating crime and violence, so a focus-group discussion with one of the foreign African immigrant groups saw South Africa as having a culture of crime unique to the country:

> *In my country, the only way up is through education, but not in South Africa. Here it is guns. If you have a gun you can move up in life. The whole South African environment is permissive to crime – there is no law against guns and therefore everyone [tries]to get ahead with his gun.*

For the most part, refugees and migrants are a silent group, never engaging with the authorities or drawing attention to themselves for fear of incurring official sanction or social wrath. A taxi driver we interviewed provided an interesting indicator of their efforts at invisibility. He said that foreigners were his best customers because they were afraid to walk the streets or use public transport, so they relied almost exclusively on taxis. Unfortunately, their encounters with the authorities are also primarily unhappy ones. The evident corruption within the police force serves to make crime pay in South Africa and also affects foreigners adversely. The focus groups that were conducted with foreign Africans all revealed experiences of constant harassment and arrests, even of legal immigrants, nearly always accompanied by requests for bribes and pay-offs. One group said that they were constant targets of criminals, as well as police raids of their homes.

While, clearly, there are criminal elements among immigrant as well as South African communities, the social exclusion experienced by foreigners who are universally tarred with this brush is a very sad side effect of the transition from apartheid. This was perceptively picked up by the focus group among Zimbabwean migrants who explained things as follows:

> *There is this culture here in South Africa based on the darkness of your skin. The white man is at the top of the scale, then the Indian, then the coloured, then the blacks and then they said: 'Hey, we need someone below us. Ah – who has a darker skin? The foreigners!'*

Respondents from the same group said that foreigners were in South Africa because of the hope for a better future: 'Everyone is moving around – it is a global trend – and all we are all looking for is a lucky break in life.'

While it may be that the foreign African communities have exclusive social networks of support and exchange, this has always been the case for immigrant communities in cities throughout the world and has not prevented such populations from becoming integrated and, in time, making significant contributions to social and economic life. Moreover, there is already a lot of social and economic interaction between South Africans and African migrants. An organizer of the Gauteng Self-Employed Women's Association (GASEWA), and a Yeoville resident, argued that despite the 'pavement wars', there is also much evidence of non-hostile engagement between South African women traders and some African traders.[4] She also pointed out the numerous informal hairdressers who have sprung up in Yeoville and elsewhere in the inner city, and that 'many of the hair salons are run by outsiders, and South Africans use these facilities'.

The Challenge of Coalition: Community Builders

Those who are adapting to the new Yeoville are struggling to find novel ways of building community. Local business is showing signs of beginning to get organized through the Rockey/Raleigh Streets Management Committee, and is thinking about developing a BID, having turned to the CJP for advice. One problem of emulating the precinct approach of the CBD is that businesses in Yeoville are not of the same order of magnitude as those in the inner city. It is not clear, for example, that Yeoville will be able to generate the R64,000 per month necessary to qualify as a BID. Furthermore, over 90 per cent of the commercial premises are owned by whites, as are 80 per cent of the businesses, so as one of the organizers argued: 'it is difficult to get people to buy into the idea'. At the other end of the retail spectrum is the Rockey Street Hawkers' Association, which has been very vocal around the issue of the Yeoville Market and the needs of traders. Although dismissed by some as 'a lot of hot air', this and other economic interest-based organizations, such as GASEWA, could well play an important role in coalition politics. If this were the case, they would certainly provide an important counterweight to the power of big capital in the inner city.

Other interest-based groups that could be rallied are the street committees. Although typical not-in-my-backyard (NIMBY) organizations, they are vocal and well-organized CBOs. They predominate in some of the better-off parts of Yeoville, where there are more houses than apartments and a majority presence of owner occupiers. Some are particularly active, having started with neighbourhood watch schemes or clean-up campaigns, and leading people to discover that they had a diverse set of neighbours whom they enjoyed meeting. However, the main organizers felt that people are, on the whole, apathetic about these things and are sceptical of efforts to broaden the street committee idea. One effort involved leafleting 300 households; but only 30 people turned up for the meeting, most of them being 'the regulars'.

Religious institutions are promising as contributors to a coalition community; they help to create and support local networks that straddle various divides. Although some churches have failed to adapt and have remained committed to their dwindling and disappearing white congregations, others have sought to embrace the new Yeoville and play an important role. as one of our interviewees explained:

> *The Anglican church has a new black minister and the church seems to be growing considerably, as a result. You can see people walking to church and this suggests they are from the area. There are also the more traditional churches, such as the Presbyterian; but about 90 per cent of the congregation do not live in Yeoville. This is evident because they arrive by car.*

Many of more adaptive churches have grown exponentially with the influx of African immigrants. For example, the Roman Catholic church now has a large Nigerian congregation, while Ghanaians attend the Pentecostal Tent church and the local Mosque is the religious focus of people from the Côte d'Ivoire. There are also numerous new and more exclusive congregations springing up, which are specifically associated with immigrant communities.

There are a number of smaller welfare-oriented organizations, which although not well integrated into the local political life of Yeoville, are active and potentially important coalition partners. They include a facility for HIV/AIDS patients, a shelter for abused women, meals on wheels, soup kitchens and the Yeoville Community School. The latter was set up in 1992 for the children of returning South African freedom fighters and now accepts refugee and migrant children. The school encourages them to mix freely and to share and be proud of their own cultures. It has played a small, but important, role in establishing the ground rules for a new community culture in Yeoville.

In general, there is more evidence of emerging integration in Yeoville through the everyday interaction of the area's residents than from formal organizational initiatives, with the exception of some religious institutions and some area-based and issue-based initiatives. For example, the Yeoville Carnival and the HIV/AIDS campaign were both widely mentioned and appreciated as events that broke down social barriers. It was suggested by one group that local councillors should take note and create more opportunities that could bring people together and 'make them forget their differences'.

At present, new forms of social organization remain small scale and often constitute exclusive rather than inclusive groups. There is evidence that social interaction is spatially confined – for example, among tenants in one building or homeowners in one street. There are certainly communities of identity – for example, among immigrant or religious groups. This, after all, is not a new phenomenon for Yeoville. Although people do come together around activities, what seems to be different from the halcyon anti-apartheid days of Yeoville is that such groupings appear to have defeated community activists and politicians. Both interest-based and identity-based groups present tremendous challenges for local governance; but this suggests working in new and different ways, including raising awareness about entitlements and educating citizens about the value of civic engagement.

CONCLUSION

In this chapter we have sought to understand the prospects for redeveloping Johannesburg's inner city. In assessing the prospects for state–society relations in the inner city, we need to assess the value of partnerships as the key basis for developing the CBD and its surrounds. At the moment, these partnerships appear to be increasingly entrenched. We would not go so far as to dismiss the concept of partnership as being hopelessly ambiguous (Mackintosh, 1992) or meaningless (Lawless, 1991). However, we did find that the discourse of partnership varies considerably in Johannesburg, depending upon whether business or residents are the city's partners in redevelopment.

In the context of fostering local economic development in the inner city, it can be argued that partnership projects have not been altogether unproductive. Formal business operating in, and on, the inner city has been successful in initiating, and participating in, urban partnerships. This very much has been driven by North American perceptions of inner-city decay and models of urban regeneration. For their part, the metropolitan council was grateful for the involvement of other players and the external motivation and resources that they brought. Together, they developed a remarkable synergy and single mindedness, manifest in what we dub their 'project-and-precinct' approach, which looks destined to be taken forward by the new Johannesburg Development Agency.

Our view on partnerships (as they have been taken up in Johannesburg, thus far) is that they are fashioned too closely on early models of urban regeneration in the north. As such, although they engage in widespread consultative processes and pay lip service to participatory democracy, the projects to which they give rise remain dominated by powerful interests, and the benefits rarely spread beyond the precinct. As a result, while the city has been able to engage successfully in circumscribed projects with coalitions of interest linked to formal business in Johannesburg, its efforts at residential urban regeneration have been less impressive.

Recent relationships, both in the north and in the south (Beall and Lingayah, 2001), have been more progressive and inclusive by coordinating coalitions of interest to develop particular areas within the city. Not simply concerned with transferring responsibility for urban regeneration to the private sector, or shifting the mandate for urban development from national to city governments, partnerships can be useful vehicles for fostering synergy in state–society relations. However, to fulfil this function there has to be some flexibility in the construction of partnerships at the local level. To date, this has been prevented by a project approach, which, in turn, limits the potential for accommodating partnerships within the context of sustained local democracy. So long as partnerships remain outside of broader political processes, they are unlikely to give rise to sustained improvement in the well-being of people in their chosen localities, let alone beyond them.

Post-apartheid metropolitan government in Johannesburg has devoted considerable energy and resources towards managing the commercial and residential development of the inner city through project partnerships with business and individual buildings or precincts. However, it has not yet found a way of adapting the processes of consultation and participation, associated with DLG, to quirky residential and idiosyncratic organizational environments such as Yeoville. One of the major problems for Johannesburg's ICO, and its successor the JDA, is that the participatory planning format envisaged by DLG in South Africa was not really designed with the realities of established neighbourhoods in mind.

Dealing with poverty, differentiation and social exclusion in established residential areas of the country's wealthiest city was not part of the vision of the RDP, which was the initial driver of state–society relations in relation to post-apartheid development. The geographical scope of the RDP in urban areas was envisioned to be the informal settlements, such as Diepsloot, discussed in Chapter 8, or the former African townships, such as Soweto, discussed in Chapter 9. A key question is whether formalized structures such as the CDFs are suitable vehicles for citizen participation in areas where full basic services exist, where communities are far from homogeneous, where it cannot be assumed that all residents are legal citizens, and where a long-term commitment to living in, and improving, the area might not necessarily be forthcoming.

Chapter 8

Participatory Planning and Informal Settlement Upgrading in Diepsloot

INTRODUCTION

We have argued that in the post-*iGoli 2002* period, uniting a divided Johannesburg hinged more than ever upon the successful operation of integrated planning and community participation. Although it was still experimental, an inclusive post-apartheid developmental planning process was operational, and participation was its leitmotif. Across the spectrum of the unequal and divided neighbourhoods of Johannesburg, the task of identifying community development priorities fell largely upon a single organizational format: the CDF. As the legacy of the anti-apartheid struggle and the South African variant of participatory forums seen elsewhere in the world, the CDFs represented a valuable instrument of state–civil society engagement. But politics cannot be straight-jacketed, and there is a danger that, through their institutionalization as a compulsory dimension of the participatory planning process, the role of the CDFs will undermine the ability of communities to engage with the local authority. Here we explore the tension between the benefits of compulsory state engagement with communities, and the lack of democracy associated with the institutionalization of community organizations.

Nowhere was the political imperative of successful participatory planning stronger, nor the need for reconstruction and development more pressing, than in Johannesburg's informal settlements. It was inconceivable that the city's IDP would not give attention to the future of informal settlements. Indeed, the imperative to address poverty and service backlogs was, and is, officially acknowledged (Monitor, 2000a). At the narrower scale, as set out in Local Area Integrated Development Plans (LIDPs), the upgrading of informal areas and their incorporation within the spatial economy of the metropolitan area is still the highest priority of the Johannesburg authorities (GJMC, 1999e; 1999f). As a result, the CDFs of impoverished areas expect a more receptive audience from city officials and politicians. But, we must ask, how well are residents able to engage in, and direct, the integrated planning process? How important are structure, agency and informal institutional control in shaping the capacity of communities to participate in negotiations over their urban futures? Given the divided nature of the urban realities of Johannesburg, we must question if the model of CDF-regulated participatory planning is a sufficient, or even useful, strategy for inclusive governance.

Diepsloot, a site-and-service settlement located on the northern boundary of the Greater Johannesburg Metropolitan Area, is the largest informal settlement in the affluent peri-urban belt that lies between Johannesburg and Pretoria (see Figure 8.1). It had one of the most actively involved residents' groups in Johannesburg in the first participatory planning process (the setting of LDOs) run by the council in 1996. The CDF was given sole responsibility for liasing with outside actors in the development processes that were unleashed by the LDO's findings.[1] Huge state resources, from local, provincial and national coffers, were directed at the impoverished area in an attempt to meet basic needs and to satisfy political demands for reconstruction. Against an understanding of the structural base of informal settlement, in general, and the particular political experiences of the communities, we assess the nature, extent and basis of the CDF's negotiating power and engagement in the reconstruction and development process.

Diepsloot has been a major site of public investment, with massive construction and obvious progress in the provision of state-funded, low-income housing, primary health clinics, roads and schools. This has not been only a top-down autocratic intervention: residents have used the CDF successfully to express their developmental priorities and concerns. The Diepsloot CDF enjoys a substantial reputation for effectively representing the interests of the poor. It is tempting, and not necessarily inaccurate, to depict formal community involvement through the CDF in this settlement as an example of 'best practice' that illustrates how the poor can influence the state's allocation of resources for development through established participatory structures, set up by local government.

However, this chapter is not a eulogy to 'good practice' at Diepsloot; although by any criteria, residents of Diepsloot have enjoyed greater access to post-apartheid reconstruction and have secured a bigger slice of the urban development pie than have the residents of many other squatter areas (GJMC, 2001b). That said, negotiating state power, maintaining civic autonomy and ensuring that the rights of all residents are embraced through democratic practice, while at the same time fending off racist and elitist interests and mobilizing infrastructural and economic investment, is never a simple matter. Closer scrutiny of the Diepsloot CDF's record suggests caution in allowing a single organization or forum to be burdened with the responsibility for giving voice to an entire community. While, in general, the achievements of the Diepsloot CDF are to be admired, we argue that their role as the conduit of inclusion between residents, developers and the state is tenuous.

We assess the challenges faced by the CDF in maintaining legitimacy as a voice of the people in the post-LDO development process at three levels. First, challenges to the CDF from within the Diepsloot community are discussed. Second, we outline the problems of a community organization engaging with technical planning processes to achieve the pro-poor development decided upon in the LDO exercise. Finally, we review the place of Diepsloot in the wider political and financial context of the city. Overall, we argue that the power of

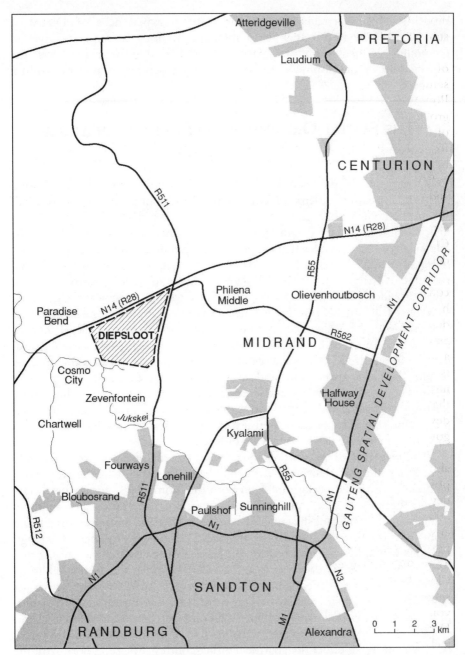

Figure 8.1 *The Diepsloot settlement and its environs*

the CDF to reduce poverty through engaging ordinary citizens in ways that influence the planning process is limited, not only by internal political contests, but also by the wider structural environment. In short, we suggest that the CDF structure is a useful but insufficient instrument for entrenching participatory planning. More particularly, even the positive experiences of Diepsloot demonstrate the importance of a medium- to long-term perspective on community consultation and participatory planning processes, lest the expectations of development and the benefits of democracy turn out to be a mirage.

THE SOCIAL ORIGINS OF PERI-URBAN SQUATTER SETTLEMENTS

The social origin of the Diepsloot site-and-service settlement is typical of other peri-urban squatter settlements in greater Johannesburg. Although peri-urban squatter settlements have much in common with other kinds of informal shelter in Johannesburg, their origin is, nonetheless, due to a very specific set of relationships and dynamics that are peculiar to the suburban periphery. All types of squatter settlements in South Africa are caused, ultimately, by the chronic shortage of affordable housing. However, this kind of long-term structural cause provides only a partial explanation for squatting. Specifically, although a shortage of affordable housing is a necessary condition for homelessness, the lack of adequate housing does not necessarily take the form of illegal squatter settlements. In order for illegal squatting to take place, some sort of social catalyst is required. This social catalyst usually has to do with the specific relationships of ownership and control over vacant land. Since these relationships of ownership and control are different for peri-urban areas, township backyards and vacant land within townships, so the social origins and the resulting social character of peri-urban squatter settlements, backyard shacks and urban shantytowns are somewhat different.

The residents of peri-urban squatter settlements are not predominantly from either rural or urban areas. Although there is generally a higher proportion of people with rural backgrounds, in both the 'homelands' and white-owned farms, there is also a significant proportion of urbanites among them (Crankshaw, 1993; Crankshaw and Hart, 1990). There is, moreover, originating from both the apartheid and post-apartheid periods, a presence of foreign migrants within the informal settlements precisely because these are places that do not require identity documents (GJMC, 2001b). What the more established residents, local and foreign, have in common is a fairly long history of employment and residence in the peri-urban areas. For a variety of reasons, peri-urban farms and smallholdings offer opportunities for housing and employment to people who are unable to secure urban accommodation and employment. First, under the apartheid influx-control laws, rural-born Africans were excluded from family accommodation within urban areas. For this reason, rural-born immigrants and immigrants from neighbouring states often sought both employment and accommodation as farm workers and domestic servants in the peri-urban districts. Second, employers in the peri-urban areas are restricted to farmers, private households and construction companies engaged in new suburban residential and office development (Sapire, 1990; Frankel,

1988). Employment opportunities are therefore restricted to mostly unskilled manual jobs and some supervisory and driving positions. Such jobs are poorly paid by urban standards, and they are filled only by people who cannot secure better-paid jobs in the urban economy. Finally, peri-urban employers often allow their employees to reside on their properties. Since employees usually provide their own housing in the form of a shack, this kind of accommodation is acceptable only to those with no other options.

For these reasons, then, peri-urban farms and smallholdings offer both employment and accommodation to poorly educated, unskilled manual workers and their families. Under apartheid, such settlements were very small and did not constitute illegal squatting. However, during the 1980s, the circumstances that provided legal accommodation and employment on these peri-urban farms began to break down. First, the encroachment of suburban residential development meant that farms were sold to property developers (Adler, Beetge and Sher, 1984; Crankshaw, 1993). This change in land use put an end to agricultural production on many farms. Although many farmers who sold their land took their farm workers with them, many did not. Consequently, many farm workers and their families were left without both employment and accommodation. Other residents, who worked elsewhere as domestic servants or construction workers, were left without accommodation. Although many displaced households may have found alternative accommodation in either the urban areas or in outlying rural districts, many did not. This transition from rural to urban land use, therefore, concentrated the peri-urban population on fewer and fewer farms.

At the same time that suburban residential development displaced peri-urban residents from farms that were bought up for urban development, it also created opportunities for illegal squatting. These opportunities took two forms. First, many developers who bought out farmland did not develop it immediately. As a consequence, many farms stood vacant for years without any supervision or control over settlement. This was especially true for large tracts of land bought by the government for the development of housing for coloureds and Indians in the south of Johannesburg, but also obtained in the north. Displaced households who settled these abandoned farms did not miss this opportunity. Second, many farm owners saw in this demand for accommodation an opportunity to make money by renting out sites to homeless families. During the 1980s, farmers charged households between 30 Rand (R30) and R60 per month for the right to occupy a site. This form of settlement was illegal under the terms of the Prevention of Illegal Squatting Act, as amended in 1988 (O'Regan, 1990), and was soon noticed by neighbouring property owners and the provincial authority, which soon launched legal action against the offending farmers. However, once these settlements had been established, the residents were very difficult to remove, even by force.

The most obvious reason for this is that these settlements grew very quickly, and within a matter of months had reached populations of over 1000 individuals. This form of illegal squatting was typical of a number of peri-urban squatter settlements on the on the south, west and north of the greater

Johannesburg area. Of particular interest to us is the case of Zevenfontein, which is the name of the squatter settlement from which many of the residents of Diepsloot were resettled. In seeking to influence their urban futures, the communities of Diepsloot have to overcome the structural exclusion inherent in their peripheral location, their labour market marginalization and other forces of exclusion, such as nationality, political affiliation or ethnicity. It is this task that has constituted the agenda of the Diepsloot CDF.

SOCIAL MOBILIZATION AND SOCIAL INCLUSION IN DIEPSLOOT

Securing development opportunities from the various tiers of the state and the private sector was a dominant activity for Diepsloot leaders. On behalf of the community, the CDF spearheaded tasks associated with greenfield development, including mediating the layout and allocation of basic services and defining the settlement's size and long-term status within the metropolitan area. Although basic services were only installed during the late 1990s, it would be erroneous to see Diepsloot as a new community: its formal status was nearly a decade in the making. The 30,000 residents living in Diepsloot (South Africa 1996), and represented by the CDF, share similar class and migrancy profiles; but they were not initially a geographically homogenous community. The Diepsloot CDF cannot, therefore, be compared with the opportunistic organizational structures that often accompany land invasion. Indeed, the Diepsloot CDF represents a second generation of community organization that replaced the initial shacklords who were associated with the land invasions that characterized the first waves of settlement (*City Vision*, 20 April 1995). The Diepsloot organization was helped in the early stages by the involvement of Planact, a powerful local urban development and planning NGO. Planact has not only facilitated and offered technical support to the CDF since its inception, but also secured the first meeting place of the CDF.

Even as a relatively new settlement, the unequal social and migratory histories of the residents were inscribed within the landscape. The west bank of Diepsloot, where formal housing with full services was first built, was undoubtedly better off than the rest of the settlement that relied on water tankers, had chemical toilets and had no formal structures. Nevertheless, there was much scope for the CDF to demonstrate its ability to improve the quality of life across the whole settlement. As one of Johannesburg's poorest neighbourhoods, housing and basic services were delivered under state subsidy programmes. Street lighting and roads were constructed. Effective social-service provision was slower and is still to be established. But visible evidence of infrastructural delivery to the poor abounds. During the time of our research, the raw landscape of dusty streets and rows of corrugated iron shacks gradually gave way to rows of identical square brick houses. Known colloquially as RDP houses, the small units are approximately 25 square metres and are financed through a home-ownership subsidy programme (see Figure 8.2).

Figure 8.2 *Reconstruction and Development Programme houses in Diepsloot*

Despite residents' attempts to create gardens with lawns and small trees, Diepsloot had the feeling of an apartheid resettlement camp. The presence of chickens and goats reinforced a somewhat rural atmosphere. In the local primary school, which was fashioned out of large steel containers, children were crammed together with four or six to a double desk – hardly adequate conditions for learning. Community frustration at the absence of an effective police force in the settlement resulted in a mob (of about 1000 people) killing the alleged robbers. Hassan Mohamed from Planact recalled that the police, stationed 40 kilometres (km) away, did not respond in time to intervene. Widespread litter, blocked drains and serious roadside erosion were reminders that urban service delivery in Diepsloot was not yet at the standard of the average Johannesburg township. Diepsloot, although a major recipient of anti-poverty investment, was still far from the suburban ideal of many of the occupants. Widespread aspiration for jobs, better services and infrastructure provides the organizational basis of the CDF.

Diepsloot and the Community Development Forum

From a sparsely furnished room that was once the main en-suite bedroom of a white-owned farmhouse on the northern periphery of Johannesburg, members of the Diepsloot CDF and officials of the Northern Metropolitan Council (NMC) deliberate on the allocation of subsidy-built houses to residents of shacks. The ward councillor, a man known by name across the area, had sent apologies for the meeting. This is a weekly site meeting for which the CDF members receive no direct payment. It is also a committee that they must leave should they accept employment in one of the job creation schemes associated with the activities of the local authority. The time-consuming commitment of the CDF members is testament to their belief in what they describe as the importance of 'grassroots government' and their ability to assist in improving the quality of life of Diepsloot residents. The issues being addressed at the farmhouse are complex, ranging from the quality control of the structures that are being handed over by the developers, to the monitoring of land invaders who try to jump the housing queue. The meeting follows committee procedures, with an agenda and minutes that are freely available for inspection. Relations between officials and community leaders are warm. This is consultative democracy; community-led development and participatory governance in action.

The organizational power of the Diepsloot CDF is legendary in Johannesburg. Local government officials, private-sector developers and local NGOs were all quick to assert the solidity of community organization in this informal settlement. The organization was born out of a community policing forum and gained legitimacy through its involvement in the widespread consultative process associated with the NMC defining its LDOs in 1996–1997 (GJMC, 1997). Formally constituted as late as 1998, the CDF had a sophisticated structure, with numerous sub-committees covering issues such as housing, environment, security and social concerns (see Table 8.1). The labours of the CDF and its predecessors were, therefore, not without achievements (see Table 8.2).

Although it was not the sole community organization operating in Diepsloot, the CDF established itself as the voice of the people and the coordinating forum of other small-sector or issue-based CBOs. Using the block committee system made popular by anti-apartheid struggles in African townships, the CDF also had a relationship with the ward councillor in order to bring matters of importance to the attention of the council. The CDF elected representatives and was accountable to both the residents and organizations in the settlement (CDF, undated). Over 18 months at the height of implementing development investment, the importance of the CDF grew. It was identified both by residents and external parties as a principal role player in the development of the area, and was seen as a potential role model for wider consultative settlement practice. The platform for this increased profile was the unquestioned legitimacy across all stakeholders of the CDF's status as

Table 8.1 *The programmes of the Community Development Forum*

CDF programmes	Issues covered
Social programme	Monitor clinic-operating times, staff inaccessibility and the failure of the clinic to employ local people for security.
Education and training programme	Negotiate the site of a private school. Liaison for the Iron and Steel Corporation (ISCOR) multipurpose training centre (unsuccessful).
Safety and security programme	Organize opposition to the Housing Support Centre and the Sizisizwe Development Trust. Community policing forums (little impact).
Sports and culture programme	Liaise for ISCOR's multipurpose training centre (unsuccessful).
Transport and infrastructure and roads	Negotiate road upgrading. Negotiate new taxi routes in Diepsloot East. Demand better litter removal from roads.
Projects, facilitation and support	Liaise on environmental upgrading (eg the floodplain development)
Finance and fund-raising programme (includes economic development)	Liaise with the NGO Planact, the province and consultants for a Diepsloot local economic development (LED) strategy
Land and housing programme	Oversee the Elcon and Mayibuye housing projects.

Source: CDF (undated)

community representative. This extract from the IDP for Diepsloot illustrates the authority accorded the CDF (CDF, undated, p4):

> *The development of Diepsloot will be driven jointly by the CDF with the government and private sector all collectively participating in, and contributing to, the ongoing development of the area. Diepsloot could be an example of how inappropriate planning and political decisions of the past may be addressed and transformed into a permanent residential area that is linked to the surrounding urban development areas.*

The Diepsloot CDF assumed prominence because of residents' recognition of its role. According to Peter Lebakeng of the well-respected planning NGO Planact, which assisted the CDF on technical matters, 'the community speaks, through the CDF, with one voice'. This positive view of the CDF was held more generally. The commercial planning consultants who drafted the Diepsloot/Olievenhoutbosch Integrated Development Framework noted: 'the community is very organized and the CDF is widely recognized as being truly representative of its people' (APS Planafrica, 1998, p4.2). Local government officials in a range of service departments happily proclaimed that their relations with the Diepsloot CDF were cordial and effective. More importantly, they acknowledged that they would do nothing in the Diepsloot area without

Table 8.2 *Community demands and development progress in Diepsloot*

Land development objective priority 1996/1997	Position in 1996	Progress in 2000
More land	Diepsloot seen as transit camp	Diepsloot's permanence secured, but a moratorium on expansion
Low-cost housing	Diepsloot West: 3800 houses	6000 houses
Clinics	Nil	Diepsloot west
Secondary schools	Nil	No state school – private informal school
Pre-primary schools and creches	Nil	CDF-run creches
Multipurpose centre or one-stop shop	Nil	Proposal under contentious debate
Police station	Station 40km away	Station 40km away, Community policing forum
Graveyard	No local facility	No local facility
Transfer of title deeds		Secure title in Diepsloot West, title pending transfer in Elcon and Mayebuye, no title in reception area or the riverbed
Apollo (high-mast) lights	No lights	Apollo lights and house electrification
Tar roads	No tarred roads	Arterial and main roads tarred
Public transport	Taxis	Taxis
Post office and telephones	Nil	Telkom public phones

Source: GJMC (1997)

consulting the liaison officer and the CDF, who are perceived as reliably reflecting the views of residents. The Northern Metropolitan Local Council (NMLC) community liaison staff and the ward councillor were widely praised for their role in facilitating communication between the council and the people of Diepsloot through the CDF.

It may well be that this close relationship between the local authority and the Diepsloot community was an artificial creation. Provincial intervention, driven personally by the ex-premier, Motole Mateshego secured the first substantial investment in Diepsloot when the NMC did very little to set in motion housing development. It is, thus, with some cause that the CDF members themselves boldly asserted their power to access and influence provincial government. As one of the executive declared: 'We have a hot line to the premier. If he can't come to us when we call, he sends someone to fetch us and we go to him.' The CDF executive members have similar confidence in their ability to lobby the local council, both through the ward councillor and directly through officials. So, the CDF occupied the lead part in negotiations about the future of Diepsloot, with commanding control of the participatory process. But were there no other competitors for the role?

Political Representation in Diepsloot: Conflict and Exclusion

In the development negotiations over the future of Diepsloot that were set in motion by the LDO process, the CDF spoke authoritatively on behalf of the community. Yet, the power base of the CDF has, at various times, been hotly contested. There is also some evidence that the modus operandi and priorities of the CDF might have excluded the core interests of marginal constituencies. Also worrying is the sense that, while the CDF enjoyed general community support, there was, at times, a passive endorsement of decisions about the allocation of resources by ill-informed residents. Against the backdrop of the unwavering official endorsement of the CDF, and widespread resident support of the CDF, it is worth establishing the parameters of the organization's legitimacy.

The role of the CDF as the sole arbitrator of development opportunities was challenged more than once, sometimes violently. The most significant challenge to the authority and dominance of the CDF was a breakaway of disenchanted members of the executive committee, who formed a rival housing support centre with an interim steering committee (ISC). ISC committee members allegedly attacked members of the CDF and the transferring attorneys and sought to prevent the handover of keys to new houses. Around the time of the 1999 elections, members of the IFP (which is supported largely by rural Zulu migrants and was involved in violent conflict with the ANC during the late 1980s) and the Democratic Party (DP) (an historically white liberal party that opposed apartheid) joined the ANC members who had defected, and sought to link the ISC to SANCO, the waning umbrella organization for civics started in the 1980s. This was not a conflict that would be resolved through the ballot box. At least two CDF members were arrested for violent behaviour and street fighting with 'the other community organization', whereupon their supporters marched to the local police station to demand the release of the arrested CDF members.

Council mediation of the conflict appears to have temporarily resolved the issue, and mechanisms for including the breakaway group back into the CDF were found, although there was evidence of ongoing tension around ISC involvement in the housing allocation process. Efforts at mediation aside, the credibility of the CDF as the sole mediator of housing delivery appeared to have been restored among residents. The alternative housing association, on the basis of a R200 deposit, promised to fast-track the delivery of subsidy houses. This was a promise it did not fulfil, and the deposits disappeared without trace. Tenants now pay tribute to the CDF for 'jumping over the other organizations' that falsely promised paid-up residents' access to the first 50 houses to be erected by the NMLC.

Even though the conflict within the CDF appeared to have been resolved, it remained a matter of concern in the neighbourhood, not only because leadership contests had resulted in recent public violence. A group of women residents complained that when the leadership of the CDF fought, residents got caught up in it and did not know which of the competing factions' meetings to attend. In significant contrast to other squatter areas where crime was seen as the major barrier to development (GJMC, 2001b), this group of middle-aged women identified community leadership struggles as the dominant tension. They gave conflict with the CDF a higher profile than even the general criminal violence or gang activity that had plagued the area in the past. Their view suggests that 1998–1999 conflict between the CDF and the ISC was not an isolated outbreak of internal political wrangling; rather, it was an episode that is indicative of ongoing conflict over control of the forum's access to resources. A more sinister reading is that the CDF and the gangs are now one.

These leadership wrangles notwithstanding, the Diepsloot CDF enjoyed exceptionally strong grassroots support, with relations between the CDF and the community described by several residents as 'outstanding' and 'excellent'. Leaders of block committees drew particular praise from both homeowners and a group of the poorest women in the area for attending to residents' complaints. Among the supportive evaluations, the following remarks made during a focus group with Diepsloot women suggest CDF engagement in the nitty-gritty of township problems:

> ... the CDF, through its involvement with the main service providers, had a number of meetings to speed up the process.

> ... the CDF is a grassroots organization that serves the community through coordination of development projects to improve their community's living conditions, and they have understanding relationships with the residents.

In the light of such forthright praise, it seems churlish to quibble about the popularity accorded to the CDF. Nevertheless, aside from the problems associated with the technocratic language and practice of planning that we discuss below, there are other areas of concern about the CDF's representivity.

Not all community views about development priorities for Diepsloot concurred with those put forward by the CDF in the formal planning processes, either in the initial LDO process, or in subsequent planning processes emanating from the LDOs. Issues of concern raised by residents that did not appear, or did not receive prominence in the consultative forums on infrastructure, economic or environmental development, were largely social in nature. For example, when asked to identify key concerns, Diepsloot youth expressed both fear of HIV/AIDS and prejudice towards those infected with the virus. A related concern came from the local primary school principal, who noted the growing problem of AIDS orphans. Neither the incidence of HIV/AIDS or tuberculosis, nor the social consequences of the devastation unleashed by the disease on poor households, were high on the CDF agenda, although HIV/AIDS awareness posters were visible in all CDF public places.

A reading of CDF documents and discussions with its committee members reveals that crime was an overriding concern of the CDF. However, in their documentation, the issues of taxi violence, gang warfare and guns take precedence over the fear expressed to us by female residents, who spoke openly of the problems of rape in the poorly lit, unsafe streets and the unprotected watercourse zone. Judging from the responses of interviews with women in Diepsloot, problems of gender-based vulnerability abound. Older women spoke of their anxiety that there was not enough food, a younger women raised her concerns about finding out that her partner had a second family in the rural area, another spoke of having to resort to prostitution to survive. Children in Diepsloot are potentially even more at risk than women. Aside from the absence of any effective recreational or sporting facilities, there is some evidence of child labour in the area, with children doing piecework for the coal merchants.

Another worrying aspect of the CDF's control over the development agenda was the fact that there were new groups arriving in Diepsloot who did not have the organization's ear, although they drew upon existing community support. For example, the CDF enjoyed widespread support, especially from unemployed male youths, for monitoring the arrival of illegal migrants who squat in the riverbed. The growth of an illegal population is seen in the proliferation of backyard shacks in places such as Diepsloot. The growth of subletting to illegal immigrants in the area suggests that, despite the xenophobic views of the youth, the R100 monthly rental received from foreign tenants is ultimately more important to Diepsloot residents' survival strategies than restricting immigration. Nevertheless, growing xenophobia across Johannesburg is a matter of considerable concern, as foreigners are socially and politically excluded from the democratic practice of post-apartheid South Africa. It must be assumed that the presence of a population who is not only disqualified from state subsidies for houses (which include water, waste and sanitary services), but is also excluded from the traditional African practice of social assistance known as *ubuntu*, will eventually generate civic strife. In the words of a Diepsloot tenant:

> *The residents have* ubuntu; *nobody is excluded from the community because of being poor or rich, and nobody likes to exclude himself from the community consultation and decision-making. However, those who are illegal immigrants are perceived as the occupiers or beneficiaries of wealth in this country [that belongs to]the real citizens of South Africa.*

The emergence of an overtly excluded and marginalized foreign population within Diepsloot seems, therefore, inevitable. The CDF has made no claim, or expressed any desire, to represent this constituency. In fact, members of the community and of Planact, some of whom were veterans of the anti-apartheid struggle, felt free to express strongly xenophobic views. In the absence of any censure, we must assume that the CDF's position received the unofficial support of the NMLC and Planact.

Not withstanding the challenges from within the community, and despite the fact that the interests of some of the poorest residents were clearly ignored, the CDF emerged as the sole legitimate and representative voice of the 'community'. Avenues of expression of non-citizens, or even of dissenting locals, were thus effectively cut off. It was clear to us that the CDF would eventually have to confront other interested parties on matters of the township's growth, but that moment had not yet come. The issues currently up for negotiation by the CDF appeared to relate to more immediate concerns of how best to develop the Diepsloot area. To this end, the CDF became a major player in the exercise of township master planning.

Community-driven Development in the Diepsloot Master Plan?

The CDF's confidence in its ability to access government, and the reciprocal confidence of local and provincial officials in the CDF, arises out of the forum members' interaction with government and the private sector over the form and character of local development. Their extensive interaction has been facilitated by involvement in the post-apartheid planning framework. Prior to the LDO accord, none of the three squatter communities from Zevenfontein, Alexandra or Rhema that were drawn together in Diepsloot had managed to successfully negotiate to remain on the land that they had first invaded. Even their eviction and forced relocation to Diepsloot did not guarantee them a secure future. Because the 1996–1997 LDO process marked the formation of the CDF structure and the start of a much more extensive process of community engagement with formal planning processes, it is worth rehearsing the major points of discussion at the time (GJMC, 1997). It was also this round of extensive LDO negotiations that were, on the one hand, held up as the basis for community participation in *iGoli 2002* and, on the other, cited by officials as the origins of the unattainable and unfocused community 'shopping lists' of demands.

Through the LDO forums, residents were able to decide on their development priorities (see Table 8.3). It is hardly surprising that an insecure settlement such as Diepsloot came up with land, security of tenure and housing as its principle demands. What may seem odd is the omission of services such as water and sanitation from the list. This is because, in post-apartheid South Africa, subsidized housing delivery encompasses the provision of running water to the house and water-borne sanitation. The total absence of waste management as a priority is noteworthy; although, again, a basic package of municipal services is assumed. Aside from recognizing the considerable gains of the last five years, it is important to recognize the changing and increasingly differentiated needs of Diepsloot residents as expressed in 1996 and in 2000 (compare Tables 8.2 and 8.3). Having secured land, housing and water, almost all residents in the focus groups that were conducted in 2000 placed jobs and improved transport highest on their lists of needs. Social services, especially policing and education, also emerged as priorities.

In 1998, the development of Diepsloot entered a second phase with the launch of a series of coordinated planning initiatives. In accordance with the post-apartheid commitment to community participation and consultation, the CDF was allocated a major role in the various technical processes aimed at integrated development. We turn now to reflect on the CDF's involvement in defining and applying the components of the master plan for Diepsloot. Although the notion of a 'master plan' is used by both the public and private

Table 8.3 *Diepsloot residents' needs, as outlined in focus groups during 2000*

Focus group with 8 very poor women (38–50 years old)	Focus group with 11 unemployed youth (19–27 years old)	Focus group with 5 women traders (28–45 years old)	Focus group with 11 Diepsloot tenants	Focus group with 11 Diepsloot west home owners
Money and jobs	Money and jobs	Access to credit	Houses	Jobs
Transport	Secondary school and bursaries	Security from domestic abuse	Schools	Police station
Road across the river	Library and hall		Proper sanitation	Educational institutions
Food	Sports centre		Electricity	Recreational facilities
Clinic	Information centre		Road	Road access across the stream
Schools	Clothes		Road across the river	
Clothes	Litter		Police station	

sector, there is, in fact, no single document. Instead, an initial report by the provincial government spawned several other linked initiatives that shaped the future of Diepsloot (see Table 8.4).

During 1995–1996, the wisdom of the Gauteng premier's intervention in providing houses at Diepsloot for the Zevenfontein squatters was not immediately questioned. Indeed, some praised him for his strategic leadership. Soon, however, officials began to review this decision, which was made in response to a crisis, pointing out that to build housing for the poor so far from the urban core was not sustainable. The director of the Department of Land Affairs in the province accepted that:

> *Diepsloot is not the ideal by any stretch of the imagination... [T]he ideal is never to do reception areas like at Diepsloot, but for local authorities to identify areas for settlement continuously.* (Sunday Independent, *24 November 1996)*

In an attempt to correct the problems caused by siting development for the poor far from jobs, and in an attempt to improve the lives of residents who were not about to move again, a retrospective integrated-development programme was launched. It brought together all of the major stakeholders for Diepsloot and was, once again, initiated by the provincial government. Significantly, members of the local community who approached the office of the Gauteng premier prompted this venture into integrated settlement planning. But it would be naive to see the master-planning venture simply as an act of community-led development. The CDF members were not alone in their petition for the future of Diepsloot to be defined:

Table 8.4 *Planning schemes pertaining to Diepsloot*

Planning scheme	Coordinating agency	Major proposals of the scheme	Role of the Diepsloot CDF
Diepsloot Integrated Development Project	Provincial office of the premier	• Launch Diepsloot CDF • Coordinate capital projects (housing, multipurpose centre, satellite police station, clinic, upgrade water supply, improve road access) • Discourage additional growth of the area • Focus on short-term improvements in social services, infrastructure, shelter and transport • Facilitate realistic and sustainable growth	• CDF given formal status • CDF accepts co-responsibility for restricting inmigration to the area by monitoring new shack development
Diepsloot/ Olievenhout-bosch Regional Development Framework or Master Plan	Greater Pretoria Metropolitan Council, Khayalami Metropolitan Council and the Northern Metropolitan Local Council	• Spatial plan for the area that confirms constraints on economic growth (see below) • Economic development and implementation of catalytic projects (see below) • Definition of deliverables for Diepsloot • Identification of environmental upgrading • Land identification for social and community infrastructure • Define links and interface with other areas	• Community involvement restricted to implementing priorities following the master plan recommendation that consolidation be pursued
Spatial Development Framework	Greater Pretoria Metropolitan Council, Khayalami Metropolitan Council and the Northern Metropolitan Local Council	• De-densification of the informal areas and re-housing into subsidy houses with tenure • Establishment of a database to determine needs • Service delivery strategy for piped water to all formal houses	• Water-borne sewerage
Economic development plan	Greater Pretoria Metropolitan Council, Khayalami Metropolitan Council and the Northern Metropolitan Local Council	• Entrepreneurial development pilot projects	• Small, medium and micro enterprise (SMME) programme • LED council • Promotion of small-scale farming
Environmental management plan	Greater Pretoria Metropolitan Council, Khayalami Metropolitan Council and the Northern Metropolitan Local Council	• Define the urban edge	• Riverbed management • Flood

Various other local and provincial departments were constantly approached by the private sector regarding the proposed development in the area. The Premier, who was involved in the relocation of the residents of Zevenfontein in 1994, was aware of other development initiatives and proposals for the area. He called a joint meeting of the various role players in the area in July 1998 in an attempt to ensure a better life for the residents through coordinating the various development initiatives. Both Provincial Cabinet and Local Council have formally approved the attempt to coordinate development at Diepsloot. (NMC, undated)

Under the impetus of the provincial government, a number of more detailed planning schemes relating to Diepsloot were devised, and the sub-committees of the CDF (see Table 8.1) actively engaged with specialist recommendations. None of the component plans departed in any significant way from the primary recommendations agreed to in the integrated development project (see Table 8.3). According to the plans, Diepsloot was to be consolidated and the area would be encouraged to have an inward development focus, making it more like 'an entire [town]in its own right', than an integrated node located on the edge of the Gauteng space economy (APS Planafrica, 1998, p5.2.1). In reality, this means that Diepsloot has been excluded from the Gauteng Spatial Development Framework, which proposes a north–south corridor of high-technology and capital-intensive development between Johannesburg, through Midrand to Pretoria (see Figure 8.1). Given the very high levels of poverty and unemployment in Diepsloot, and the settlement's potential proximity to major economic-growth nodes – especially if public transport links were enhanced – it is not unreasonable to query why the CDF agreed to the consolidation and containment proposals.

In the planning documentation, the rationale for limiting expansion at Diepsloot and curtailing its links with the wider area are couched in the most overtly pro-poor terms. The settlement's economic and physical marginalization are primary factors given for the moratorium on further settlement, as is the perception that Diepsloot is a dumping ground for the urban underclass. The potential for competition for scarce social resources, such as schools and clinics, is noted. In practice, however, the factor that appears to have carried the most weight in the rationalization of the development impasse placed on Diepsloot is the capacity constraint on bulk water supplies (APS Planafrica, 1998).

So, was Diepsloot being limited for the perceived good of residents, or was the technical capacity constraint a ruse to protect rich landowners in the Dainfern area from inheriting a growing low-income settlement in their backyard? There were contradictory indications that suggested shifting coalitions of influence behind the Diepsloot master plan. Nevertheless, the move to confine the growth of the Diepsloot settlement through the master plan can be viewed as a sinister manipulation of the participatory planning process. The evidence that restricting Diepsloot may have been in the interest of other wealthier and more influential actors is suggested by two comments. Firstly, there is the observation that the expansion of Diepsloot would prevent further development in the vicinity; secondly, there is the comment that the economic development potential along the R511 and R28 routes and the intersection would be diminished (see Figure 8.1). On the other hand, the authorities can be seen to have negotiated a win–win situation with the CDF support. There is no question that Diepsloot was perceived by a second group of wealthy landowners at Bloubosrand as a viable alternative to a proposed mass low-income housing development that was being planned for their backyard called Cosmo City. It is therefore plausible to suggest that the restrictions and associated focus on upgrading was the best option for the existing poor of Diepsloot and their better-off commercial and residential neighbours. Clearly, this was the decision of the CDF. Members were actively involved in a campaign to destroy the shacks of new arrivals and to ensure that only established residents were given housing.

Until 2000, the policy and implementation phases of the Diepsloot master plan were characterized by remarkably high levels of cooperation and consensus. Nevertheless, there were incidents that defied the order of idealized structure plans and community participation frameworks. Having, at great cost, removed illegal squatters from the riverbed, local politicians were alleged to have condoned and even encouraged their immediate return to the floodplain. Unfortunately for these squatters, 2000 was a year of unusually heavy rain in Johannesburg, and some 1500 Diepsloot residents lost their shacks and possessions in heavy flooding.

The demand for land and money from rental or bribery in Diepsloot is only one of the factors that may break the accord on containment between the CDF and other interested parties. Demographic, social and economic realities and political dynamics will play out over the next few years, determining the impact of the Diepsloot master plan consensus. Having been a major player in its formation, the test of the CDF's strength will be the extent to which it is able to continue to hold support and influence the future of Diepsloot.

Local Participation in City-scale Development Politics

The ability of the CDF to deliver land, housing and services to its constituency hinged upon resources (such as having access to a council-sponsored cellphone) and processes (for example, who is served notification of meetings). Under the current participatory planning dispensation, the CDF is allocated a central role (and limited resources) in negotiating the terms of development. Yet, as we have seen, Diepsloot was a politically contentious settlement. Its strongly ANC identity belies the fierce undercurrents that shape political allegiances. Allegedly an area of (ANC) local-government neglect in the mid-1990s, the settlement was adopted by the controversial (ANC) Provincial President Matole Matshego to provide him with a popular support base. At least one resident who participated in the focus groups was deeply appreciative of the provincial administration's intervention in Diepsloot West:

> *On our arrival, we saw what one could have said 'promised land' [sic]; there were water taps in every yard, roads were tarred, houses were electrified… roughly everything we never had before was there.*

As a presidential lead project, the Gauteng Department of Land and Housing facilitated the single largest housing development (3800 units) and became directly involved with the CDF, even though, in theory, the local authority should have initiated housing delivery. The provincial leader's intervention was attributed to his fragile position within the ANC and the imperative of securing a support base among the poor. Afterwards, the Diepsloot site became the object of close scrutiny by the NMLC, in part because the local council had to assume responsibility for managing the servicing of the units delivered by the provincial government. Since the departure of Matsego as provincial leader (a story of political intrigue), Diepsloot has ceased to feature as prominently as a political football within the local or provincial ANC structures. Recent evidence, where thousands of displaced people were moved to Diepsloot from the flooded riverbed of Alexandra in 2001, even suggests that the area may have fallen right out of political favour.

There is, undoubtedly, more to the politics of Diepsloot than a vote-catching exercise or a party squabble. The future of Diepsloot is also tied up with external actors interested in environmental protection and land speculation. As we have already seen, both these constituencies have strong interests in a well-managed, but limited-scale, settlement at Diepsloot. Thus far, this agenda of containing the low-income urban sprawl has been upheld through the IDP process; therefore, no conflict of interest has been manifested. The CDF was part of a successful development regime. But the demographic profile of the area (with a large youthful population), as well as the evidence of ongoing in-migration and even forced resettlement, suggest that this will not always be the case. It is, thus, a matter of time until the social composition of the population changes, and the politics of party leaders dictates high-profile interventions elsewhere in the city. When this happens, the CDF will find itself confronted by hostile rather than supportive forces.

The Diepsloot development is located along the urban edge in an area of potential natural beauty, in the otherwise overdeveloped *highveld*. Gauteng is poorly endowed with recreational or agricultural opportunities; and so the vacant land to the north of Diepsloot is, according to environmental officials, being jealously guarded for agriculture and eco-tourism. The fact that there is already a master plan for Diepsloot is testament to the sensitivity of its location. Whereas, at the micro scale, the impact of environmental concerns has been a major boost for improvements in water catchment management, litter campaigns and dust regulation, there are also more general green environmental issues at stake that might influence the future of the area. When asked during the focus groups to identify the major players in urban development in the city, metropolitan officials singled out the deep northern suburb ratepayers' associations and the environmental lobby (see Figure 6.1 in Chapter 6).

Thus far, the council's strategy for appeasing all of the interest groups has been to assert the importance of restricting the scale of settlement at Diepsloot, due to its peripheral location and to the serious constraints on the delivery of bulk services. This technocratic rationale for limiting the settlement to its present size has been accepted by all stakeholders, and the CDF has gone along with measures to restrict in-migration. However, one cannot but ponder the consequences of the rupture of this consensus. Even assuming that the objective of consolidating Diepsloot is preserved by the partnership of the CDF, the private sector and local and provincial government, there remains the uncontrolled aspect of the pent-up demand of the newly arriving poor, who seek to access the city to the north through Diepsloot. The most likely scenario seems to be that their demands will not be taken up by the CDF. Rather, the new urban poor will be forced to seek alternative strategies for improving their lives, even if this means keeping their heads down and noses clean and staying outside of formal participatory politics and planning.

CONCLUSION

Over the five years of the phase of interim local government, significant gains were made in improving the quality of life of some, but not all, of Johannesburg's poor residents. In the far north of the city, this was, in great part, thanks to the efforts of the Diepsloot CDF who worked alongside the new government to promote development in the area. The consolidation of the Diepsloot settlement is an excellent example of delivering the priorities demanded by the poor and meeting the expectations of the post-apartheid transition. Under the LDO/IDP process, a major effort was made to secure community involvement as part of an alternative approach to urban planning and development.

For DLG to presuppose and depend upon a single structure as a channel for residents' participation is, however, unrealistic. Structures, such as the CDF, that can be corrupted, influenced, overpowered or rendered ineffective through internal tensions are flawed instruments for eliciting the views of citizens on the role of the state in their own future. But does this mean that the noble desires of participatory planning are ill founded? Setting aside the ongoing role of elected councillors in the various stages of the planning process, there is much in the CDF structure to recommend it as a creative force in the planning process. An important advantage of the CDFs includes their institutional position, which allows community members to access both politicians and officials while forging coalitions with other interested parties, such as NGOs or businesses. However, if the municipality, civil society and organized political structures are to optimize the power of CDFs, there are several lessons to be drawn from the Diepsloot case.

Throughout the process of post-apartheid reconstruction, the Diepsloot CDF played a vital, if potentially unsustainable, role. The sustainability of the CDF intervention relates, among other things, to the fact that the conditions and experiences of the poor change over time, especially in consolidating urban areas. We have thus questioned the uncritical assessment of the success of the CDF in the ongoing participation of the poor in developing their neighbourhood. Central to our reservation is the increasingly dominant role of the CDF in mediating policy, service delivery and ongoing urban maintenance. There are three dimensions of this hegemony and the silencing of alternative political voices that create the conditions of instability. First, while the CDF has become the only mouthpiece for residents, its efficacy is eroded by the fact that it does not have absolute community support. Second, the reality of the urban development process is that the Diepsloot CDF is an unequal player in both the technical and political decisions about city-wide planning priorities. As the interests of commerce, the local authority and the community begin to diverge over the inevitable expansion of the area, the CDF is going to face increasing opposition to its role as gatekeeper and in freezing the settlement's size. Third, as the community of Diepsloot matures and becomes demographically and economically more differentiated – with women's interests in security, youth concerns for jobs and recreation, and an aged focus on welfare – the probability that a single community structure, such as the CDF, will survive in the way that it has done over the past five years is low.

Even in places such as Diepsloot where there is an unusually high degree of community coherence and support for one prominent organization, the circuits of political influence are not static. In Diepsloot, there is evidence that the support base of the CDF has been, and will continue to be, challenged. In addition to the ever present threat of those who wish to capture the power of the organization for their own ends, there is a (growing) constituency within Diepsloot who is the object of discrimination or whose needs are badly represented by the organization. Thus far, the CDF has managed these tensions with aplomb. In order to maintain its legitimacy as a voice of the people, it must continue to do so. Institutionalized and unresponsive community participation, as in the case of the Diepsloot CDF, may undermine flexibility and representivity, thus contributing to the exclusion of marginalized groups.

While institutional flexibility and fluctuation in the personalities of the leadership and the priorities of the organization are good for bottom-up representation, they are probably counterproductive for interfacing with state- and private-sector developers. The imperative of ensuring that the poor direct, rather than endorse, the decisions that surround the implementation of development means that the voice of the poor in accessing resources and power needs to be couched in the technical language of suppliers. In the case of Diepsloot, the CDF has displayed considerable skill in this regard, admittedly with NGO assistance. However, where professional blind spots exist, as in the areas of social development, the community representatives have not found a way for independently inserting their own priorities onto the agenda.

A relatively untested realm of the CDF's power in Diepsloot is their ability to confront the wider context that regulates city management. For example, without a city-wide superstructure that champions the interests of CDFs (such as SANCO), it is hard to see how residents of Johannesburg can engage in the privatization debates or other key questions covered by the city-development strategy process.

Overall, then, we argue that institutionalized community representation though CDFs has some strengths and some worrying limitations for achieving participation in the planning process. Where the deliverers of development depend upon the same group to speak for the community at the design, implementation and assessment phases of development, there are real threats to democracy. If the laudable goals of the post-apartheid planning frameworks are to be realized, more nuanced approaches to the participatory process will have to be encouraged that recognize the structural constraints on local organizations.

The task of facilitating participatory government does not lie exclusively with local government. Indeed, it is the place of CBOs, political parties and civil society also to question the CDF structure and to challenge the local authority to adapt its stated commitment to inclusive planning. It is not, as Friedman warns (2001), for the local government to reconfigure the tools of negotiation – this would perpetuate the regulation control and centralization of the political process, which is antithetical to both development and democracy – but also for civil society organizations to fashion the process.

Chapter 9

Housing and Service Consumption in Soweto

INTRODUCTION

Urban services in Johannesburg are of a comparatively high standard, so service delivery in contemporary Johannesburg has much to do with overcoming past inequities and integrating low-income citizens within the network of infrastructure and services enjoyed by better-off residents of the city. As such, the whole area of service provision is in some need of reform. At a macro level, there has been external pressure to seek private solutions to service delivery (Bond, 2000b, pp49–182), and at a meso level, there have been efforts to marry these imperatives with the aim of poverty reduction. Service improvements, especially water, electricity, policing and housing, are seen as key mechanisms for creating greater equality in Johannesburg (Beall, Crankshaw and Parnell, 2000). Chapter 6 provided a background to some of the structural and institutional dimensions associated with improving infrastructure and extending service *provision*. We argued in that chapter that the debate over *iGoli 2002* and the privatization of services had taken the urban restructuring debate up a basic-needs *cul de sac*. In seeking to advance the services debate in Johannesburg, the focus of this chapter is on differential *access* to urban services in Johannesburg, with particular attention being paid to the challenges posed by different patterns of service *consumption* in Soweto. Specific reference is made to the area of Orlando East, the heart of sub-tenancy in Soweto and an area of contested service provision and consumption.

This chapter is important in two key respects. First, it shows the impact of apartheid's legacy on access to, and control over, services by showing how the experience of service provision was structured by race and housing type. Second, it demonstrates to policy-makers and planners the importance of taking into account not only the formal organizational and institutional arrangements involved in the delivery of urban services, but also the informal institutional dynamics that go to make up the social relationships and micropolitics of everyday life. As we show below, these hold significant implications for the sustained delivery of urban services.

SERVICE PROVISION IN JOHANNESBURG

The provision of services and the construction of infrastructure to meet the basic needs of low-income South Africans is the widely accepted priority of the post-apartheid government (Khosa, 2000). In meeting this goal, the first major task of the GJMC has been to rectify the imbalances in services and infrastructure inherited from the previous dispensation. There are three respects in which the legacy of apartheid impacted directly on the current crisis in levels of services in Johannesburg. The first was the well-known policy of providing inferior quality services for blacks. Thus, standards of social and physical infrastructure were intentionally set lower than they were for whites. In public education, health, housing and transport, racially defined standards of construction and service gave tangible expression to the political and economic hierarchy upon which white supremacy depended.

The second explanation for poor levels of service across large parts of Johannesburg relates to the 1968 decision to stop the development of African areas in 'white' South African cities. The metropolitan outcome of the policy of separate development, which insisted that African development be restricted to racially defined 'homelands', or '*bantustans*', was a massive backlog of housing and infrastructure development in the old township areas. As explained in Chapter 4, rigid restrictions on tenure rights and individual housing construction prevented African people from effectively providing for their own shelter in white-controlled urban areas.

The third aspect of service provision directly affected by apartheid policies was the problem of differential, and unequal, billing systems for urban services in black and white areas. Cross-subsidization from wealthy citizens to the poor was not a feature of apartheid Johannesburg. Rates paid in white-occupied residential areas invariably went towards servicing white areas, and these were supplemented by industrial and commercial rates. As the background paper on poverty, housing and urban development prepared for the *Speak Out on Poverty Hearings in South Africa* put the urban case:

> *Poverty in South Africa is more than usually associated with the high cost of household expenditure. The irrationality of the segregation-driven location of the residential areas of the poor has increased costs such as transportation. Moreover, because of the system of financing townships, there is a legacy of the unfair cross-subsidization of rates to rich white neighbourhoods instead of poor African residential areas. In common with other Third World cities, residents of informal settlements pay the highest per-item costs on basic commodities such as water and fuel.* (SANGOCO, 1998, p15)

Clearly, then, in the context of South Africa, it is difficult to address the issue of urban services without considering inequality, not least for political reasons.

It is not just apartheid South Africa that has provided adequate and reliable services to only a minority of its urban citizens Across many cities of the South, mains water and sewerage connections are concentrated in better-off areas, while new investment has tended to be in existing serviced areas. Thus, it is common for local governments to subsidize the elite heavily in terms of urban services, and this is compounded by the fact that new investment in low-income areas is characterized by cost-sharing or community participation. As with much else in South Africa, differential service provision took on racial dimensions. Moreover, the rates and service boycotts of the last two decades, in townships such as Soweto, mean that the metropolitan council has inherited a deep-seated culture of non-payment for services. This, together with increased trends towards illegal piracy of services, such as electricity, means that any normalization of the delivery system, even with subsidized rates and reduced service charges, may well represent an increase in living costs for the city's poorer citizens.

Not all of Johannesburg's infrastructural challenges can be ascribed to racist policies. Johannesburg is over 100 years old, and as it continues to grow, some of the contradictions of past planning and servicing are beginning to emerge. Water supply, sanitation and electricity are infrastructure investments that are favoured by government for political reasons. Such services, therefore, seem to receive greater attention than bulk sewerage repairs, and this may threaten water quality across the city, especially in low-income neighbourhoods. The most important new demands on infrastructure are densification of neighbourhoods across the city and the dramatic expansion of low-income areas on the periphery. Approximately 10 per cent of the area of Greater Johannesburg has some spare bulk-infrastructure capacity, and a further 60 per cent would be able to cope with limited densification (GJMC, 1997). However, shortages in capacity are already apparent, and there are also uncoordinated patterns of infrastructure provision across the city. Moreover, sewerage and water supplies are not necessarily strong in the same locations. The imperative of committing resources to extending services to the poor has, ironically, seemed to raise awareness of the deteriorating condition of the ageing infrastructure in the rest of the city. Thus, in practice, there is a technical as well as a political tension emerging between the maintenance of established service levels and the extension of services to new, and historically under-serviced, areas.

As in many cities, there are concentrations of poverty in Johannesburg that merit special attention. However, a worrying tendency, explained, in part, by the need for the new government to demonstrate immediate and tangible delivery, is the focus of service and infrastructure provision in unsustainable informal settlements. By managing the city in such a way that poverty and inequality are reduced, the metropolitan council cannot adjudicate the competing demands between new service provision and the maintenance of existing investments in isolation. Areas of extreme infrastructure stress or neglect are often geographically congruent with neighbourhoods that house the population who is most adversely affected by changing occupational and employment opportunities in the city. This is certainly the case for Soweto.

Physical infrastructure, although often funded with national funds, is organized and initiated by local government. Housing, infrastructure and service provision comprise a major, if not the major, fiscal commitment to poverty reduction in Johannesburg. Although the metropolitan council does not control the capital budget for most of these projects, its operating budget maintains the services, and its planning and environmental departments coordinate project planning and implementation. The tariffs generated from services, either as rates or user charges, enter the municipal purse. At this stage, therefore, the demand for retrospective delivery means that the metropolitan council's attention has been focused on finding capital to provide new services to all of those who were deprived under apartheid, with a particular concern for people without any services, usually those living in informal settlements. What we see in places such as Soweto is frustration over the low levels of existing service provision, combined with poor maintenance in a context of increasing densification.

The nature of the infrastructure challenge in Greater Johannesburg was widely debated in relation to the planning process linked to defining LDOs, discussed in Chapter 5. An impressive list of individuals, NGOs, CBOs, ratepayers' associations, civics organizations, and political party stakeholders participated in a series of workshops to define the city's development priorities. The development of acceptable and affordable standards, the insistence on service equity, the development of new service areas, the redress on service backlogs, and the enforcement of equitable spatial development were all identified as key objectives for infrastructure delivery in Johannesburg. The real challenge, however, is how to reverse generations of inequality and to translate these laudable policies into effective practice on a tight budget. This issue is discussed in Chapter 6.

RESIDENTS' ACCESS TO SERVICES IN JOHANNESBURG

In looking at the post-apartheid challenge, what emerges from Tables 9.1, 9.2 and 9.3 is that, when access to services is used as an indicator of poverty, even the poorest urban residents of Johannesburg are better off than many other urban dwellers across the continent. In Africa, 36 per cent of the urban population are thought to be without an adequate water supply and 45 per cent are not covered by sanitation (Beall, Crankshaw and Parnell, 2000). It should also be pointed out that the situation of Johannesburg's poor compares well with national figures. For example, it has been estimated that for the country as a whole, in the immediate post-apartheid period, only 21 per cent of households

Table 9.1 *Main source of domestic water by race in Johannesburg, 1996 (percentage distributions)*

Source of water	African	Coloured	Indian	White	All Races
Piped water in dwelling	53	94	98	99	67
Piped water on site	31	3	1	0	22
Public tap/borehole/tanker	16	3	0	1	11
Total	100	100	100	100	100

Source: authors' analysis of 1996 Population Census results

Table 9.2 *Type of sanitation provision by race in Johannesburg, 1995*
(percentage distributions)

Type of sanitation	African	Coloured	Indian	White	All Races
Flush toilet in dwelling	50	89	94	99	70
Flush toilet on site	38	11	6	1	23
Toilet off site (all types)	4	0	0	0	3
Other toilet on site					
(chemical and bucket)	5	0	0	0	3
Pit latrine on site	2	0	0	0	1
Total	100	100	100	100	100

Source: authors' analysis of 1995 October Household Survey results

had access to piped water and only 28 per cent to sanitation facilities. Over 80 per cent of rural households had no access to either (May, 1999, p138).

Nevertheless, intra-urban inequalities along both racial and class lines do exist, and this is undoubtedly the most startling picture that emerges within Johannesburg. Whereas coloured, Indian and white households live almost exclusively in formal houses or flats, African households are distributed across a much wider range of informal and formal types of accommodation, which, in turn, have more variable access to services (see Table 9.4).

Water Provision

There is official and constitutional commitment to the right of access to safe and sufficient water in South Africa. In its 1994 White Paper, the Department of Water Affairs and Forestry (DWAF) translated the general constitutional obligations into the practical goal of providing access to basic water and sanitation services to all within seven years (DWAF, 1994). Responsibility is located with the local- or third-tier of government, which has a constitutional obligation to provide for basic needs. In respect of water supply, this is defined by DWAF as 25 litres per person per day of good-quality water, provided at a maximum distance of 200 metres on a regular and reliable basis.

Table 9.3 *Main energy source for cooking by race in Johannesburg, 1996*
(percentage distributions)

Type of energy source	African	Coloured	Indian	White	All Races
Electricity direct from authority	79	95	96	96	85
Electricity from other source	0	0	0	0	0
Gas	2	1	4	4	2
Paraffin	17	3	0	0	12
Wood	0	0	0	0	0
Coal	2	0	0	0	1
Total	100	100	100	100	100

Source: authors' analysis of the 1996 Population Census results

Table 9.4 *Type of dwelling by race in Johannesburg, 1995*
(percentage distributions)

Type of dwelling	African	Coloured	Indian	White	All Races
Formal house or apartment	62	97	100	95	77
Formal house or room in backyard	20	2	0	4	13
Shack in backyard	3	0	0	0	2
Shack in squatter settlement or site-and-service scheme[1]	10	0	0	0	6
Hostel	4	1	0	1	3
Other	1	0	0	0	0
Total	100	100	100	100	100

Source: authors' analysis of 1995 October Household Survey results

Most survey research suggests that the vast majority of Johannesburg's residents have access to piped water (see Table 9.5). These findings are based upon specified criteria, such as the distance of a household from a tap or other water source. Case studies of water supply based upon qualitative research reveal greater differentiation in terms of access to piped water. For example, a recent survey of informal settlements in Greater Johannesburg showed that as many as 12 per cent of residents in clusters of poorly serviced land depend upon non-piped water (CASE, 1998a).

In a recent household survey of Soweto, the variations between housing types emerged as a reliable predictor of access to water. Although almost all households have access to piped water, residents in squatter settlements and site-and-service settlements were much more likely to rely on a communal standpipe in the street (see Table 9.6). In contrast, most of the original houses that were built by the local authority during 1950s and early 1960s were supplied with a tap outside the kitchen door (Morris, 1980). This means that today, most backyard tenants have access to a tap in their own backyard (see Table 9.6). Hostel residents have water that is piped into their dormitories, but only to

Table 9.5 *Main source of domestic water by type of housing in Johannesburg, 1995*
(percentage distributions)

Source of water	Formal house or apartment	Formal house or room in backyard	Shack in backyard	Shack in squatter settlement or site-and-service scheme[1]	Hostel	All housing types
Tap in dwelling	90	65	0	4	100	80
Outside tap on the stand	10	34	55	78	0	18
Public tap/kiosk/ borehole	0	2	45	18	0	2
Total	100	100	100	100	100	100

Source: authors' analysis of 1995 October Household Survey results

Table 9.6 *Main source of domestic water by type of housing in Soweto, 1997 (percentage distributions)*

	Council house	Private-sector house	Shack or room in backyard	Shack in squatter settlement	Hostel	Site-and-service scheme	Total
Outside tap in backyard	62	2	99	11	0	59	65
Tap inside formal house	36	98	0	2	100	6	28
Communal tap	0	0	1	84	0	33	6
Missing data	2	0	0	3	0	3	1
Total	100	100	100	100	100	100	100
Sample size	1101	361	378	368	360	379	2947

Source: authors' analysis of Soweto in Transition Household Survey results[2]

communal kitchens and toilets. The only other households that have water piped into their houses are those who have renovated their council houses or those who have bought their own homes (see Table 9.6).

In Johannesburg, the metropolitan government is acutely aware that the extensive and generally very effective network of water coverage is not universal across the city. For example, it does not reach the new development nodes to the north and south of the city adequately (GJMC, 1997). Moreover, in a pattern that is repeated across many services, standards of water delivery vary enormously according to both the original racial occupation of the suburb and the type or generation of housing in which a household lives. In practice, the worst supplied are the more recently urbanized African households or children of established urban dwellers who have moved from formal housing stock in townships into informal settlements. There are limited cases where water is trucked into informal settlements, and a small fraction of the population depends upon water from rivers and streams. However, taps in houses or on the stand provide most of the population with safe and drinkable water.

Compared with other cities of the South, direct purchase of water from private vendors is relatively uncommon in Johannesburg. However, as is made evident by our study of Orlando East, in townships such as those of Soweto, rental arrangements mean that tenants share service charges with landlords and therefore indirectly pay for water. In many informal settlements, on the other hand, 'shacklords' control access to water sources, such as communal standpipes. Consequently, many of those paying for water in the province of Gauteng, of which Johannesburg forms a significant part, are not necessarily paying the service provider but an intermediary. What this signals is that the politics of water supply are not confined to who gets what at the level of the city. They also involve vested interests at the local level that may well oppose improvements in delivery because they are making a profit from the current unregulated supply of water.

Table 9.7 *Type of sanitation provision by type of housing in Johannesburg, 1995*
(percentage distributions)

Source of water	Formal house or apartment	Formal house or room in backyard	Shack in backyard	Shack in squatter settlement or site-and-service scheme[1]	Hostel	All housing types
Flush toilet in dwelling	79	54	0	0	98	70
Outside flush toilet on stand	20	43	55	13	2	23
Toilet off site (all types)	0	3	40	19	0	3
Other toilet on site (chemical and bucket)	0	0	0	50	0	3
Pit latrine on site	0	1	4	18	0	1
Total	100	100	100	100	100	100

Source: authors' analysis of 1995 October Household Survey results

Sanitation

The standard of formal sanitary services in Johannesburg is very high, with flush toilets the norm (see Table 9.7). Nevertheless, as with water, the same patterns of uneven service delivery are reflected. The GJMC is the sole agent responsible for bulk sewerage. Water-borne sewerage and wastewater treatments predominate, covering almost 80 per cent of the metropolitan area. No separate charges are levied for sanitation in Johannesburg, and the costs form part of the rates. In low-income areas, sanitation charges are part of the flat rate system. A key debate in post-apartheid Johannesburg relates to the issue of standards and technology choice, specifically the extension of water-borne sewerage versus the provision of pit latrines or chemical toilets. There are both political and environmental issues at stake in this choice. Issues of affordability and appropriateness aside, water-borne sewerage was the norm for historically white areas and formal African townships. There are, therefore, expectations that this level of service should be extended to informal settlements and new developments, even if this puts pressure on the city's water supply. In some informal settlements, such as Diepsloot, the extension of a water-borne sewerage service is feasible because of the proximity of the settlement to existing trunk sewerage lines. However, this is not always the case and alternative arrangements have to be made.

Levels of service differ dramatically across different settlement and housing types. Formal housing has a high level of service, while newer informal areas are poorly supplied. For example, in the informal settlement of Diepsloot, private operators under contract to the municipality provide chemical toilets and tank water. They are strictly managed and monitored by the Diepsloot CDF. However, there are important variations within settlements, as well. In Soweto, for example, flush toilets inside of the house are a feature of homes in wealthier areas only, with most houses having an outside flush toilet (see Table 9.8). However, qualitative studies reveal the importance of going beyond statistics to understand the micro politics of service use and consumption. For example, in Soweto's hostels there are flush toilets; but these essentially communal facilities are associated with the worst humiliations of abject living conditions (Pirie and da Silva, 1986).

A study of Alexandra, a township to the north of Johannesburg, found that the proportion of households sharing toilets with other households was as high as 87 per cent (CASE, 1998b). In the same study, backyard shack dwellers complained that not only did flush toilets not work, but that access was restricted because landlords locked up toilets at night to stop them being used by squatters and other non-tenants in the area. Tensions over sanitation are one of the issues that some squatters voiced as the reason for their move away from backyard shacks into the informal settlements (Crankshaw, 1993). Another study, however, showed that a large proportion (40 per cent) of squatters in Gauteng also reported having to share their toilets with other households (CASE, 1998a). Thus, the issue of service standards has as much to do with the number of people per toilet and the relations between them, as with the technical quality of the service.

Results from the Soweto in Transition Household Survey (Morris et al, 1999) show very clearly that it is only in the elite, new private-sector developments that flush toilets inside of the house are the norm. Almost all council stands were provided with outside toilets connected to a water-borne sewerage system; and, so, both house residents and backyard tenants have access to a flush toilet. Nevertheless, it is interesting to note differences in access to toilet facilities across different housing types in Soweto (see Table 9.8).

Electricity

Apartheid's African townships were electrified only after the 1976 Soweto uprisings. Among the reasons for this belated initiative was the hope by the Department of Mineral Affairs and Energy (DME) that power supply to low-income areas would stimulate local economic development. Initially, the cost of electrical power was higher in the townships than in the white suburbs because the BLAs responsible for implementing it tried to recoup the costs of installation. It was this levy that, above, all fuelled the rent-and-rates boycotts that characterized the 1980s and beyond, and that fuelled the fiscal problems of the GJMC discussed in Chapter 6 (Swilling and Shubane, 1991).

Since the electrification of many of the townships in the 1980s, there have been various efforts to promote increased consumption. Progress has been steady, but a recent survey of informal settlements in Gauteng (CASE, 1998a) suggested that only 11 per cent of informal residents used electricity as their major source of power. Our figures on energy use for cooking, which are drawn from the October Household Survey, suggest that consumption for backyard shacks (29 per cent) and informal settlements (59 per cent) is substantially higher than this study suggests, although they reflect similar trends of low electricity usage. Once power has been made available, the major reason for low consumption is affordability.

Table 9.8 *Type of sanitation provision by type of housing in Soweto, 1997 (percentage distributions)*

	Council house	Private-sector house	Shack or room in backyard	Shack in squatter settlement	Hostel	Site-and-service scheme	Total
Flush toilet in backyard	75	1	95	0	0	1	65
Flush toilet inside dwelling	25	99	4	0	0	2	17
Communal flush toilet	0	0	0	10	100	0	9
Pit latrine	0	0	0	23	0	8	2
Chemical toilet	0	0	0	67	0	0	4
Septic tank toilet in backyard	0	0	0	0	0	89	3
No toilet	0	0	1	0	0	0	0
Total	100	100	100	100	100	100	100
Sample size	1101	361	378	368	360	379	2947

Source: authors' analysis of Soweto in Transition Household Survey results

The average bill for households with electricity in Soweto was found to be 97 Rand (R97) per month in 1997 (Morris et al, 1999), almost UK£10 at that time, and a sum substantially beyond the means of many African households.

One factor thwarting efforts to increase consumption is the fact that traditional methods of cooking continue to be favoured by many low-income households. This is especially the case given the fact that people are fearful of their ability to control the use of electric power. They are also mistrustful of the ability of the ESKOM (the para-statal that undertakes bulk electricity generation for metropolitan Johannesburg) to levy the correct charge for the service (White et al, 1998). Traditionally, credit meters were used to measure consumption; but this system began to break down because of tensions between ESKOM and consumers in areas such as Soweto. Residents were incensed by high electricity bills and alleged corruption among ESKOM employees. ESKOM officials, in turn, were frustrated by non-payment of bills by consumers and the practice of many poor consumers simply to pirate power from overhead cables (Meintjes, 1997). This has led to a slow reassessment of delivery methods; following unsuccessful experiments with traditional credit meters, there is now a greater focus on pre-paid electricity meters. However, by 1997 only 5000 pre-paid meters had been installed in Soweto (Meintjes and White, 1997), and there is a long way yet to go in establishing trust between ESKOM officials and workers, on the one hand, and electricity consumers, on the other.

Table 9.9 *Electricity supply by type of housing in Soweto, 1997*
(percentage distributions)

	Council house	Private-sector house	Shack or room in backyard	Shack in squatter settlement	Hostel	Site-and-service scheme	Total
Mains supply with a credit meter	98	100	4	0	0	1	44
Mains supply with pre-paid card system	0	0	0	0	0	90	3
Mains communal supply	0	0	0	0	92	0	7
Illegal electrical extension cord from formal house	0	0	87	1	0	1	35
Other	0	0	0	1	0	1	0
No electricity supply	1	0	8	98	8	7	11
Total	100	100	100	100	100	100	100
Sample size	1101	361	378	368	360	379	2947

Source: authors' analysis of Soweto in Transition Household Survey results

Soweto houses were not electrified until the late 1970s; but by 1988, all formal houses were supplied with electricity (Mashabela, 1988). Although very few backyard households have a legal connection to an electricity meter (4 per cent), almost all backyard households in Soweto (92 per cent) have some access to electricity. Most get their electricity through an illegal extension cable from the main house (87 per cent) (see Table 9.9).

SOCIAL DIFFERENTIATION IN SOWETO AS SEEN THROUGH HOUSING

The vast disparities in the built environment of Johannesburg are legendary and are laid out in Table 9.10 for easy reference. Images of Soweto's barrack-like hostels and endless ranks of 'matchbox' houses are symbolic of the apartheid state's regimentation of peripheral African townships, while the irregular landscape of shantytowns and informal settlements are increasingly the leitmotif of the post-apartheid urbanization challenge.[3] Within former African townships, too, there has been growing social differentiation, reflected often in the changing urban landscape of areas such as Soweto, where a closer look overthrows any notion of housing uniformity.

Table 9.10 *Types of dwellings in Johannesburg, 1995*

Type of accommodation	Description of the accommodation	Percentage distribution of accommodation types
Formal house	In white and Indian areas, these are generally privately built detached houses. In African areas, these are the public housing units known as 'matchboxes'. In coloured areas, formal units are a mix of publicly built detached housing and limited private construction.	71.7
Apartment in apartment block	In white areas, flats are of a very high standard; in coloured areas, multi-floor public construction of a poor quality abounds. Some Indian housing in the inner city is in flats.	9.3
Backyard house or room	These are formal brick structures, often registered as garages.	10.6
Backyard shack	These are informal, less permanent structures.	1.4
Shack in shack settlement	These are informal, generally corrugated iron structures.	3.9
Hostel	These comprise single-sex units of shared accommodation, built either for miners or municipal workers.	2.5
Other	These include boarding and lodging houses. This figure is too low to reflect the very common shelter of domestic servants' quarters, where many African women live on the properties of their employers.	0.4
Total		100.0

Source: authors' analysis of 1995 October Household Survey results

The bulk of Soweto is a relatively new creation, with most of its townships established during the 1950s. From this time on, Soweto became a major reception area for African families in Johannesburg. The number of houses in the area rose rapidly, from 11,000 in 1948 to over 62,000 in 1965 (Lewis, 1966; Parnell and Hart, 1999). Today, there are about 127,000 formal houses and some 24,000 hostel rooms in Soweto (Crankshaw, Gilbert and Morris, 2000). The original 'matchbox' houses were built in three slightly different designs (Morris, 1980). The most common type, measuring 40sqm, is the '51/6', so named after the date (1951) and the number (6) assigned to the prototype. These houses comprised two bedrooms, a kitchen and a living room and were often built as semi-detached units.[4] The original houses were built to rudimentary standards, with only earthen or ash floors and without internal doors and ceilings.

During the 1950s, the vast bulk of Sowetans had no choice but to accept the standard 'matchbox' council house. By the 1990s, however, state reforms had privatized the provision of housing so that Sowetans now live under increasingly differentiated conditions. On the one hand, reforms that introduced home ownership offered a better-off minority the opportunity to purchase housing of a comparatively high standard at a relatively reasonable rate. On the other hand, the withdrawal of the state from low-cost housing provision led to overcrowding of formal houses and the proliferation of shacks in backyards

Table 9.11 *The population of Soweto by housing type, 1997*

Type of dwelling	Frequency distribution	Percentage distribution	Average number of residents per dwelling	Percentage distribution of residential units
Council houses	611,350	57	6	37
Private-sector houses	91,924	9	5	7
All backyards	212,015	20	2	37
Informal settlement shacks	66,976	6	4	6
Site-and-service shacks	44,471	4	4	4
Hostel rooms	40,901	4	2	8
Total	1,067,637	100		100

Source: Crankshaw, Gilbert and Morris (2000)

and on open land. In Soweto for example, only 57 per cent of the population live in ex-council houses (usually four rooms), while as many as 20 per cent live in single-roomed backyard structures (see Table 9.11 and Figure 9.1).

Moreover, many of the original 'matchbox' houses in low- to middle-income areas of Soweto, such as Meadowlands and Orlando East, have been altered often beyond recognition. Common changes include the installation of larger windows, smart front doors, garden walls and even electronic gates. Additions to the houses themselves are not common, and multiple storeys are even more rare. However, the backyard of almost every Soweto house has shacks or formal outbuildings, housing-extended family or paying tenants, mostly the latter (see Figure 9.1). They have been described elsewhere as follows:

> *Designed and built by the residents themselves, these backyard shacks are made of wood, zinc and even plastic and canvas sheeting. With their variety of materials, design, position and orientation, these backyard shelters stand in stark contrast to the serried ranks of uniform matchbox houses. These backyard shacks never intrude on the clean lines of the streetscape. Front yards are never built on. However, from the vantage point of even a small hill, the densely packed roofs of the backyard shacks are clearly evident. From the air, the visual impact of this informal building is even greater: the sheer volume of backyard shacks creates the impression of a residue of formal matchbox houses floating in a sea of shacks.* (Crankshaw and Parnell, 1999)

What this picture of Soweto suggests is that although better-off people are leaving, many who are less well off are staying, either through choice or because they have no option. As a result, pressure on accommodation continues, both from sustained population growth within the area and as people carry on moving into Soweto.

There are very marked sociological differences across housing types in Soweto. In income terms, the private-sector houses are characterized by higher earnings, followed by council housing, backyard shacks, site and services and

Figure 9.1 *Formal houses with backyard structures in Soweto*

hostels (Morris et al, 1999). The age profile of residents in the different housing types also varies considerably, with council houses demonstrating older profiles. Indeed, the owner-occupiers of Soweto's 'matchboxes' represent Johannesburg's quintessential Fordist working class: ageing and often unemployed and caught in the poverty trap of Johannesburg's very own 'city of the south'. Moreover, like other cities of the South, Soweto is experiencing internal population growth, as well as acting as an important reception area for migrants from elsewhere in the country and from countries in the Southern African region, many of whom find accommodation as tenants in backyard shacks.

Backyard shacks are a fairly recent phenomenon in Soweto. During the 1970s, the main response to the pressure of ever increasing numbers of people moving into the area was for families to share council homes. It was only during the 1980s that there was widespread construction of backyard shacks, coinciding with popular resistance in the townships and the collapse of municipal government in Soweto (Crankshaw, 1993; Sapire, 1992). Since the first fully democratic election in 1994, there have been significant changes in housing policy. One important change has been the introduction of a housing subsidy for low-income families so that they can buy a serviced stand and build a basic home. However, progress has been slow, particularly in Johannesburg, and there is still a lot of pressure on families to remain in Soweto, with backyard shacks remaining an important accommodation option because of traditional difficulties with land invasion and no tradition of private rental in former African areas. Moreover, the fact that 97 per cent of backyard accommodation is on ex-council properties, rather than in new privately built dwellings, suggests that landlords are not necessarily well off themselves and need backyard tenants to supplement their incomes (Crankshaw, Gilbert and Morris, 2000). Until recently, very little was known about backyard tenants, themselves. However, recent research has shown that they have some distinct characteristics. One of these is that a higher proportion of in-migrants who live in backyards are foreign born compared with in-migrants in Soweto, as a whole. Backyard households are also characterized by their comparative youth. In general, backyard households are likely to comprise unmarried youngsters, and young married couples without children or with relatively young children (Crankshaw, Gilbert and Morris, 2000).

Backyard shacks, such as those that predominate in Soweto, constitute a critical policy issue for the GJMC in its management of housing and urbanization, both in terms of the physical and service challenges they present, as well as the social issues that emerge from this tenure arrangement. Since the political transition to democracy in South Africa, Johannesburg's Metropolitan Council has struggled to define its policy towards unregulated settlement, in general, and to backyards, in particular (Monitor, 2000a). The proposed Soweto Development Plan seeks to address the issue; but in the case of backyard shacks, the goal of regulating subletting arrangements is ambitious, given the sale and transfer of the bulk of Soweto's council housing stock to sitting tenants. This is particularly the case when there are ongoing transfers and it is not always clear who the registered property owner should be. In addressing the backyard phenomenon today, there are complicated issues of standards, bylaws, private land rights and service-delivery strategies. Unlike the case of informal settlements, such as Diepsloot, there are no national guidelines to assist the metropolitan council in defining its position.

SERVICE STORIES FROM ORLANDO EAST

Against this background, we turn to our micro study of Orlando East.[5] It is an area that continues to host the greatest concentration of backyard accommodation and sub-tenancy in Soweto (Morris et al, 1999) because of its convenient location and relatively larger plot sizes compared to elsewhere in Soweto (Parnell and Hart, 1999).[6] We are not concerned, here, with the bricks and mortar, tin and packaging that make up the structures of backyard units. Rather, we focus on the social and institutional relationships, underpinning access to, and consumption of, services in Orlando East. In particular, we focus on how the poorest among its residents, the backyard tenants, are marginalized by the political and administrative workings of the GJMC.

Orlando East is a multi-ethnic neighbourhood that, in addition to a wide range of South African ethnic identities, is home to residents from other African countries, including many who have been in Johannesburg for decades. Interestingly, while there is a significant representation of foreign migrants from the Southern African Development Community (SADC) region, particularly those with a history of labour migration to South Africa, more recent foreign African migrants from further north in the continent, on arrival, have targeted the more accessible and less insular inner city, rather than the backyards of Soweto.[7]

The currently cosmopolitan nature of Orlando East represents a shift from the population patterns of the past. Under apartheid rule, Orlando East was zoned for Nguni occupation (Pirie, 1984) – that is, largely isiZulu- and isiXhosa-speaking people from present-day KZN and Eastern Province, respectively. Today, however, there are no area-based patterns of clustering of linguistic groups in Orlando East, although the impact of ethnic zoning remains in evidence in Greater Soweto. Gilbert and Crankshaw (1999) explain later patterns of ethnic clustering by housing type in terms of the different arrival times in Johannesburg, rather than by ethnic groups staying together solely for reasons of social bonding. While this is not the case for ethnic communities housed in hostels, backyard rooms in areas such as Orlando East have been a primary housing choice for local and regional migrants over an extended period of time, and this is clearly important in explaining its current diversity.

The emergence of backyard shacks testifies to the failure of the apartheid housing system to adequately provide accommodation to Johannesburg's poor African residents. Occupants of backyard shacks in Orlando East have still not made it into the formal housing system; as such, they are also a reminder of the failures of the new housing dispensation. Indeed, many of the tenants have had their names on the lists for RDP houses since 1995, but have not yet been informed of when, or where, they may expect re-housing. However, not everyone living in Orlando East in backyard accommodation is waiting for an alternative, or for government to intervene. There is a significant proportion of illegal immigrants who have no papers and therefore cannot expect to apply for houses. Others are circular migrants with families in other places. Still more are young people who have left home but have not yet settled down and who prefer the flexibility of rental accommodation. Finally, there are the extended families of house owners for whom backyard shacks provide relief from the cramped confines of the 'matchbox' houses. Thus, while the majority of informants desire and would accept RDP housing, not all tenants can be seen as unhappy or unwilling occupants of the backyards.

One reason for this is that the provision of services and the quality of accommodation available to the residents of backyards are significantly better than those available in the squatter camps. While almost half of all backyard structures in Greater Soweto are crudely built wood and corrugated-iron shacks, a majority (54 per cent) are formal structures made from bricks and cement. What varies little is the number of rooms; virtually all backyard structures comprise only one room (Crankshaw, Gilbert and Morris, 2000). What survey results do not show is that backyard rooms range greatly in size and the quality of the shacks also varies. Some are built with old and rusty corrugated-iron sheets (with many holes from previous constructions), whereas others are quite pristine (see Figure 9.1). Given the limited size of backyard accommodation, it is not surprising that there is a great deal of overcrowding. However, there are no significant differences between the occupancy rates of backyard shacks and formal rooms, with severe overcrowding in both of these forms of accommodation (Crankshaw, Gilbert and Morris, 2000).

Although very few backyard households have a legal connection to an electricity meter (4 per cent), almost all backyard households have some access to electricity (92 per cent). Most get their electricity through an illegal extension cable from the main house (86 per cent). Similarly, because backyard taps were originally fixed to the outside wall of all council houses next to the kitchen, almost every backyard household (99 per cent) has access to water. With few exceptions, neither the residents of the main house, nor the backyard tenants, have water in the house unless they have had it piped in at their own expense. In addition, because almost all council stands were provided with outside toilets, all backyard tenants have access to a flush toilet. Thus, backyard shacks are popular precisely because they offer amenities that are not found in informal settlements. This is what tenants are paying for, rather than living in equivalent quality shelter under more autonomous conditions in squatter camps. As one informant remarked: 'People who stay in informal settlements suffer because they have to walk a long distance to fetch more water.'

Moreover, the whole relationship of tenancy is based upon the purchase of services. In theory, payment of rental includes water and sewerage, but not electricity. But not paying for electricity is not really an option for tenants. The tendency seems to be for the electricity bill to be split among all yard occupants, even when the consumption is unequal. While rents for backyard rooms and shacks have remained remarkably stable over recent years, service charges imposed by landlords are reported to have increased. As a result, backyard tenants are paying privately for services, albeit indirectly, by sharing costs with homeowners. Those who cannot afford to do so move to informal settlements. However, they are not receiving an adequate service. We found that across all categories of local-government service delivery to stands in Orlando East (water supply, sanitation, waste collection and electricity), insufficient attention was paid to the specific needs and realities of the backyard population.[8] We explore this in more detail in relation to a number of specific on-plot services.

Electricity

At the time this research was undertaken, electricity was the most contentious service as no backyard shacks are legally wired. Most tenants pay for power consumed through illegal lines extended from the main house, although a number have illegal electric-power connections drawn straight from mainline cables. Apart from being extremely dangerous, reliance on informally erected cables running between the main house and backyard shacks is inadequate in a number of ways. From the perspective of backyard tenants, supply is limited and erratic as only one or two appliances can be used at a time or the overloaded switches trip constantly. Moreover, the cost of power is unpredictable and often excessive. In the focus-group discussions, tenants spoke enviously of the pre-paid card system for electricity that operates in RDP houses, 'so you know where you stand'. Tenants do not see the electricity bills, which go to homeowners, and so they have no control over what they consume and what they pay for. Because they split the bill with landlords, tenants often are made to pay excessive amounts for the unpaid consumption of power of other households. Landlords control payment for electricity by cutting off power to backyard shacks; because connections are illegal and unearthed, serious safety problems emerge. Human exposure to unprotected lines, interior pollution resulting from the use of candles, paraffin lamps and stoves, as well as the prevalence of shack fires, are common consequences.

The individual costs of such accidents are enormous. However, the GJMC also faces the consequences from the incomplete electrification of backyards. One impact is increased air pollution, with Greater Soweto being one of the worst affected areas in this regard. Others include below-par cost recovery on bulk electricity, increasing health costs from pollution-related diseases, such as asthma, and growing reliance upon health and emergency services, not least of all for domestic accidents.

Water Supply

In the case of water supply, once again the official figures suggest that the legal requirements of the water department have been achieved (Monitor, 2000a), and indeed, access to water is not generally a problem for landlords or tenants. It is not clear whether access to water for tenants will remain unproblematic once the metropolitan council introduces free allocation of water to meet basic needs. Under these circumstances, landlords may begin to charge tenants for water consumed over and above the allotted amounts provided free of charge, as they currently do with the supply of electricity to tenants. At the time of this research, however, the main issue for backyard tenants was not about supply – access to on-stand taps means that no backyard residents do without water – but about being notified of cuts in the supply. Because backyard tenants do not pay their water bills directly to the GJMC, but rather as part of their rent to the landlord, they are not included in the council's communications with users. As one tenant put it: 'the landlord receives water and so do I, too; but my problem is when they close water and (we) are not notified'.

Sanitation and Drainage

The conventional argument that the original bulk sanitation designed for a low-density neighbourhood is inadequate for the new higher densities of unplanned backyard shacks holds true for Orlando. The fact that the original 'matchbox' houses had outside toilets means that there is a flush toilet in every yard, and it is this facility that all residents use, including backyard tenants. As in the case of water, they are piggybacking on a service designed and installed for fewer users, which is problematic. Officials were clear that it was general overuse, and not specific misuse, that caused problems that were linked to densification and the high levels of sub-tenancy associated with the backyard shacks.

Pressure from heavy use of the sewers is only one consequence of backyard accommodation. Other issues relate to drainage problems arising from the greater coverage of the stand by shacks, and presumably insensitive locating of the structures for runoff. As a sanitary official noted:

*When it rains, the down-flow is quiet high. Water dams up in the yard. People
break the gullies and drain water through the galleys. Sand and paper and
other rubbish drain into the system, which causes blockages.*

Our study of Orlando East also suggests that problems of drainage and sharing
toilet facilities often give rise to conditions of tension and conflict. For example,
many tenants are obliged to pay 'in-kind' rent by sweeping the yard, clearing the
drains and gullies and cleaning the toilet and around the tap, an issue that is
widely resented.

Solid Waste Management

Orlando East is an area that enjoys regular waste collection services, which are
provided by the metropolitan council through the waste collection agency that
used to fall within the remit of the Southern Municipal Council. Under the
general waste performance indicators of the city, it features as fully serviced
(Monitor 2000c). However, the aggregate statistics hide incomplete and
inadequate service delivery for some of Orlando East's residents, notably
backyard residents. The loudest refrain to emerge from these quarters was 'not
enough plastics'. The problem is simple. A waste-bagging system operates in the
area and only two plastic refuse bags are allocated to each plot because backyard
shacks are not officially recognized. On stands with three or more distinct
households, this is inadequate and tenants lose out to landlords in the
competition for bags. Where the service that landlords provide is inadequate, as
in the case of waste removal, residents either buy plastic bags by clubbing
together to purchase communally, or resort to informal methods, such as
dumping or stealing bags from other people. Alternatives include using official
dumpsites on street corners; but the reality is indiscriminate littering.

Effectively, however, there is no institutionalized waste-collection service
catering for backyard residents. There are a number of ways in which the failure
of the GJMC to fully confront the presence of the backyard population, and
the conditions under which tenants live, undermines the effectiveness of the
solid-waste management system in Orlando East and in similar areas in Soweto.
Inadequate distribution of plastic waste bags has already been noted as a central
problem resulting from the exclusion of backyard residents from municipal
service-delivery strategies. However, it is also the case that the technology choice
for waste collection in the area may be inappropriate for the nature of the waste,
particularly waste disposed of by backyard residents. For a number of reasons,
most backyard residents use coal or paraffin rather than electricity for cooking
and heating. First, backyards do not legally have electricity. Second, it is rationed
by many landlords; and thirdly, poorer households often opt for non-electric
sources of power, which are considered cheaper. This means that residents have
to dispose of hot coal, and plastic sacks were not made for materials such as
this. As a result, they melt and spill their contents.

To cope with the failures of the plastic-bag collection system, the Southern
Municipal Local Council, under which Soweto fell prior to the formation of the
GJMC, initiated a large container bin system. However, as with the plastic bags,

the larger containers are issued to rate-paying homeowners. Backyard residents were then expected to take their waste to the owner's bin or, more commonly, to general collection points on street corners. In other words, they are only indirectly serviced by the council and are certainly not provided with an on-plot service. Some of our focus-group discussions suggested that the introduction of the large bin system had rendered their position worse because this had been accompanied by a reduction in the number of street containers. This led to increased dumping and littering on the part of backyard residents, who then had nowhere to dispose of waste.

In a laudable effort to deal with the problems of waste, a local forum has been established in Orlando East. However, it is not clear that the forum includes specific representations from backyard residents, those most challenged in terms of waste disposal and, as a result, those likely to be responsible in part, at least, for many of the problems. All too often, officials declared that they treated tenants and homeowners in the same way; but there was limited acknowledgement that their needs clearly differed and that the issues facing backyard residents were less likely to be addressed through the normal planning processes associated with the delivery of this service, no matter how consultative, in respect of homeowners.

LOCAL POLITICS AND STATE–SOCIETY RELATIONS IN ORLANDO EAST

By pointing up some of the conflicts and tensions that arise in relation to differentiated service provision in Orlando East, we do not mean to suggest that there are vast and irreparable social cleavages in the area between landlords and tenants. On the contrary, unlike many of the inner-city areas reviewed in Chapter 7 and the hostels discussed in Chapter 10, Orlando East deserves its reputation as 'the melting pot of Soweto'. Without being over-reverent about what is often, clearly, a difficult and contested relationship between landlord and tenant, there is also widespread evidence of sound integration and remarkably little mutual prejudice. The persistence of low rentals and a sense of obligation to fellow victims of the housing shortage seem to feed something of a united consciousness among Orlando East residents. Tenants themselves said they felt more comfortable in Orlando East than elsewhere:

> *People are comfortable in the environment of Orlando because they are accommodative towards the people who live in their backyards… [Elsewhere] you feel as a tenant and people pointing fingers at you, and they'll say 'you are a tenant in someone else's house', and you feel out of place as you are an outcast.*

Moreover, many of the backyard shack occupants are family members who are related to occupants of the main house, which also serves to undermine a collective chasm between owner-occupiers and backyard residents.

Unlike other parts of Soweto, where political divisions often parallel differentiated settlement patterns, and where homeowners tend to dominate local branches of the ANC and the CDF (Beall, Crankshaw and Parnell, 2002; Everatt, 1999), in Orlando East there is considerable evidence of integrating both tenants and migrants within mainstream political, social and economic life. Nevertheless, the dominance of the ANC, street committees and the link between these bodies and the CDF by homeowners means that tenants can be excluded from participation in political structures. Indeed, it is interesting that SANCO has defined its local agenda around issues such as domestic disputes, rents and services precisely in order to preserve its popular base among the poorest and most disadvantaged people in the area: the tenants.

Insofar as SANCO is doing this, and is also playing a role in establishing norms and procedures for evicting tenants, it must be seen as a voice of backyard residents.[8] However, although SANCO is alert to tenants' issues and takes them up actively and with great political astuteness, it is primarily doing this directly with landlords, rather than by raising the more fundamental issues – the solutions to which lie with the local authority. In the words of a SANCO spokesperson:

> *So, basically, most of the time there is a dispute between the landlord and the tenant around the services they get, or around the payment. If one tenant is no longer working, so sometimes they don't pay the rent when they are expected to do, then they come to the office for assistance and we help them to resolve their disputes... Some of the landlords, they really don't have respect for these people. They just say they must go out of his or her yard without notice... As SANCO, we put a time frame of three months' notice they must give... in most cases, they have a success rate and they adhere to our three months' notice.*

Thus far, then, the approach of SANCO has been to deal with conflict resolution and support mobilization rather than to take on the more developmental problems underlying landlord–tenant relations. Nevertheless, the organization is beginning to be recognized as taking a lead in what the GJMC now acknowledges to be a priority issue: the regulation of landlord–tenant relations (Monitor, 2000a).

The fact that SANCO has taken up, on a systematic basis, the specific issues faced by tenants suggests that collective action will not necessarily continue to be harmonious in places such as Orlando East. Furthermore, the fact that the council is aiming to formalize secondary-dwelling structures, that it supports the transfer of house ownership to the names of those living in the formal houses, and that it is tightening up on the payment of service charges are all factors that are likely to increase the obvious divisions between landlords and tenants. It seems unlikely, therefore, that the symbiotic and consensual relationships between them will persist indefinitely. Indeed, a focus group of women tenants expressed alienation with respect to community-level political structures – specifically, the CDF but also the street committees. One woman who had only arrived in Johannesburg after 1994 said:

> *I think there is one [CDF]; but we don't really know about community issues
> as backyard renters, and when there are meetings the council writes letters or
> holds meetings for our landlords, not for all of us. Everything they talk about
> excludes us all. It is for the landlords, so we don't know it.*

The practical implications of local government's tendency to liaise with
landlords in the process of consultation over services was summed up by a
Mozambican-born tenant:

> *We get the service because the owner of the house is the one who goes to the
> meetings and he must report back to us and give us the waste bags that the
> council gives him.*

Overall, then, it seems that the backyard residents of Orlando East, while feeling
free to engage in formal local politics, are one step removed from the interface
with the GJMC and its officials in their dealings with 'the community' or with
'clients'. As such, it may be useful to draw a distinction between collective action
and participation in local politics, and participation in participatory or
consultative processes initiated by the council. This awkward and, for the
metropolitan council, inefficient dichotomy between uniting tendencies in local
politics, and divisive tendencies in engagement with local authorities, is a direct
result of the informal and unrecognized status of tenants as sub-tenants, and
the failure of the metropolitan council to think laterally about developing a
rental housing market in Johannesburg.

CONCLUSION

Present housing policy promotes home ownership and ignores the fact that
many low-income and younger residents in Johannesburg are found in rental
accommodation, much of it unregulated. Since the political transition to
democracy, the Greater Johannesburg Metropolitan Council has struggled to
define its policy towards informal settlements and, in particular, towards
backyard accommodation, despite an obvious need for the city to broaden its
housing strategy. Unlike the case for informal settlements and hostels, there are
no national guidelines on unregulated backyard renting to assist the
metropolitan council in defining its position. National urban strategy documents
are virtually silent on the backyard rental phenomenon, and urban poverty is
generally depicted as being concentrated in informal settlements and hostels,
where policy attention is mainly directed. However, given the evidence on
backyard rental within Soweto and the dynamics of the associated relationships
discerned in the case of Orlando East, we suggest that the issue will assume
increasing prominence in local, if not national, policy debates. In this regard, we
would join Crankshaw, Gilbert and Morris (2000) in making a plea for the GJMC
not to intervene in order to remove this affordable, if imperfect, shelter option.
The reality of Johannesburg is that a large proportion of the city's poorest

citizens live in backyard accommodation; the metropolitan council has to find ways of dealing with the status quo rather than embarking on a de-densification strategy.

The imperative of coming to terms with the reality of backyard accommodation is nowhere more pressing than in relation to service provision. In addressing the backyard question today, the GJMC must face the formal institutional issues associated with standards, bylaws, legal complications associated with the transfer of housing titles, service-delivery strategies, and questions of private land rights, not to mention the often higher costs of extending services in existing, but densely and informally settled, areas of provision when compared with putting in new services in informal settlements. This is particularly the case when the level of services in informal settlements is designed to ensure 'appropriate technological choice' and to meet 'basic needs', which would be considered unacceptable in areas of formal housing, such as Soweto.

What becomes clear from the focus on access to, and consumption of, services in this chapter is that different tenure arrangements must be considered in the future development of service provision. This has been done, to some extent, for informal settlements but not for backyard shacks or for private inner-city rental, where landlords play a critical role in mediating service consumption and payment. Moreover, when considering the most appropriate forms of infrastructure and service provision, the choice of technology should take social as well as spatial and physical factors into consideration. The number of, and relationships between, service users are critical in terms of issues ranging from the maintenance of services, to the payment for facilities.

From the perspective of managing and financing services, while the metropolitan council has recognized that, for some time to come, the informal settlements and hostels will require a level of subsidization, even for basic services, and while it has focused much attention on reversing the culture of non-payment among occupants of formal housing in African townships, little attention has been paid to backyard rental accommodation. One policy conclusion to emerge from the present research, and reinforced by that undertaken in the inner city, is that direct billing in rental accommodation may well improve payment levels and service satisfaction because service fees will be related directly to service consumption. Second, the neglect of tenants and the current low level of services to backyard shacks not only serve to reinforce the culture of non-payment in Soweto, more generally, but also militate against cost recovery. This is despite the fact that there is obvious evidence of ability to pay: backyard tenants are already paying privately for services by sharing bills with landlords.

While political engagement and collective action currently remain a possibility in Orlando East for most residents, despite its very heterogeneous and socially differentiated population, it would be a mistake to expect this relatively unified front to continue automatically and infinitely. Even now, these patterns of organization have not given rise to increased civic engagement, as Putnam (1993) might suggest, or effective state–society synergy in relation to the co-production of services, as Evans, (1996a; 1996b) or Ostrom (1996) might predict. On the contrary, in the absence of alternatives provided by the local authority, illegal electricity connections are common, and the potential exists for increasingly anti-social relations to emerge between landlords and tenants over water supply and sanitation.

It would also be foolish to rely on current consultative practices, such as CDFs, since our research suggests that this form of civic engagement is not necessarily functional to all communities or to all constituencies within a given community. In places such as Orlando East, access to local-level decision-making and local government interventions is most likely to involve the better-off homeowners. These individuals, having obtained water supply, sanitation and electricity in the past, are now concentrating on issues such as improved community-level infrastructure, waste collection and social services. These issues, in turn, will ultimately lead to raised property values, while for poorer residents, such as backyard tenants, they may well, in time, serve to raise rents and other charges imposed by landlords. Furthermore, the issues found to be most pressing among poorer residents are difficult for local government to address on its own. They either lie more closely to the ground (for example, landlord–tenant conflicts), or are issues that concern competing grassroots organizations and constituencies. Alternatively, they fall into the terrain of provincial or national government – for example, the provision of new greenfield site housing. This said, our conclusions are not licence for the local authorities in Johannesburg to abdicate responsibility for responsible governance in respect of service provision in the city. Instead, they reinforce the plea that the medium-term city-development strategy is one that provides a sustained and sustainable process of participatory development, and ensures a commitment to flexible and targeted service provision for residents across all of Johannesburg's shelter options.

Chapter 10

The People Behind the Walls: Insecurity, Identity and Gated Communities

INTRODUCTION

The carefully manicured lawns of Los Angeles's Westside sprout forests of ominous little signs warning: 'Armed Response!' Even richer neighborhoods in the canyons and hillsides isolate themselves behind walls guarded by gun-toting private police and state-of-the-art electronic surveillance... We live in 'fortress cities' brutally divided between 'fortified cells' of affluent society and 'places of terror' where the police battle the criminalized poor. (Davis, 1990, pp223–224)

Delete the word 'Los Angeles' and the above quote from Mike Davis's celebrated book, *City of Quartz*, could apply as well to Johannesburg as to California's most notoriously divided city. Former white suburbs, now home to a predominantly white, but increasingly non-racial post-Fordist, middle class, range from ranch-style houses on large stands, to the more recent phenomenon of compact and often overpriced 'cluster homes' in secure housing complexes. What residents of both forms of housing share in common, with each other and with Davis's picture of Los Angeles's Westside, are the ubiquitous 'armed response' signs and a collective paranoia about 'security'. However, whereas Davis presents a picture of 'fortress LA' as a city where there is 'civil warfare' between those who can afford to protect themselves from the urban jungle and those who cannot, our picture of Johannesburg suggests that, in a city fractured by past divisions and reeling under the onslaught of new ones, it is not only the wealthy who find ways to barricade themselves behind protective barriers.

Using different means of cutting themselves off, we identify, in the case of Johannesburg, 'gated communities' among some socially disadvantaged communities, as well. Sometimes for reasons of fear and insecurity, sometimes for purposes of their informal and occasionally illicit livelihood strategies, they opt to exclude themselves. Teresa Caldeira (2000, p297), in the picture she paints of urban segregation and fortified enclaves in São Paulo, Brazil, recognizes that:

'Residents from all social groups argue that they build walls and change their habits to protect themselves from crime.' However, like Davis, she moves swiftly from this realization to an analysis of public space and urban design. By contrast, we were as curious about the lives of the people living behind the walls, and how their voluntary self-exclusion may be undermining efforts by the city's new progressive planners to challenge the apartheid legacy of socio-spatial segregation.

In this chapter, we explore perceptions of insecurity and processes of social exclusion across two very different types of location in Johannesburg, and our analysis draws upon two sets of fieldwork. The first was conducted among the multiracial, but still mainly white, residents of two gated communities in Johannesburg, one self-contained cluster-home complex in an affluent suburb to the north of the city and another in a lower middle-class suburb to the west. Second, we conducted research among the mainly isiZulu-speaking migrants of a hostel complex in Soweto.[1] Our analysis is set against an account of the realities and perceptions of crime and public safety in Johannesburg, a city renowned as a national 'crime capital' and one that enters the international public consciousness almost invariably by virtue of the dramatic crime statistics and horror stories on violence and crime reported by the media. We show how issues of crime, violence and insecurity are invoked to create fortress enclaves, both by the well-off and the less well-off. We explore the relationship between space and social identity, and how both are mediated by 'who you are' and 'where you are'. We make this case on the grounds that space and the built environment, on the one hand, and social relations and institutions, on the other, are closely bound together (Harvey, 1973; Massey, 1999). Finally, we conclude the chapter with a discussion of what these trends mean for urban governance, particularly in a context where the ability of Johannesburg's metropolitan government has been hamstrung by the nature of the decentralization process in South Africa.

CRIME CITY

It is increasingly acknowledged that rapidly expanding crime rates in cities of the South have negative consequences for economic development. With the notable exception of a number of recent authors who focus on the relationship between crime and urban social development (McIllwaine, 1999; Moser and Clarke, 2001; Moser and Holland, 1997), it is the impact of crime on urban productivity and efficiency that has given rise to much research in this area (Ayres, 1998; Fajnzybler et al, 1998; Vanderschueren, 1996). Globally, most urban crime is property based – for example, burglary – or violent inter-personal crime, such as assault, rape and murder (Vanderschueren, 1996, pp98–99). South African statistics follow this pattern (Kane-Berman, 2001), even though crime data can be ambiguous. This is because there are differences depending upon whether reporting is by the victim or by witnesses, and depending upon the quality of police records – problems that are aggravated by (often justified) public mistrust of the police. For example, crime surveys reveal 60–70 per cent more crime than official statistics (Schönteich and Louw, 2001, p1).

Shaw and Gastrow (2001, pp235–237) observe that South Africa is 'riddled with violent crime' and that this leads to 'an exaggerated fear of crime'. This is fuelled by the national and international media, which has become obsessed with the subject of crime. South African society is increasingly characterized as one exhibiting levels of lawlessness, violence and crime that match or exceed those of Pakistan, Brazil and Venezuela, countries often thought to be at the top of the public-safety blacklist. For South Africa, as a whole, we know that between 1994 and 1999 the incidence of crime increased by 15 per cent. Moreover, serious and violent crimes have increased faster than average, notably rape, assault, robbery with a firearm, car hijacking, housebreaking and common robbery, with one third of all recorded crimes being violent. It is also common knowledge that South Africa now has the highest per-capita rate of reported rape in the world, with 115.6 cases for every 100,000 population in 1998 (Monitor, 2000b).

So, how does the situation in Johannesburg compare with the rest of South Africa? Johannesburg is seen as South Africa's crime capital.[2] Moreover, there is no doubt that the city experiences high levels of crime.[3] A number of surveys reveal that for Johannesburg, itself, crime is not only lower than in many comparable developing countries, but for some crimes, the statistics are lower than for other South African cities (Louw et al, 1998). Commensurate with the concentrations of wealth in the province, most national property crimes occur in Gauteng and more than 50 per cent of the vehicles stolen nationally are stolen in Johannesburg. Fraud and computer crime are also concentrated in Johannesburg, as are many crime syndicates. In addition, residents of Gauteng Province are more likely to have experienced a crime than South Africans living in other provinces (Monitor, 2000b). Furthermore, Johannesburg experiences high levels of *violent* crime. Between 1993 and 1997, two-thirds of Johannesburg's residents were victims of crime, most commonly burglary, with nearly one quarter of the respondents (24 per cent) reporting this crime to a victimization survey conducted in Johannesburg in 1997 (Louw et al, 1998, p3). The second most frequently reported incidents were violent crimes: mugging and robbery (17 per cent) and assault (16 per cent). Most of the assaults were of a serious nature, with 84 per cent involving a weapon (Louw et al, 1998, p17). However, here it should be noted that although a large proportion of violent crimes committed nationally occur in Johannesburg, the statistics are worse elsewhere. For example, it is Cape Town that has the dubious reputation of being the nation's 'murder capital' (Camerer et al, 1998). Police records suggest that Johannesburg's murder rate is the second highest of all police areas in the country. Nevertheless, second place for attempted murder goes to Soweto, which falls under a separate jurisdiction for the South African Police Force, although it is located within the boundaries of the GJMC (Louw et al, 1998, p29).

Moreover, crime does not affect all residents of Johannesburg equally, and the main victims of crime are not the affluent white population whose fears are so widely publicized, but rather the African poor. There are a number of different interpretations provided to explain this. They include the argument that the institutional violence perpetrated by the apartheid government, and the political violence that characterized the fight against it, led to high levels of domestic and interpersonal violence. An alternative view is based on socio-economic explanations that point to links between rapid urbanization, a slow-growing economy, poor levels of education and high expectations on the part of historically disadvantaged groups, especially the young. More contingent explanations include high levels of gun ownership, uncontrolled levels of alcohol consumption in an environment of poverty, and the perception on the part of offenders of impunity from prosecution. The latter relates to problems in policing, which include poor community–police relations, high levels of police corruption, and the fact that police resources remain unevenly spread across the country.

Not surprisingly, property crimes disproportionately affect areas that offer the greatest opportunities for theft. These are the historically white and Asian residential areas. However, the use of violence in the course of property crimes is more common when Africans are the victims than for other groups (Louw et al, 1998, pp17–18). The occurrence of car hijackings, which is considered to be a serious crime as it is often armed, is highest in the north-east of the city where there are high-income residential environments. In this area, there is a high percentage of car ownership and it is also an area very accessible between two major highways. The 1997 Johannesburg victims' survey reported that over 12 per cent of respondents were subject to car theft between 1993 and 1997; of these, as many as 6 per cent experienced violent car theft in the form of hijacking. Of this latter group, however, 73 per cent of victims were African (Louw et al, 1998, p17). Police records show that the highest occurrence of murder in Johannesburg occurs within a crime corridor that stretches from Soweto, in the west, through the CBD, to the high-income residential areas to the east. This corridor also corresponds to the mining belt, which contains vacant land that is often not secured or occupied on a 24-hour basis; most hostels and deprived residential areas are also located in this belt (GJMC, 1998d, p22).

In terms of gender dynamics, the 1997 victims' survey found men to be most at risk of violent crime in Johannesburg. However, this probably relates to the fact that sexual attacks and domestic violence are likely to be under-reported in a street survey (Louw et al, 1998, p22). More recent data suggest that middle-class men are the most common victims of crimes perpetrated by strangers with guns. However, taking all victims of crime in Johannesburg together, it is most likely to be young black men and women who are victims, with 38 per cent of firearm deaths being in the 24- to 34-year age group.[4] While the proportion of middle-class whites in Johannesburg affected by crime is unacceptably high, it is nevertheless the case that the types of crime to which they are exposed are less serious than those experienced by other population groups. Moreover, a significantly large proportion of Johannesburg's victims are women in the home (Monitor, 2000b). Just as murder is the crime most likely to be reported, domestic violence and rape are those known to be most under-reported. Despite under-reporting, official figures still point to 2.27 rapes per 1000 population as the average for Metropolitan Johannesburg.[5]

Despite almost certain under-reporting, more than one in five Soweto women across all age brackets admitted to being a victim of marital violence, while one in ten women were victims of routine or serious abuse (Morris et al, 1999). A study conducted by the Johannesburg Sexual Offences Forum in 1997, which sought to overcome the bias imposed by under-reporting of rape, found that over 70 per cent of the 786 victims interviewed from people reporting to district surgeons' offices in hospitals and clinics across Johannesburg were African women, with the majority aged between 13 and 30 years (Louw et al, 1998, p22). According to official police reports (GJMC, 1998b), the highest incidence of rape reported to police stations was in Greater Soweto (849), followed by the densely settled area of Alexandra in north-east Johannesburg (314) and Hillbrow in the inner city (311).

However, the most significant crime statistic, given our focus on 'gated communities', is that shown in Table 10.1: in Soweto, one of the most common sites of crime was at home. Similarly, for Johannesburg, as a whole, it has been shown that most inter-personal crime is likely to take place at home or in a bar, tavern or *shebeen*, with heavy involvement of guns and alcohol (Monitor, 2000b). With these statistics in mind, it is both sad and ironic that the response to insecurity is so often a retreat into the home. This reinforces the view that insecurity is as much about the fear of crime than crime itself, and that fear of crime can serve to mask fear of race and social difference.

Table 10.1 *Sites of crimes experienced by Soweto residents, 1997*

Location of crime	Percentage distribution of crimes experienced
In your home	39
On the street	47
At school	0.2
At work	1.0
In the Johannesburg CBD	7
In a taxi or at a taxi rank	0.4
On the train	3
Other town	1
At relative's house	0.4
At hostel	0.1
Total	100

Source: authors' analysis of Soweto in Transition Household Survey, 1997

WALLS, MALLS AND TREADMILLS: JOHANNESBURG'S MIDDLE-CLASS FORTRESS ENCLAVES

One of the most remarkable things about Johannesburg is that, when in public spaces, middle-class people are most often seen behind the wheel of a car. Alternatively, they confine themselves to relatively protected public spaces, such as clubs, schools, coffee shops and restaurants. In this respect, not much has changed since the latter days of apartheid except that now the middle class is increasingly racially mixed. One observable change over recent years is that you are less likely to see the once ubiquitous suburban jogger. In a country obsessed with sport and fitness, men and women of the middle classes have replaced pounding the suburban streets with pounding the treadmills of membership gymnasiums. Such spatial enclaves are a frequent response to fear of insecurity and social difference and are not confined to Johannesburg or South Africa. Ranging from shopping malls to office complexes, from business parks to sports clubs, these fortress enclaves include gated residential communities. A familiar image in the city's suburbs are the high walls, electric fences, boom gates and lugubrious security guards lolling in their post-modern 'keeps'. Less obvious is a sense of who lives behind these barricades. What is certain is that the arrival of these gated communities in Johannesburg's landscape predated the end of apartheid, as described by Mabin (1998, p16):

> *While pseudo-suburbia sprouted on the fringes of townships, the form of the white suburbia, which it imitated, itself began to alter. As white population growth tailed off in the 1970s, the population aged; other conditions change, the nature of the property market altered. Rising land prices (though they remain relatively low by world standards) and security concerns, as well as departures from high-rise apartment land, drove a new form of development in the 1980s: the so-called 'townhouse' complex, really not much different from row housing, and usually developed in the furthest flung sections of suburbia... They are the new compounds of urban South Africa, representing tightly defended social segregation.*

The two middle-class townhouse complexes we researched were both built in 1994, the year of the first democratic elections in South Africa. Both complexes were multiracial, although residents remained predominantly white. The research conducted in these townhouse complexes involved both white and black residents.[6] While the research is neither statistically reliable nor generalizable, the lifestyle patterns identified, and the perceptions elicited, are interesting and indicative.[7] One complex was located in an affluent northern suburb where the majority of residents were homeowners and comprised mainly young couples, a few families with young children and a number of retired people. The complex comprised 74 units. The majority had two bedrooms, but there were also one- and three-bedroom homes. Each had its own garage or garages, a walled garden and individual intercom connections to the central gate. Communal facilities included a squash court, a large and well-maintained swimming pool, a pool-side recreation area, a clubhouse, a games room with a pool table, and a well-equipped children's play area. The complex, as a whole, was fully walled with an electric fence, had automated electronic gates at the central entrance and 24-hour access control by a security guard. All maintenance services, such as painting, gardening, pool care and security, were contracted out to professional service providers. They were paid through a monthly levy and were coordinated by the managing agent. Only day-to-day issues were in the hands of the elected residents' association.

The other complex was located in a lower middle-class, former white area to the west of the city and close to the Westgate Shopping Centre, which is the largest mall serving Soweto. The majority of residents were owners, with households comprising a mixture of retired people, young couples and families with school-going children, including a number of women in single-parent families. The complex comprised 72 units with either two or three bedrooms. Units were allocated covered parking spaces rather than garages, walls did not separate individual units, and residents shared a communal lawn and swimming pool. The complex itself was fully walled and had an electric fence, but this was not in working order at the time of the research. There were automated security gates at the central entrance; but these were operated by the 24-hour access-control guard rather than from the house by individual householders, so there was less control over who came in and out in comparison with the complex to the north. There were countless complaints from residents about the inefficacy of the arrangements and the failings of the professional security company charged with looking after the complex. In addition, the complex exhibited generally poor maintenance; this was surprising because, although the purchase prices of these homes were considerably lower than those for the complex to the north, the monthly levy paid per unit was double.

Mabin (1998, p20) has made the point that during the late 1990s, there was a shift in civil-service managerial positions being occupied by blacks from 22 per cent to 60 per cent. When combined with increased employment of blacks in the private sector, and the movement to Johannesburg of former '*bantustan*' elites, this suggests an enormous new demand for middle-class housing. That such people tend to choose townhouse accommodation was confirmed in an interview with a young African computer specialist working in a multinational company, who moved into a townhouse after a frightening experience of armed robbery, leaving his new free-standing house, which had also been in a former white area. He explained his reasons to Beall and Lawson (1999) as follows:

> *Before, it used to be more on the whites you know, because in the townships you got this thing of saying: 'The white man has got money and that's my forefather's money'. Ja, if you are a black they never used to bother you. And now, because you are staying in the northern suburbs, you are just like a white man. 'You think you are a white man now? Why are you staying in the white suburbs?' So if you are a professional, if you have got a proper job and people know you have got a proper job, then you are also under threat. It's now equal. Whether you are a white man or a black man, as long as you've got money.*

Interestingly, and as illustrated by Table 10.2, for most residents this kind of living was not part of a process of upward mobility, en route to a larger or grander free-standing house. Indeed, most informants had moved to a townhouse complex from a free-standing house, and most intended to stick to protected cluster-home living. Not all had experienced crime; but a number of the discussants and interviewees knew of someone close to them who had been a victim of crime.[8] Without exception, everyone gave fear of crime and the search for safety and security as their reasons for moving.

Table 10.2 *Residential profile of 12 residents in two townhouse complexes*

	Upper-middle class complex to the north		Lower-middle class complex to the west	
Place of previous residence	House/flat in ex-white area:	5	House in ex-white area:	5
	House in ex-Indian area:	1	House in ex-African area:	1
Next anticipated place of residence	This or another complex:	5	This or another complex:	5
	Overseas:	1	A safer town in South Africa:	1

Insecurity and the Fear of Outsiders

When we asked why they had opted for cluster-home living, without exception all the people we engaged with offered safety and security as their main reason. In the responses, there were similarities across class; but there were also interesting gender differences. With men, there was some reluctance to admit fear on their own account; instead, they professed fear for their families. As one of the discussants put it:

> *I fear for my wife and son. I feel that I can take care of myself. Sure, I'll most probably lose a lot if that happens; but I feel I can do a better job than what my wife and my son can. So, I fear people who threaten my family.*

By the same token, women mainly expressed fear on behalf of their children. One said her biggest fear was being hijacked with her child in the car; as a result, she had stopped putting her toddler in a child's car seat and relied simply on a seat belt so that it would be easier to get him out:

> *The way we live in Johannesburg is not nice. They don't care if they shoot you. They don't care if they take your car with your child in it. They don't care about other people... They have no value for life.*

The racism associated with insecurity was often thinly veiled, and it did not take much probing to uncover who 'they' were perceived to be. Articulated in terms of 'those guys', 'strangers' and 'outsiders', it was clear who was meant. According to the men, they feared:

> *People walking around here. In this area especially, there are a lot of people walking around.*

> *The thing is with guys around here... if you show them you're, afraid that's when they look at you and they say this guy is vulnerable. That's why you don't show your fear.*

> *All the unknown people outside.*

> *I love the country to bits; but I don't know what's going to happen. It's not knowing – that's what I fear.*

Fear of crime is often used to justify spatially separate urban forms in ways that disguise other motivations (Amin and Graham, 1999, p17). Judd (1994, p161) goes as far as to suggest that fear of crime is a 'code word' for fear of race. Certainly, a sense of insecurity was offered as a synonym for fear of difference by most of the townhouse residents we interviewed, fuelled by 'everyday talk of crime' (Caldeira, 1996, p201). Among the women, they were more explicit about which strangers frightened them. However, one of the many 'silences' we encountered concerned the fear of sexual assault: but the fear of rape was almost palpable:

> *People you don't recognize – not actually strangers, but threatening strangers – one that's standing sizing you up or watching.*

> *Men. Black men. But even some of their black ladies. Some of them can be very arrogant. They've got far more strength than we've got, you know, if they decided to take you.*

When it was pointed out that the woman in question had black neighbours, she said:

> *Yes, but the type of black people that we get here are well-educated, well-groomed people. They are not the sorts of people that you will be afraid of. They dress well and drive nice cars and everything.*

Thus, for the predominantly white women living in this affluent townhouse complex, class replaced race as the badge of inclusive membership. It allowed them to erect physical and symbolic 'walls' in order to reduce interaction and mixing in shared public spaces. Furthermore, an architecture of fear legitimized a deepening segregation that was based not upon an apartheid of race, but upon new articulations of social difference.

Exclusion and the Anomie of Insiders

Retreat into bounded spaces, such as townhouse complexes, is seen by some as encouraging community, especially among minorities (Marcuse, 1995; Blakely and Snyder, 1997). However, in neither case, in our research, was there much evidence of a sense of deep community resulting from proximate living. People found the uniformity and rule-bound environment stifling, although this was less the case in the north, where its more affluent residents were afforded more privacy. Here, discussants agreed that although they were not close friends with their neighbours, they felt good about being part of the complex. They enjoyed access to the communal facilities and the occasional get-together organized by the residents' association, such as the Christmas party and the annual *braaivleis*.[9] This reinforced a sense of community without being oppressive. However, in the less affluent complex to the west, which exhibited less privacy and individual household space, there was much less enthusiasm for neighbours. As one of the women put it: 'It's more that you know a few people and the rest just stare into your place when they walk past.' Among the men, some reported occasional mixing, such as playing darts or watching rugby together; but interactions were described as those between acquaintances rather than friends. As one of the residents put it: 'When Leon moved in… I said: "I'm so and so", and I got a bottle of whiskey and said: "Come and have a drink." We had a drink and since then we've been chatting. Every time I see him, it's "howzit".'

One clear consequence of fear of crime and generalized moral panic is that people spend more time at home. This was less cause for remark in the case of women, for whom it was probably less unusual. But men discussed how their lives had changed. Not classifying going to work as going out, they talked about how their evenings had changed and how they were 'in bed by 9.00 at night'. As one of the male discussants in the western suburb complex explained:

> *People are scared, so they are not going out… They go to work and they come home. And now with computers you can get things through the Internet, so you don't really have to leave your house. You feel safe there and you can build your nest. This is when a complex comes into its own because it is a safe haven. You feel safe there, and why in the world would you want to go out? You can even phone 'Mr Delivery'.*[10] *Why would people want to go out? People are not lazy, they are comfortable. If you don't believe it, just look at the cars. They don't want to go out because if you do, you might get hijacked.*

Another elaborated by telling of a friend of his who sold vacuum cleaners door-to-door. In order to catch people in, his appointments were made for the evening and he often found himself urged to stay for food or a drink as 'people are so hungry for relationships that you can spend five hours there – they don't want to just watch TV'. The fact that this was more of an issue for people in the less well-off western complex suggests that there may also have been family and financial constraints to an active social life. Nevertheless, enclave living has clearly served to foster what, in South Africa, is termed a *laager* mentality, referring to the defensible space created by the circular pattern in which the *voortrekkers* arranged their ox wagons during the 19th century, when poised for conflict with the African populations whom they encountered. Commenting on fortress Johannesburg, one male informant mused that:

> *I think it's taken away the community… People used to go to parks, drive-ins, drive in the streets. They don't get out as much… But at the same time, I'd rather stay here without that community and stay alive.*

For all the sense of being beleaguered, the vast majority of informants were committed to staying in South Africa and, for most of them, in Johannesburg. Among the more affluent, the impression was given of a sense of capability and a commensurate willingness and desire to make a difference. As one of the men assured us: 'We will be the last ones to leave and put the lights out!'; or as one of the women put it: 'Our lives are here – our work, our family, our children – and there is no guarantee that it would be better elsewhere.'

It could not be argued, by any stretch of the imagination, that the two gated communities we studied were politically engaged in any way. For example, no one knew the name of their councillor, although, in the north, they knew it was a 'woman from the DP'.[11] Even when frustrated with the inefficiencies of the metropolitan council, there was a reluctance to engage and a belief that, one way or another, services would be provided. Indeed, many of the services that these residents enjoyed were, in any case, privately paid for. Among the lower middle-class discussants, by contrast, there was a feeling of increasing financial pressure, fewer and diminishing options and a notion that they had been forgotten by local politicians. One of the western complex residents put it this way:

> *In my opinion, they don't make the effort to come to us, to come to this complex... we don't have those guys coming to us and saying: 'Look here, I'm your Democratic Party or your ANC', or whatever. Nobody comes here and says: 'Look, let's get together.'*

Nonetheless, fear of crime and the various social antipathies for which it stands has given rise to an aversion to public spaces and engagement with the city. The wistful resentment and sense of anomie echoed by this statement should not distract us from the fact that the residential urban form chosen by this informant and his neighbours is working against creating a diverse and integrated city, and is perpetuating apartheid-like socio-spatial segregation.

COUNTING US IN OR COUNTING US OUT? SOWETO'S HOSTELS AS 'GATED COMMUNITIES'

It is commonly assumed that gated communities are only a feature of affluent populations and that poorer communities protect themselves through other means, such as vigilantism or commanding public spaces. Here, we take issue with this view by demonstrating how isiZulu-speaking rural migrant workers have utilized their socio-spatial identity to secure the hostels as defensible spaces in the city. Hostels have housed unskilled African migrant workers in Johannesburg since before World War I; but they were entrenched under apartheid and came to symbolize the worst exigencies of racial Fordism. Although they have been transformed demographically and, indeed, physically since the twilight years of apartheid and the transition to democracy in South Africa, migrant hostels remain much as they ever were, separately demarcated and controlled social arenas. They were built to house a temporary and captive male labour force and remain caught in the legacy of their design, described by Robinson as follows (1992, p296):

> *Certainly, in the planning of single sex hostels, matters of control were explicitly considered. High surrounding walls were usually required and doors were restricted to the inward facing walls. Only one entrance was allowed, in order that residents and visitors could more easily be supervised.*

Thus, hostels remain highly institutionalized places even today, and as Crush and James (1995, pxi) have argued, although they no longer serve the same purpose, the bounded nature of hostel accommodation continues to 'exclude outsiders and insulate insiders'. As such, they stand in contradistinction to a democratic society's values of freedom of movement, particularly a society keen to leave behind the migrant labour system – since it is such an infamous legacy of segregation and apartheid.

At the height of the apartheid period, the government wished to racially segregate the inner city and sought to relocate hostels from within 'white' Johannesburg out to the townships (Parnell and Pirie, 1991). The government hoped that hostels for migrants would become an increasingly important component of housing in African townships; and it did, to an extent, although only 11 hostels were ultimately constructed in Johannesburg itself, 9 of which were located in Soweto (Pirie and de Silva, 1986).[12] According to the Soweto Household Survey, these hostels provide 24,000 beds and house 40,901 residents (Morris et al, 1999). No longer comprising single-sex accommodation (apart from one hostel, which is for women only), today 23 per cent of hostel household members are women (Morris et al, 1999).

Although many people living in hostels are long-time residents of Johannesburg, most are migrants from other parts of South Africa, notably the province of KZN, home to the majority isiZulu-speaking population of South Africa and to the largely rural support base of Chief Mangosuthu Buthelezi's IFP. Towards the end of the apartheid era, a ferocious struggle for power ensued between the ANC and the IFP. Before the 1990s, ethnic mobilization by the IFP had been largely confined to rural KZN. From the early 1990s, the party turned its attention to the cities. In its attempts to enhance its national and urban power base, the IFP used Zulu-speaking migrant workers in the hostels to ferment conflict, sometimes with state backing (CASE, 2001; Everatt, 1999). The hostel dwellers shared a language, culture and sense of alienation, which presented an ideal opportunity for rapid mobilization. The fact that Inkatha increasingly articulated the political position of Johannesburg's hostel dwellers served to fuel the violence that erupted between hostel dwellers and township residents during the 1980s and 1990s. The period claimed a total of 9325 deaths, and of these, 4756 took place in present-day Gauteng and 1106 in Greater Soweto. Of the latter, the Human Rights Commission linked 483 deaths, or 44 per cent, to the hostels (Xeketwane, 1995, p17).

According to the 1993 Goldstone Commission of Inquiry into the Prevention of Public Violence and Intimidation, the bloody conflict between township residents and hostel dwellers led many 'to view the hostels as a key problem within the much larger context of protracted violence in South Africa' (Oliver, 1993, p1). Moreover, the civic organizations, which had constituted the backbone of ANC support in Johannesburg during the anti-apartheid struggle, made it clear that they saw the upgrading of the hostels to family accommodation as a priority. From the time of Nelson Mandela's release from jail in 1990, the former Nationalist government tried to demonstrate a break with apartheid by attacking its worst symbols, including single-sex hostels. The provincial administration at the time, the Transvaal Provincial Administration, agreed in principle to abolishing Johannesburg's hostels and to selling them off to private buyers for conversion into family flats (Coovadia, 1991). However, except in a few cases, this did not arise.

A crucial reason for this was that the migrant workers themselves were vociferously opposed to, what they saw as, plans to displace them from the urban areas and, most importantly, from what constituted affordable accommodation within the city. After all, the coming of democracy had not put an end to poverty. State-funded research conducted during the phase of political transition suggested that, for reasons of affordability, there were clear imperatives to retain aspects of the single-sex hostel system (Minnaar, 1993). Ultimately, it was this position that prevailed, reinforced by the fact that hostel–township relations had been so acutely politicized during the 1980s and 1990s. It was felt that untimely change to the hostel system would potentially threaten a peaceful transition to democracy in South Africa and the important, but fragile, rapprochement between the ANC and IFP, considered crucial to its success. Thus, a compromise position on the hostels was reached. The policy adopted was to opt for short-term emergency upgrading, putting on hold any longer-term development strategy.[13]

The hostel complex where our research was undertaken had not been converted into family accommodation; instead, single rooms had been constructed with communal ablutions, although today many rooms are, in fact, used for multiple occupancy. The complex was developed in accordance with broader development strategies at the time, notably the IDP process, in a spirit of commitment to participatory decision-making. Decisions about hostel upgrading involved representatives of the hostel dwellers and the other residents of the Soweto ward, of which it formed a part. During the initial phase of upgrading, there was a local negotiating group, which included representatives from the hostel, the local civic organization and the Council. Often fiercely contested, the resulting conversions reflect the preferences and victory of the *indunas*, or customary leaders, in the hostel – those men with status and connections to traditional authorities in the rural areas who control most of the decision-making processes within the hostel complex. Nevertheless, despite extensive upgrading, the hostels we researched were still profoundly affected by the character of their original design, the legacy of their historic social and economic function, and the memory of their involvement in a recent violent past.

Hostels – on the Outside Looking In

Ironically, the first point of exclusion for hostel dwellers is a statistical one. For our study, according to the 1996 Population Census, the population of the part of Soweto in which the hostel is situated stands at around 18,000; but this figure excludes the largely migrant hostel population, which is estimated to stand at around 7000. Instead, the census identified individuals in relation to their rural homes, a fact that was not necessarily to their detriment, as we demonstrate below. Second, although many rural–urban migrants are long-time residents of Johannesburg, and although we found many hostel dwellers to be urban born, it was clear that hostel residents had long been excluded from the social life of their immediate neighbourhood. This is beginning to change. As one woman hostel resident described it: 'I feared going to church – I used to fear but I used to go – I just prayed to be safe there and back. But now everybody is free. Now everyone is free to go as he pleases.'

As a result of the involvement of many hostel dwellers in earlier episodes of political violence, all hostel dwellers are still regarded with suspicion by many Sowetans. An example was provided by a hostel resident who claimed that when anyone from the hostel went for treatment at the Chris Hani Baragwanath Hospital, which serves Soweto, they gave the administration a false address. If they declared themselves to be from the hostel, they would not be attended. While other township residents who were also involved in the political clashes of the 1980s and early 1990s between the ANC and IFP, notably the youth, have been able to move on from the resulting abuses and excesses, it has been more difficult for hostel dwellers to do so. This is not only because of their ethnic identity (who they are), but also because they live in a place associated with violence and crime (where they are). The hostels are stigmatized zones, associated with social pathologies and violence, and are not integrated within the wider community, although prejudices and fears are abating. This is illustrated by the following comments from one of the council's community liaison officers, working with representatives of both the hostel and the community:

> *People thought that they were troublemakers, but when you come closer to it, then you see it is not true. At some stages, during the times of violence – I am also from the township – the youngsters, they became aggressive against them, the people from the hostel. They swore at them and provoked them, but we the representatives said: 'Look gentlemen, these are kids, they don't know what they are doing. There is something behind them. They are being pushed and influenced by somebody else.' The migrants are very polite people.*

This view was endorsed by one of the political leaders within the hostel who said:

> *At first, the people in the community used to look down on the people who were staying in the hostel, saying they were vermin, but now things are changing. There is cooperation between us.*

Whatever rapprochement has occurred between hostel dwellers and other township residents, a cultural and attitudinal divide remains that will take a long time to overcome. This can be discerned from the following comments made in relation to the hostel dwellers by the local ANC councillor:

> *The majority of people here come from KwaZulu–Natal and they have their own type of life that they lead, which is separate from the general community here in the township... They come from a structured society back home where there are structures in place. They've got a king and their* indunas, *and here*

the same kind of system is operating except that here there is no king. They've got leadership here. The first two meetings that I had prior to this Saturday they had sent the juniors – the [Inkatha]Youth Brigade. Like they sent me their Youth Brigade! But on Saturday they came – right up to the top – the real induna. *Although they are not that problematic... there is still that element of not trusting each other – we view them with suspicion and the same thing happens with them – they perceive us differently. Now it is my duty to try and bring the ordinary people in the township and the hostel together and say: 'Look, you are one ward. You cannot remain this way because it creates a division within the ward itself and it makes it difficult for development.'*

The fact that the councillor has cause for optimism can only be understood by exploring some of the shifting social dynamics within the hostel itself, notably those between the older and younger male residents.

Hostels – on the Inside Looking Out

Social exclusion can result not only from others doing the excluding, but also from groups choosing to exclude themselves from broader social participation. Self-exclusion can be exercised not only in response to prejudice and stigma, but also in order to preserve or protect existing resources, or to access potential new resources. Both issues applied in the case of the hostels studied here. Under apartheid, the *indunas* successfully used their Zulu identity in order to ensure continued contact with, and access to, resources in the rural areas of KZN, while retaining, at the same time, a foothold in the urban areas through their control over the single-sex migrant hostels. Social linkages, such as kinship, clan and friendship networks, reached across to the rural areas, small towns and cities of KZN from which many residents or their families originated. Within the hostel compound, people living within a particular hostel building invariably heralded from the same area, and many maintained links with 'home boys' or 'home girls' living in other hostels in Gauteng.

When the whole process of hostel upgrading was debated, the older male hostel representatives, the *indunas*, opposed the idea. As the ward councillor put it:

There was a problem with the hostel people there because the inmates [sic]said: 'No! We want to remain as we are. Just leave us alone, we are fine as we are!'

However, once they saw the upgrading process in other hostels, the leadership became keen to participate and developed a well-rehearsed position in opposition to full-scale conversion to family units on the grounds of affordability. By doing so, they managed to retain access to cheap urban accommodation without having to forfeit new state transfers, such as the housing subsidy, which they receive at their rural homes. However, it must also be said that even the younger men and women without connections in the countryside emphasized, as positive, the low rents or 'staying for free' in hostels.

Additional advantages of hostel life, emanating from focus-group discussions included:

A lot of us come for work to stay in the hostel, and we go back home.

We have our own homes back home.

We just feel comfortable and used to the place.

I am used to living at the hostel. I use this place as home now.

It is a place to go at the end of the day.

We like it, the fact that there is convenient transport.

Now there is security; this is your place and you belong here and you can have your family come and visit you.

However, there was not a wholly positive vote for the hostels, with some residents saying that they lived there only because they could not afford to live anywhere else. Negative responses came particularly from the women. Upon being asked what they liked about living in the hostel, a focus-group discussion among women finally concurred: 'Nothing!' The list of what upset them was long, but at the top of it was the fact that the upgrading of the hostels had not involved or accommodated women in any way. They found access to ablution facilities difficult, and said that the men prevented them from using the toilets and showers, so that they had to 'go to the veld near to the railway station'. Moreover, the women complained that the hostels were violent, frightening places. Women feared rape and were constantly anxious on behalf of their children because of the high level of child abuse, particularly on the part of unemployed men who hung around the hostels in the afternoons when mothers were working.

Other hierarchies in the hostel related to length of residence. Upon asking informants and discussants how people came to be in the hostel, the answer was invariably because they already knew someone there. Those with the most status and privilege within the hostel complex were those who had been there longest. They occupied the best rooms in the upgraded hostels. The most recent arrivals, and those who were least well off or connected, occupied the older buildings that had not yet been converted. These were without piped water, sewerage and electricity connections. Despite extremely reasonable charges, even for upgraded rooms, the vast majority of residents did not pay rent, with the hostel manager estimating those paying as no more than 5 per cent. For some residents, there were real issues of affordability, addressed either through non-payment or various forms of sub-letting. For example, people shared their rooms, getting sub-tenants to pay their rent and sometimes actually surviving on rents. Thus, while the council enjoyed only a 5 per cent payment rate, an informal private-rental market was operating within the hostels, over which there was very little council control.

Services in the hostel were poorly maintained, with things in a state of disrepair or functioning on the basis of makeshift repairs, undertaken by hostel dwellers themselves. Although it was clear that there were obvious differences in the hostel's standards, compared with the surrounding townships, culpability did not lie exclusively with the service providers. For example, although hostel residents justifiably complained of power cuts, water shortages and blocked sewers, the maintenance crews reported difficulties in working in the hostels. The *indunas* tried to control everyone who entered the hostel, and this extended to a reluctance to allow service workers into the hostel compound. For example, the official in charge of water supply and sanitation reported that:

> *Inside [the hostel], they did not want to accept our people in to do the maintenance – it was a cultural thing, or something; I am not sure. Then we brought a contractor in and he first needed to meet the* induna *and talk to him, and after that it was fine… it seems to be sorted out now the contractor is someone who lives in the area.*

However, even those crews acceptable to the *indunas* were afraid to go into the hostel to execute repairs. The same official said in this regard:

> *The major problem that we are struggling with at this stage is just the crime issue. They get hijacked, their stuff gets vandalized – it's a big problem. It is at a stage where people do not want to go in there anymore – especially at night. We do not go in at all at night – they are very reluctant to go in.*

Electricians, too, were afraid of going into the hostel; as a result, repairs were rarely undertaken, even with regard to the overhead mast lights, which are essential for providing some counter to the lack of public safety in the hostel. Even the ambulance service refused to go beyond the hostel gates because the drivers and paramedics were afraid. One of the male residents said that the failure of ambulances to enter the hostel compound was problematic, particularly when people had been stabbed or shot, which was often. The women emphasized that there was a problem when women went into labour during the night and could not get to hospital.

Confirming that it was not only women who were vulnerable and fearful, young men mentioned the following when asked what they disliked most about hostel living:

> *It's the crime that happens, killing each other, mugging of cell phones.*

> *It is thugs – especially the ones who carry guns.*

> *There are a lot of them – you can't just point them out.*

> *Gunmen.*

> *They kill.*

They take our money and you won't say a thing – you just keep quiet.

They kill, so you see him killing and you won't say a thing because even if you go to the police, they have been paid too, to keep quiet.

It's the rape and being tortured by policemen when they have nothing to do.

It's the random shooting at night.

If you tried to take them out of the hostel you would not even make it to the exit gate.

A major source of fear was a gang that either comprised police officers or was masquerading as police officers. They entered the hostel at night on the pretext of a tip-off and stole property, especially cell phones, and caused panic and mayhem. The police were generally seen to be corrupt and often violent, colluding with the gangs that operated from, and within, the hostels. Of all the relations between hostel residents and outsiders, those with the police were at the lowest ebb, with no evidence of trust at all.

Although it is difficult to say whether levels of crime and violence are necessarily higher in the hostels than elsewhere, they are certainly more highly concentrated. It was also clear that within a bounded socio-spatial environment, a majority of hostel residents were held to ransom by a minority of powerful anti-social elements, both within and without the compound, while at the same time being branded as violent criminals themselves by people outside of the hostel. It seems, too, that the hostels have served to foster and reward patron–client relationships that lie outside of the rule of law and that will prove difficult to dislodge. In this, the role of the hostel *indunas* in limiting engagement with the outside world cannot be discounted.

Curiously, these hostels were a lot less 'porous' than the middle-class fortress enclaves of Johannesburg. This stemmed from the fact that the more affluent residents of the latter seemed unable to do without the manual labour supplied by Johannesburg's working poor. The irony of the situation was captured by a townhouse resident who complained that strangers found their way into what was supposed to be a secure complex, while readily admitting to picking up and bringing home 'guys looking for piece jobs' whenever he needed his car washing. The hostel *indunas*, by contrast, allowed in no strangers, not even to provide municipal services. Instead, residents were self-servicing, relying on informal solutions or none at all.

When the hostel focus groups were asked who were the 'big guys' in their community, the *indunas* invariably came up and they clearly acted as gatekeepers in all sorts of ways. The *indunas* also tended to keep themselves apart from local governance issues, although they did participate fully in local electoral politics, largely behind the IFP. However, they have increasingly been drawn into local governance processes. The *induna* committee comprised representatives from the various hostel buildings and was the most conservative and inward-looking committee in the hostel. It comprised older residents who were elected by virtue of their rural status and their links in KZN. Ostensibly concerned with social issues, such as the resolution of domestic disputes and hostel conflicts, their power appeared fairly pervasive. There was also a hostel residents' committee that was formed in 1991, which included younger political leaders, as well. This committee was formed specifically to relate to the council and was the official interface between hostel residents and municipal officials. Third, there was the local IFP branch that overlapped in terms of membership, influence and connections, both with the *induna* committee and the hostel committee, as well as with Inkatha supporters elsewhere. This political network also included branches of the Inkatha Youth Brigade and the Inkatha Women's Brigade.

Both the *induna* committee and the hostel committee were male dominated, as were all the decision-making bodies; and hostel women were not represented in any serious way. In terms of local governance processes and decisions, therefore, the views, perceptions and priorities of hostel dwellers were overwhelmingly biased towards those of the male residents. During the initial phases of hostel upgrading, there was, in addition, a local negotiating group that was formed as part of the IDP process. During negotiations, the metropolitan council tried to include within this structure and within its processes a broader range of hostel residents, including women, with limited success. The ward councillor explained it this way:

> *Change is always difficult. Some of them actually resist it. They just don't like that life and the way we live in Jo'burg. They feel it is not right, like here you talk about women's rights and stuff like that, but back home it's not an issue, it's not negotiable. A woman knows her place and a man knows his place. It's a cultural and moral issue, and some of them still resist it and still believe it's unheard of.*

Interestingly, women, who represented a significant proportion of hostel residents, appeared to be among those most willing and able to build links with the broader township community, of which the hostel was a part. However, they were excluded from important social networks and decision-making arenas within the hostel and between the hostel and other organizations.

Nevertheless, the male hostel leadership was not homogeneous, and there were observable differences of approach between the older, more rural, *indunas* and the younger political leaders. The latter had come to see challenging the older *indunas* as justifiable, particularly because they appeared ineffective against the criminals and gangs who made their lives a misery within the hostel complex. Moreover, there were also many hostel dwellers who did not have connections and resources in rural areas, and were increasingly committed to living their lives in Soweto and engaging more fully with surrounding Sowetan communities. Thus, the older leadership was beginning to face challenges from younger political leaders who saw benefit for themselves and their generation resulting from greater cooperation with township residents and the metropolitan council.

The hostels are a sad reminder and a pernicious symbol of the apartheid era. Over the years, they have served to devalue and oppress people in ways that are not compatible with South Africa's democratic constitution. Although politically inconceivable in the short term, given the delicate peace between the ANC and IFP, there is something to be said for a future transformation of the hostels to expunge the stigma and exclusion associated with them. There are also equity issues associated with the council continuing to heavily subsidize the housing costs of urban hostel dwellers. This has allowed some hostel dwellers, who may well be income poor in the urban areas, to become asset rich in the rural areas. This is as a result of their being able to take advantage of two post-apartheid transfers, effectively benefiting from the housing subsidy in the countryside and from access to cheap or free accommodation in the city. This is in a context of more generalized and widespread need in Johannesburg itself. In making this argument, we are not suggesting that hostel dwellers are wealthy or that they have untold choices. Indeed, the implications for policy suggest hard choices – for example, conversion to family accommodation or greater fostering of a private rental market – and these options would not be universally popular. Nevertheless, there is a necessary process of social healing that needs to occur, which looks set to be undermined by the continuation of the hostels in their current physical form.

CONCLUSION

In this chapter, we have shown how people have chosen to live in closed compounds and to exclude themselves from wider city life. Our analysis of these communities contradicts the dichotomized thinking that suggests that the affluent barricade themselves in fortress enclaves, while poorer citizens roam the streets at the expense of being criminalized by society and pursued by the police. We present a more complex and nuanced picture that suggests that, irrespective of different dimensions of social difference, many of Johannesburg's residents fear crime and, particularly, violent crime. This, in turn, affects how and where residents use public space and at what cost; this has been the focus of much of the Northern or Western literature on the subject of fortress cities (Blakely and Snyder, 1997; Davis, 1990; 1998; Fyfe, 1998; Marcuse, 1995). However, we argue that it impacts, as well, upon how people create and use private space, and at what cost.

In the case of the self-excluded middle- and lower middle-class residents of the suburban fortress enclaves, many experienced problems associated with the break-up of old communities, the forming of new ones and the isolation imposed by segregation. While residents put themselves through this voluntarily, it should not be forgotten that, under apartheid, many black people experienced similar upheavals as a result of forced removals and pernicious influx-control laws in the cities, and they did so in far less comfort and security. The position of the hostel residents is more ambiguous. The migrant labour system of which they were a part was not slavery, although the choice to come to the city to look for work was often no choice at all. Nevertheless, they made virtue of necessity. While for many younger and poorer hostel dwellers, pursuing livelihoods across the rural–urban divide may still be a matter of necessity rather than choice, for more senior residents the hostels, while dismal dwellings, have served them relatively well. They have provided them not only with affordable urban accommodation, but also with livelihood opportunities, sometimes quite lucrative, if not always legal.

In the case of both townhouse residents and hostel dwellers, social identity played a crucial role in reinforcing socio-spatial separation, but in quite different ways. For the hostels, it was their own shared ethnic identity, overlaid and intertwined in complex ways with a violent political history based upon hostel living itself, that served to exclude residents from broader Soweto life and to reinforce their claim on affordable space in the city. And this they did without having to relinquish citizenship rights and the transfer of state assets in the countryside. In other words, it was not Zulu ethnicity alone that was the source of their social exclusion: there are many Zulus in Soweto, and a majority of Sowetans speak isiZulu. Rather, it resulted from a combination of 'who they were' and 'where they were'; for the more powerful among the hostel dwellers, it allowed them to collude in this socially constructed identity and exclusion to their own political or pecuniary ends.

Among the predominantly white, but racially mixed, residents of the affluent townhouse complex, there was a shared collusion to abandon race-based identity and to emphasize a shared class position. These residents are seen as rich and privileged by those on the outside, while they perceive themselves as having joined the ranks of the international, post-Fordist middle class. While class and status underpinned 'insider identity', the identity of unknown outsiders was more opaque. However, fear of crime and strangers clearly often stood in for race-based fear and stereotyping. The residents of the cluster-home complex to the west are much closer to Soweto, both physically and structurally. While still undoubtedly privileged in comparison to the African working class of Soweto, in the new post-Fordist Johannesburg the predominantly white residents of this failing fortress are, nevertheless, part of the sunset rather than the sunrise economy, and are profoundly alienated from the local polity and society. If they opt, like many hostel dwellers, to evoke race and ethnicity and to take recourse in identity-based politics, they may well carve out for themselves a relatively secure, if very lonely, place in the South African sun. If they are prepared to put their heads above the parapet, and are encouraged by the council to do so, they may yet engage with the wider urban community and become a part of a new non-racial Johannesburg.

However, for this group of residents, as with the others studied here, the geography of fear (when combined with exclusionary mind-sets and the socio-spatial legacy of apartheid) mitigates against this. As Saff (2001) has argued, racially divided apartheid cities have been replaced by cities that are organized upon the basis of insider–outsider exclusions. In this context, the biggest challenge facing governance in Johannesburg is the fact that responsibility for spatial exclusion rests more and more upon private citizens rather than upon the state. This stands as a real constraint to council efforts to involve a majority of its citizens in addressing social exclusion, both their own and that of others.

Chapter 11

Conclusion: Lessons from a Uniting City

JOHANNESBURG AND THE PREREQUISITES FOR UNDERSTANDING DIVIDED CITIES

For many in South Africa, Johannesburg is the test case of post-apartheid urban reconstruction. But the experience of Johannesburg also has wider significance for how we understand and respond to divided cities across the world. In the introductory chapters, we argued that the success or failure of efforts to manage complex urban change in Johannesburg constituted something of a litmus test for urban reconstruction in divided cities everywhere. In this concluding chapter, we make the point that, as a prerequisite for uniting divided cities more generally, it is important to understand and address not only the political but also the economic, social and demographic processes that shape individual cities. Furthermore, and fundamental to the task of uniting divided cities, there is a need to understand the challenges involved within historical and geographical contexts. The approach to understanding urban change that we have developed in this study simultaneously captures the dynamics of structure, institution and agency. The first task in this regard is to understand the particularities of context.

Important to our understanding of Johannesburg as a divided city is the characteristic feature of the apartheid era in South Africa: the total absence of democracy. From this fairly unique vantage point, it is fitting that, in the immediate post-apartheid period, a critical task of transition was to put in place democratic political processes, structures and institutions of governance. Moreover, given that political exclusion under apartheid was based on race, it was appropriate to make race the case for the post-apartheid political transition. However, the lesson of Johannesburg suggests that forward-looking strategies require taking into account social, economic and political factors that reach beyond racial divisions. The business of establishing broadly acceptable institutions and mechanisms of governance in the city has involved complex relationships. These relationships are informed by intersecting inequalities and intertwine with, but extend beyond, a history of race-based exclusion. Thus, uniting the divided city of Johannesburg means not only looking back at the injustices of apartheid, but also understanding the current interplay between structural and institutional forces and the actions of people, and the way that this affects the nature of governance in the city.

The protracted political transition in Johannesburg provided an extraordinary opportunity to unite one of the world's most divided cities; but it has not yet successfully created a transformative dispensation that is able to tackle the structural problems facing the city. We argue that a sound foundation for inclusive governance has been laid by the new democratic municipal system. However, progressive policy formulations and reformed institutional structures do not automatically ensure justice, especially when there are such complex and contradictory interests within a city. Democracy in Johannesburg throws into sharp relief this challenge, which is perhaps more pronounced than elsewhere but is generally in line with that of other large metropolitan areas. Here, under conditions of rapid change, the priorities and actions of city leaders are continuously being tested.

Admittedly, in *Uniting a Divided City*, we have explored only the interim phase of democratic local government (1994–2000) in any depth. While the formal political transition is now complete, institutional change will take longer to consolidate than the five-year period of interim government. The accompanying global and economic restructuring is, of course, ongoing. In its wake, and as Johannesburg consolidates its City Development Strategy and entrenches post-apartheid practice by implementating the *iGoli 2002, 2010* and *2030* visions, the city's ability to maintain committed to the redistributive and unifying goals of DLG will be closely scrutinized. There is widespread concern that the goals of equity espoused in the interim period have already given way to greater emphasis on efficiency and growth.

Additionally, our analysis of Johannesburg has unpacked the challenges created by the conditions of structural change for urban government and described the responses of local residents. Over the period of 1994–2000, which constitutes the main empirical emphasis of *Uniting a Divided City*, the structural forces most evident in Johannesburg include the impact of post-Fordist economic change, the reconfiguration of the inter-governmental political dispensation, and ongoing urbanization and urban growth. Institutionally, the ending of apartheid saw a massive restructuring of central government, but, more dramatically, the creation of the first-ever comprehensive and inclusive system of local government for Johannesburg. With the end of apartheid, civil society also underwent substantial realignment. In response to the rupture of state–civil society relationships that were once defined primarily by opposition politics, new patterns of organization and social movements have emerged – with varying degrees of impact and effectiveness. As the city of Johannesburg enters the 21st century, and positive social change remains elusive, the big questions are: can the infamous divisions of the past be mended and can new divisions be prevented?

The Metamorphosis of Johannesburg's Political Economy

Addressing the democratic deficit in Johannesburg, as in South Africa more generally, was a necessary but insufficient condition of post-apartheid reconstruction. As we have shown, political inclusion has proved easier to achieve than economic redistribution or inclusive social change. Johannesburg is a place where nascent and new patterns of urban inequality have been swift to emerge. In particular, the twin cleavages that signal a fracture with the apartheid past and a continuity with global processes of social change are, first, the growing chasm between the increasingly multiracial middle class and the rest of society, and, second, the expanding gap between the regularly employed urban working class and the largely African unemployed and working poor.

As with other divided cities, these changing patterns of inequality are reflected in Johannesburg's social geography and built environment, giving rise to a spatial order that has been shaped by economic transition as much as by apartheid planning. In this context, we demonstrate that the patterns of social differentiation and polarization emerging in Johannesburg today have much in common with shifts in production processes globally, and have provided examples of some of the city-level impacts of macro-economic change. Most notable has been the spatial reconfiguration of the city, with a clear post-Fordist geography based upon class, not race; this is already evident in the map of Johannesburg. The accompanying patterns of social differentiation and exclusion, as well as the multiple axes of inequality that underpin them, constitute the threads running through our analysis and provide the structural context for our examination of agency and institutions in Johannesburg.

In other words, we argue that a prerequisite for uniting divided cities is to understand the structural nature of urban change – in this case, largely in terms of macro-economic dimensions – within the country, the region and the global economy. Johannesburg is undoubtedly the industrial and commercial heartland of South Africa, and its success or failure as an urban centre will create ripple effects way beyond its immediate boundaries. It is also an important economic hub for the Southern African region and a magnet for the continent's more peripatetic inhabitants. The challenge Johannesburg confronts is to find an appropriate niche in the regional and global economy, while at the same time addressing domestic imperatives. Understanding the factors affecting divided cities such as Johannesburg requires an understanding of the inter-urban scale of economic restructuring, as well as the internal economic dynamics of a city. For Johannesburg, the rise and fall of economic sectors has had a crucial impact on the spatial development of the city. Instead of the physical integration of the post-apartheid ideal, a more extreme pattern of class segregation is emerging. The spatial polarization induced by post-Fordist changes in production and consumption are reflected in the increasingly bifurcated politics of the city. We have demonstrated how changes in the labour process and market have given rise to a class of well-off and demanding post-Fordist winners, and an increasingly long tail of disaffected, poorly qualified and often unemployed post-Fordist losers.

Because of economic shifts, the city now has to engage with a more diverse range of businesses and enterprises than ever before. A distinction needs to be made between capital that operates 'in the city', including the much wooed foreign-business interests that generally have less commitment to the city of Johannesburg, and capital that is much more 'of the city', which is more likely to be local, national or regional. But even local interests are increasingly complex and no longer come simply in the form of a single 'chamber of commerce'. They now include illegal traders, hawkers' organizations, taxi associations, drug syndicates, criminal gangs, absentee landlords, and movements such as the Self-Employed Women's Union. Moreover, by the nature of their illegality or informality, many of the new commercial interests remain willfully invisible and largely escape scrutiny by the city.

Economic restructuring is also a significant social force – for example, in changing gender relations in Johannesburg, with women increasingly likely to be in low-paid but stable work while men face growing unemployment. This shift in employment profiles has consequences for domestic relations, the development of informal and illegal economies and for crime. At the structural level, we have argued that there are also important demographic issues, not least of all urbanization trends and the inexorable increase in HIV/AIDS. In Johannesburg, the socially excluded are most often new arrivals in the city. We have shown how the failure of the state or long-time residents to incorporate and include migrants (whether local or foreign), is undermining the citizenship prospects and social inclusion of many migrants. The reality of ongoing urbanization, however, means that the governance structures of the city cannot afford to ignore the often illegal, poor and sometimes disenfranchised constituency of migrants, for reasons both of equity and efficiency.

In addressing the problem of divided cities, the case of Johannesburg also demonstrates that macro-level political interventions are extremely important. South Africa's re-entry into the international political arena meant that the country signed up, for the first time, to progressive declarations and treaties. These, together with the new national political dispensation in South Africa, particularly the ideals of social justice and human rights as laid out in the country's constitution, have provided the city of Johannesburg with the scope to mediate not only poverty, but also a range of inequalities through the restructuring of local government. The constitution, moreover, has provided some protection to foreign refugees and migrants, and it has been significant in addressing gender inequity and promoting the whole issue of socio-economic rights. Specifically, it has given women in Johannesburg access to housing and services, and for the first time has made it imperative that city government engage continuously with all manner of constituencies – an important counter to some of the vastly powerful and influential interest groups that remain dominant in the city. Thus, the broader legal and institutional context of city government is critical to defining the opportunities and imperatives of local government action for unity.

Reconfiguring the Institutions of Urban Governance

Like many cities in fragile states, Johannesburg's recent and impressive efforts towards democratization have taken place in the context of a centralizing national state and a partial process of decentralization. The most obvious aspect determining Johannesburg's capacity to unite a divided population lies in the inter-governmental distribution of powers and functions, and in the resources available to city government. As part of this, the birth of developmental local government (DLG) in South Africa has also unleashed a swathe of unfunded mandates, giving rise to privatization initiatives and the casting around for multi-sectoral partnerships. In Johannesburg, municipal officials and politicians, alike, have struggled to keep up with the extended responsibilities of government. Civil society, too, has been stretched in its capacity to monitor municipal action, a pattern especially evident among poor, historically disenfranchised communities who have no legacy of local political engagement. Democratic DLG has thus created the space (but not necessarily the resources or the expertise) for an engaged civil society.

Equally familiar to a global audience is the story we tell of the fiscal crisis facing the city of Johannesburg during the transitional period of post-apartheid local government. Without doubt, the Johannesburg crisis was 'talked up' in politically opportunistic ways in order to legitimize increasing neo-liberal tendencies within the council, and to pander to vocal and articulate middle-class interests within the city. That said, the imperatives of a balanced budget and sound financial management were, and are, widely recognized as the basis for redistribution and inclusive government in Johannesburg. What is clear from Johannesburg's experience is that the relative health of the city's finances are pivotal in determining policy, politics, legitimacy and power.

We have made the point that democratic urban governance is a two-way street; and in addition to evoking an accountable, transparent and responsive state, democracy also requires engaged citizens and their active representatives. The current form of local government in Johannesburg is, in very crucial ways, the product of a robust civil society and popular mass struggle. Indeed, the strident call of ordinary people in Johannesburg for a unitary, non-racial city government with a single tax base for all citizens was successful and provided the institutional possibility for cross-subsidization and redistribution across the city. However, while many middle-class area-based groups have effectively engaged with, and utilized, the new structures and avenues for local democracy in defence of their interests (whether through the establishment of gated communities or active ratepayers' associations), the picture is less clear among poorer and more excluded residents of the city. Here the experience of Johannesburg is by no means unique and follows patterns of collective action evident in urban communities elsewhere, where periods of intense local-level activity and oppositional political engagement are followed by periods of inertia or regrouping.

Although it seems certain that, for constitutional reasons at least, local government in Johannesburg will continue to seek out community-based consultation, we point to an element of cynicism among some city officials and to participation fatigue among some local residents, particularly in low-income local constituencies in Johannesburg with a long and difficult history of anti-apartheid struggle. While participation remains a pillar of neighbourhood-level investment and development, direct engagement by citizens is far more limited when it comes to defining the medium-term strategic direction of the city. In the absence of metropolitan representatives of civil society in matters of city-wide planning and policy, the responsibility of representing ordinary people falls almost exclusively on elected officials, many of whom are relatively new to the role.

Crucial to genuine democratic decentralization is a robust civil society that has voice and purchase beyond the community level. Successful and sustainable city-level organization can be scaled-out for greater legitimacy and scaled-up for greater impact. Despite an impressive and celebrated history of opposition to apartheid, it is by no means clear that umbrella organizations such as SANCO, which represents the collective interests of CBOs in low-income and historically disadvantaged neighbourhoods, will remain effective or representative. In terms of efficacy, service delivery and advocacy, NGOs are valuable in supporting and bolstering the role of membership organizations, such as SANCO, and CBOs, committed to transforming their neighbourhoods and, indeed, the city.

At the metropolitan scale, it is important to recognize that historic alliances between SANCO and organized labour are not necessarily sustainable because the interests of their members are not always coterminous. This is true in spite of the fact that the civics supported the trade unions during the anti-apartheid struggle – for example, through 'stayaways' and consumer boycotts. Divergence in their interests was signalled when, unlike COSATU, SANCO did not join the political alliance with the ANC. At a more localized level, there are other fractures. Within the civics and the CDFs, in particular, there is the danger of local elites dominating these organizations to the detriment of the interests of more excluded residents. For the unions, there is the danger that bread-and-butter issues take precedence over broader urban political issues. The most stark example of this is that, despite the rhetoric of unions such as SAMWU that municipal workers are 'in and of' their communities, in reality, the interests of workers as providers of municipal services, and those of community members as users, do not always coincide. This conflict of interests suggests the potential for community friction in the longer run. This, too, is a picture familiar to readings of other urban contexts and a perennial problem in the reform of urban governance.

Regrouping Social Movements for Effective Democratic Governance

The third level of our analysis suggests that a prerequisite for addressing divided cities is to understand the micro level of households and communities, and the way in which impacts and responses at the micro level are constitutive of social and political change in the city, and even at national level. For example, agency at the household level has led to rural–urban migration into Johannesburg, and the influx of foreign migrants into the city. Similarly, local-level agency has determined the pace and nature of civic engagement and DLG in many areas, which, in turn, has affected the nature of local governance in Johannesburg.

A key lesson to emerge from our research is that, especially at the micro level, cities are not homogeneous. People have different interests, priorities and capabilities across class, race, ethnicity, age, gender and length of residence in the city. Crucially, men and women, as well as younger and older people, are differently affected by macro-economic changes; but the lines of social, political and economic exclusion do not always follow the same faultlines. For example, our analysis of Johannesburg counters the stereotype of women as the most economically vulnerable; in some contexts, our analysis suggests that women constitute the main breadwinners and provide the social glue at community level. However, their relative political marginalization should be noted, alongside their particular susceptibility to sexual abuse and physical violence. The youth, though better educated than their parents, are more likely to be unemployed and socially marginalized, especially boys and young men, and are as likely to be victims as perpetrators of crime.

Coming out of our micro-level analysis is the fact that, in the absence of adequate social services and social security from national and provincial levels of government, ordinary people are involved in providing home- and community-based care, particularly in the context of HIV/AIDS. Whether this takes the form of child care, care of the elderly, traditional medicine or protection against crime, the development of a community level care economy has crucial implications for local government. Yet, it is an area that is very poorly understood or resourced. For some excluded and self-excluding communities in Johannesburg, we know that rural linkages provide support and an adjunct to forging an urban base. Moreover, shared identity, however fluid, is an important component of neighbourliness. A crucial challenge for city officials is to recognize, understand and operate equitably and openly within these diverse and separate constituencies.

Precisely because constituencies are diverse and the nature of local-level responses multifarious, another important lesson from our research is the need to recognize the value of flexible and fluid grassroots organization, and to allow for the potential of coalition politics to flourish among differently organized groups at different times. There is a danger of essentializing single aspects and sites of urban struggle, whether workplace or neighbourhood-based activities. Increasingly common are identity-based, area-based or issue-based coalitions. Here, issues can be as diverse as women's rights, HIV/AIDS, NIMBY concerns, or community policing. In Johannesburg, this has implications for the durability and aptness of the current preference for public consultation through the dual medium of CDFs and trade unions, both on the part of the city and on the part of many residents and workers, themselves. However, alternatives imply a demographically stable and politically sophisticated citizenry, and it may be that a more socially inclusive style of free-for-all urban governance is a long time in the making in a city such as Johannesburg.

LESSONS FOR INCLUSIVE URBAN GOVERNANCE

Building on our analysis, which covers structure, institutions and agency, what, then, are the lessons for urban governance that can be drawn from Johannesburg as it transforms itself from a city fractured in multiple ways to one where the local authority (together with the various constituencies with which it engages) can address the cleavages that have threatened to tear the city apart? We draw a number of lessons from contemporary Johannesburg as an urban centre that is axiomatic of 21st-century cities. First, we showed how

Johannesburg, as with many other cities in the North and South, is an unequal city. Thus, a focus on poverty outside of an understanding of inequality is inappropriate and inadequate, particularly in a metropolitan context. Although a very large percentage of Johannesburg's population is poor, it has a substantial middle class who compete in global financial and trade markets, and who adhere to international norms of urban consumption and culture. Elite expectations of what constitutes a well-run city permeate the aspirations of the GJMC and must be set against the demands of the city's disadvantaged populations. Balancing the state's commitment to global competitiveness alongside poverty reduction, when the current political and policy juncture means that both objectives carry moral weight, is therefore, an essential component of urban governance in Johannesburg.

Second, we have explained how Johannesburg is a city where the economic base is in transition. The economic transformation of Johannesburg goes well beyond the decline of traditional mining and manufacturing sectors during the mid-1970s, although these patterns are evident in the city. Economic change in Johannesburg is also about deliberate economic restructuring, which saw a shift from import substitution to export-led growth from the late 1970s. In the post-apartheid era, restructuring involved the search for an economic future for the city and its environs, based upon the development of a high-tech hub for the regional and sub-Saharan African market. As we have shown, economic transition is not exclusive to South Africa, nor are the social impacts of this process. As we point out in relation to the international literature on social exclusion, across the North–South divide, economic transition has eroded job-for-life and cradle-to-grave patterns of employment and social security. This has given way to insecure dynamics where the majority of individuals are increasingly excluded from formal labour markets and social security systems, with particular ramifications for city economies and the mandates of local government.

While neo-liberal economic reform was forced upon many cities of the South through the imposition of IMF and World Bank structural adjustment programmes, such direct intervention was unnecessary in South Africa, which embarked on its own voluntary process of economic liberalization, along with many cities of the North. Less deliberate, but equally constitutive of economic transition in Johannesburg (and more in synchrony with cities of the South), has been a growing economic informality. With this in mind, coordinating and managing, rather than controlling and marginalizing, the unregulated economies of the poor is an imperative of 21st-century governance, and one that is not confined to South Africa. Increasingly, it is also a feature of cities in the North.

Third, we have illustrated how Johannesburg is a multilingual, religiously diverse and polycultural city and a thriving cosmopolitan centre. The city's diverse population hails from across South and Southern Africa, the African sub-continent, Europe and Asia. Many of its citizens maintain strong rural or small-town links; through these links, as well as through the bonding networks of ethnic and national groups, social relations and the care economy are fostered and sustained. As we have shown, and as the authorities in Johannesburg are aware, the bonds are crucial to the welfare of poor and excluded urban dwellers, so that negotiating difference is a crucial aspect of managing urban social cohesion. Local government in Johannesburg, as elsewhere, confronts the need to foster social inclusion without creating a rigid and conforming social and political process, and one that fails to respect the choice of some groups to exclude themselves and remain outside of mainstream trajectories.

In terms of social development, it can be efficacious to recognize the social benefits associated with bounded communities, but much depends upon the ability of the council to support and build on existing social networks and support structures, rather than simply abdicating responsibility to households and communities for care and social support. In many respects, getting the social development agenda right will constitute the making or the breaking of the decentralization process in Johannesburg, something that hinges as much upon support from and coordination with other tiers of government as it does upon the metropolitan council's response to social issues.

Next, unlike most internationally atypical cities of the North, Johannesburg's population is expanding. More akin to cities in Africa, Asia and Latin America, it lies at the centre of a rapidly urbanizing region and must face the challenges of sustainable urban growth. Among these challenges are employment creation and the provision of services, alongside the simultaneous maintenance of the urban fabric and the rural hinterland. Furthermore, as we have demonstrated, Johannesburg is a city in which the public and private sectors are embroiled in an ongoing process of renegotiating their relationship. As elsewhere in the world, it is a city that is experiencing a move towards private solutions, not just to infrastructure and services, but also to land development regulations, building codes and social services. The privatization debate is in its infancy in Johannesburg and needs to be understood in these terms. It must also learn from the international experience, which has had greater opportunity to play itself out. What is very clear is that the debate in South Africa has become very narrowly focused, and is tied either to conditions of employment or the debate over standards of housing and services. Our findings suggest that the issues are more complex and nuanced than this. The impact of privatization on the poor of Johannesburg, and issues of conditions of employment, affordability for residents and overall social justice, constitute central challenges to democratic urban governance that need to be understood in a wider context of redistributive planning and management where a one-size-fits-all approach is inadequate.

Finally, in terms of the responses of citizens to urban change, Johannesburg straddles a potential divide between the opportunities presented by an impressive legacy of popular democracy and the constraints imposed by political and civic disengagement by an increasingly fragile and disillusioned populace. As in many other urban contexts globally, what this means is that the inclusive forces of active advocacy, accountable government and participatory planning processes have to compete with the divisive forces of political apathy – for example, where voter turnout is derisory. This occurs in a context where public–private–community relations are being renegotiated at the local level. The ruling ANC party in South Africa has been unapologetically centralist; but a combination of pragmatic imperatives, political sleight of hand and international influence is seeing elements of decentralization penetrate urban planning in Johannesburg. As elsewhere, city officials are coping with the problems of unfunded mandates as the responsibilities of local government grow disproportionately in relation to the resources they are allocated and the revenue they are able to collect. Local communities are witnessing elite capture of community organizations in efforts to control access to resources and decision-making.

The fact that urban residents, workers and communities are not homogeneous or mutually exclusive groups, places particular strains on local authorities, who are moving towards, or are committed to, consultative and participatory practice. Singular structures and mechanisms, such as CDFs, are important but should be recognized as failing to embrace the full complement of citizens and residents in a city as complex and cosmopolitan as Johannesburg. Compounding the issue is the fact that members and organizations of civil society can be decidedly 'uncivil', a familiar scenario in cities where streets and public spaces are no longer safe or inclusive places. Democratic and inclusive local governance is a major challenge in cities beset by violence, crime and a disregard for the rule of law. These are problems that characterize Johannesburg not only because of the abuse of law under apartheid, but because liberalization and globalization have brought to the city both positive and negative investment.

CONCLUSION

Much of the contemporary literature on urban South Africa focuses upon racial inequality and its relationship with the economic, social, demographic and spatial legacies of apartheid. In *Uniting a Divided City*, we argue that although race issues are unequivocally important, social differentiation, social polarization and social exclusion also operate along a number of different axes of inequality. Clearly, the legacy of racial segregation constitutes a heavy historical stamp on the city; but Johannesburg is not alone in being a city that is divided spatially and socially along racial lines and is increasingly experiencing other faultlines.

The challenges to inclusive urban governance, with regard to Johannesburg, in particular, and divided cities elsewhere, are described in our analysis of structure, agency and institutions as they operate in the urban environment. We argue that these tensions serve to underpin and reinforce urban social exclusion, and constitute the most critical challenges of contemporary urban governance as it strives for inclusivity and social cohesion. These tensions, in addition, provide some sense of why Johannesburg, although having been caught up in the specificities of the post-apartheid transition, increasingly represents the trials of governance in divided cities everywhere.

Notes

CHAPTER 1   INTRODUCTION TO A DIVIDED CITY

1   When we commenced research for this project, we were concerned whether our resources would cover interviewing and focus group discussions across all of the nine local languages spoken in Johannesburg. We did not initially anticipate that we would also have to cover French and Portuguese, as well. It is appropriate at this juncture to extend warm thanks to the staff of Progressus, a Johannesburg-based research company, who assisted us in conducting the field research for this ambitious endeavour.

2   The book draws upon the following three research reports, which detail the methodologies used and which are themselves more extensively illustrated and referenced than this book: J Beall, O Crankshaw and S Parnell (1999) *Urban Governance, Partnership and Poverty in Johannesburg*; J Beall, O Crankshaw and S Parnell (2000) *Towards Inclusive Urban Governance in Johannesburg*; City of Johannesburg (2001) *Social Capital and Social Exclusion in the City of Johannesburg*. It also uses primary research material on the inner city collected by Jo Beall in the production of a Radio Four programme and Open University audio cassette: 'Smart Johannesburg' (Beall and Lawson, 1999).

3   Research methods included the examination of primary documents, newspapers, statistical analysis of census information, social surveys, key informant interviews, focus group discussions, in-depth interviews, field observation and participatory research techniques. Interviews were conducted with government officials, policy-makers and political and community leaders, while focus group discussions were held with diverse groups of citizens selected according to social identity (for example, gender, age, employment status) and residential status (for example, migrants, tenants, homeowners).

4   Recognizing the many problems associated with the term 'Third World' (for example, that it homogenizes the majority world and is now an anachronistic concept), we use it over and above the equally normative distinction between 'developing' and 'developed' countries. We do so because the term retains political purchase in the countries of Africa, Asia and Latin America, although our preferred dichotomized nomenclature refers to cities of 'the South' as opposed to 'the North', which is used to refer to advanced industrialized economies.

5   Methodologically it should be noted that as case study research, the city of Johannesburg constitutes our case. However, within this broader research framework we also conducted a number of micro-studies that also constitute case studies. The area or settlement-level case studies were undertaken during three separate phases of research endeavour. Studies of the informal settlement of Diepsloot, the inner-city area of Yeoville and Meadowlands in Greater Soweto were conducted as part of the initial work we undertook on urban poverty and urban governance. The study of the inner city formed part of the research undertaken

towards the radio programme 'Smart Johannesburg'. The cases pursued as part of the study on social capital and social exclusion on behalf of the Metropolitan Council of Johannesburg included the informal settlement of Hospital Hill, Orlando East in Soweto and the hostel community of Dube in Soweto. We financed the work on white communities ourselves.

CHAPTER 2   REVERBERATIONS FROM A DIVIDED CITY

1   For example, the Natives (Urban Areas) Act of 1923, the Slums Act of 1934, the Black (Urban Areas) Consolidation Act of 1945 and the Group Areas Act of 1950.
2   Although poverty is severe and social differentiation extreme, it should be noted that when compared with other cities in Africa, Johannesburg's poor are better off than many urban dwellers across the continent. It should also be pointed out that the situation of Johannesburg's poor also compares well with national figures.
3   Gauteng is one of the nine new provinces of South Africa. It is a predominantly urban province comprising Johannesburg and the conurbation of which it forms a significant part, and which includes the area formerly known as the Pretoria–Witwatersrand–Vereeniging, or the PWV, region.
4   Recent work on urban politics operates at a higher level of abstraction than urban governance – for example, the debates related to regulation and regime theory to explain the political economy of urban development (Fainstein, 1994; Jessop, 1990; Lauria, 1997) – and has not yet really entered discussions on Third World cities.
5   For North (1990), institutions – which he defines as 'the rules of the game' – are distinct from organizations, which he defines as groups of individuals bound by some common purpose to achieve objectives. Thus, institutions can operate at the micro-economic level (for example, the rules of contract or exchange at the level of the firm or the bazaar) or the macro-economic level, whereby the market itself constitutes an institution, as does the state and the plethora of legal and contractual mechanisms to protect their operation. How 'the rules of the game' are defined is what is important to us.
6   The anthropologist Mary Douglas (1987) shows how social institutions form and cement social bonds within a wider social context that includes both self-seeking and public-spirited individuals. She sees institutions as comprising both a transactional element (the utility-maximizing activities) and a cognitive element (the individual demand for order, coherence and control of uncertainty), which she describes as a thought world, shared by its members. She warns of the tendency to anthropomorphize institutions, instead of seeing them as products of the fact that 'individuals really do share their thoughts and they do, to some extent, harmonize their preferences'.
7   We stress that this bias is a matter of degree, as both of these authors would probably protest their categorization as writers who do not take into account structural factors.

CHAPTER 3   BEYOND RACIAL FORDISM: CHANGING PATTERNS OF SOCIAL INEQUALITY

1   We use the term 'Johannesburg' to refer to the area that falls under the administrative authority of the present GJMC. The GJMC is a relatively new

    metropolitan authority and includes the erstwhile local authorities of Johannesburg, Randburg, Roodepoort, Sandton and Soweto.

2   Wieczorek's (1995) findings are based on an analysis of employment trends in Hong Kong, Israel, Korea, Turkey, Venezuela, Panama, the Philippines, Ghana, Kenya, Sri Lanka, Zambia and Zimbabwe.

3   The extent to which this period (1945–1975) was characterized by a stable regime of accumulation is subject to debate. Specifically, Nattrass (1992) has shown that the manufacturing sector was characterized by a falling rate of profit during this period. This finding suggests that racial Fordism was not sustainable and was therefore not a stable regime of accumulation. In spite of its downward trend, Nattrass's findings showed that the manufacturing profit rate in South Africa was nonetheless over twice that which was obtained in Europe until 1981.

4   We have broken down service-sector employment into three categories. The first category is community, social and personal services. The most important areas of employment within this category are:

- government administration;
- the defence force;
- public and private educational services;
- public and private health services; and
- personal services (particularly domestic service).

The second category is what is often classified as commerce. This sector includes:

- all wholesale and retail trade;
- the repair of motor vehicles, motor cycles and personal and household goods; and
- the hotel and restaurant trade.

The third category, which is self-explanatory, is financial intermediation, insurance, real estate and business services (CSS, 1993).

5   The sharp decline in employment in these two sectors between 1991 and 1996 is due to a drop in the enumeration of the white population in Johannesburg. This decline in the number of whites is too large to be explained solely by the emigration of middle-class whites because of rising crime levels and political anxiety about their future under a black government. A more likely explanation is that white households were under-enumerated in the 1996 Population Census.

6   The population and employment trends presented in this chapter are based upon data from the population censuses of 1946, 1951, 1960, 1970, 1980, 1991 and 1996. Population and employment estimates are published for each magisterial district. Although these magisterial districts often bear the same names as local authorities, their boundaries do not necessarily coincide with the boundaries of local authorities. The population and employment estimates for metropolitan Johannesburg are the sum of the estimates for the magisterial districts of Johannesburg, Randburg and Roodepoort.

7   This section is based on the work of Cassim, (1988), Edwards (1998), Millward and Pillay (1996), Nattrass (2001), Piazolo and Würth (1995) and Roberts (1997).

CHAPTER 4   POST-FORDIST POLARIZATION: THE CHANGING SPATIAL ORDER OF THE CITY

1   These figures exclude other townships that were to become part of Greater Soweto, built under the authority of the Roodepoort Council.

CHAPTER 5   DECENTRALIZATION BY STEALTH: DEMOCRATIZATION OR DISEMPOWERMENT THROUGH DEVELOPMENTAL LOCAL GOVERNMENT?

1   This was the case until 1988, when the reforms to adopt a tri-cameral parliamentary system created separate legislatures for coloureds and Indians respectively, a move widely rejected by these constituencies and the mass democratic movement, and boycotted by the majority of coloured and Indian voters.
2   One of the most controversial aspects of the negotiated settlement was the 'Sunset Clause' that allowed civil servants of the old regime to remain in their positions. See Beall, Crankshaw and Parnell (1999) for a discussion on the outworking of this policy in Johannesburg.

CHAPTER 6   THE POLITICS OF FISCAL AUSTERITY IN CREATING EQUITABLE CITY GOVERNMENT

1   In other words, ratepayers were required to pay 6.45 cents per annum for every Rand of the assessed value of their land.
2   The discussion in this section is drawn directly from Beall, Crankshaw and Parnell (2000). Nick Devas and Sue Parnell researched and wrote the chapter on municipal finances for that report. In addition to the material reproduced in this section, there is discussion on the city's revenue sources and expenditure patterns, the state of the capital budget, the city's debt and its alternative sources of revenue, as well as proposals for financial restructuring within the new uni-city. We are very grateful to Nick Devas for allowing us to use this extract of his text and for his insights on municipal budgets.
3   The RSC levy is a local tax on businesses levied at the rate of 0.25 per cent of payroll and 0.1 per cent of business turnover. It was introduced by the apartheid government some years ago as a way of capturing tax on businesses in black areas, and the revenue is supposed to be used to finance infrastructure. Assessments are based on self-declaration by the business. The local authority has no legal right to make assessments or to challenge them, or even to require registration. The only action that it can take is to refer the matter to the commissioner of income tax. In order to try to improve yield, some local authorities have employed agents to visit businesses with what purports to be an assessment, but which is carefully worded to avoid legal challenge.
4   The GJMC is the main (but not sole) electricity distributor within its jurisdiction, and generates some of its own power, but also buys bulk from ESKOM. In the past, surpluses from electricity sales have represented a significant source of revenue. In gross terms, it is still the largest single revenue source; but after deduction of all costs, the net contribution is quite small.

5   With the financial crisis, the capital budget was cut back dramatically. The 1997/1998 capital budget of R1.7 billion was cut back to R580 million once the financial crisis struck. As part of the restructuring programme, a Capital Development Fund has been established to ensure that resources from the city's recurrent budget are set aside for capital investment. For 1999/2000, the fund is set at R106 million. This fund is financed through contributions from the recurrent budgets from the service departments and is, for the most part, used to finance capital projects from those departments.

6   These figures relate to the current year's budget, rather than to actual results from the previous year. The latter would normally be considered a more accurate guide to the real situation; but these figures were not available in a sufficiently disaggregated form in order to make this analysis. However, in the case of Johannesburg, budgets tend to be adhered to, so budgeted figures are a reasonable guide as to what will happen. For example, actual expenditures in 1998/1999 were 100.2 per cent of the budgeted figure, while actual revenues were 99.2 per cent.

7   This is a phrase used by officials to describe the Hunter/Gordan/Fihla appointments. Formal remarks in our focus groups and loose remarks made by several officials during interviews and focus groups suggest that the appointment of the three appears to have generated energy and commitment to making Johannesburg work.

8   The Venn diagram is a research tool used in ethnographic and participatory research. The size of the square or circle represents the strength and importance of the actor or organization. The distance from the informant or focus group, in this case local government officials, represents the degree of interaction or engagement.

CHAPTER 7   THE INNER-CITY CHALLENGE: LOCATING PARTNERS FOR URBAN REGENERATION

1   The field research in Yeoville was conducted for Beall, Crankshaw and Parnell (2000). In this regard, we are grateful to Kirsten Harrison, who conducted extensive key informant interviews during the first quarter of 2000, and to Kirsten Harrison and Progressus for conducting the focus-group discussions. The chapter also draws on the field notes and interviews undertaken for the production of an audio-cassette on Johannesburg for the Open University (Beall and Lawson, 1999) and refers to the research undertaken for the city on Hillbrow (GJMC, 2001b).

2   The inner city is defined by the GJMC as the area bounded by, and including, the neighbourhoods of Vrededorp, Pageview and Fordsburg in the west, Braamfontein, Hillbrow and Berea in the north, Bellevue East, Judith's Paarl, Troyeville and Jeppestown in the east, and Marshalltown and city and suburban in the south.

3   The website is: www.pcb.co.za/yeoville/Pages/press.htm

4   This is an organization that works with South African women traders in the survivalist sector in Gauteng and is a sister organization to the Self-Employed Women's Union (SEWU) in KwaZulu–Natal. Both drew inspiration from, and model themselves on, SEWA in India.

CHAPTER 8   PARTICIPATORY PLANNING AND INFORMAL SETTLEMENT UPGRADING IN DIEPSLOOT

1   We are especially grateful to members of the CDF who gave generously of their time to assist us in our research. We would also like to acknowledge the formal assistance of the NGO Planact in conducting many of the focus groups and key informant interviews for our field research. We also acknowledge Kirsten Harrison, who played a key role in liaising and organizing field research.

CHAPTER 9   HOUSING AND SERVICE CONSUMPTION IN SOWETO

1   In South, Africa shacks are found in formally planned site-and-service settlements, which have low building standards but are serviced, and in illegal and unplanned squatter settlements.

2   The results presented in this table are based on a household survey of the African townships of Greater Soweto that was conducted during February 1997. Altogether, 2947 households were sampled, using a stratified cluster sample. Employment and demographic information was collected for each household member. For a detailed discussion of the sampling method, refer to Morris et al (1999). The authors are grateful to the members of the Soweto in Transition Committee (Sociology Department, University of the Witwatersrand) for their permission to use the results of the Soweto household survey. We also acknowledge the financial contributions made to the Soweto household survey by the Johannesburg Metropolitan Council, the Anglo American Chairman's Fund and the Human Sciences Research Council.

3   It would be an error to assume that poverty in Johannesburg is confined to former African areas because coloured areas in particular, exhibit some of the worst residential conditions in the city (Lupton, 1993).

4   A later design, the '51/9' incorporated a small bathroom (with basin, bath and lavatory) and was slightly larger, at 44sqm.

5   The research findings are based upon a study conducted in Orlando East in early 2001. The investigation included a number of observational and participatory research methods, as well as ten key informant interviews, interviews with residents, both landlords and tenants, and five focus-group discussions.

6   Even though it is the heart of sub-tenancy in Soweto, Orlando East still has much lower densities than the overcrowded stands of other, more densely settled, townships such as Alexandra (CASE, 1999b; Monitor, 2000a). As such, the findings from Orlando East can only be seen as indicative of sub-tenancy issues that prevail in many areas of ex-council housing in former African townships of Johannesburg. Nevertheless, as we argue elsewhere (City of Johannesburg, 2001), some of the service issues thrown up by the living and tenancy arrangements associated with backyard shacks in Orlando East offer interesting lessons to the GJMC in terms of managing the future of backyard shelters and service provision in the city.

7   Our informants all identified foreign migrants as coming from Lesotho, Swaziland, Mozambique and Zimbabwe, and not from other African countries.

8   The position was less ambiguous with regard to local government services that were provided at the community, rather than at the plot, scale; for these, the

distinction between the needs of landlords and tenants was less obvious and important. Most positive responses from backyard residents to local government service delivery were related to clinics and social services. Transport facilities also received general endorsement, although issues of cost and safety raised anxiety. An exception was the area of crime prevention and policing, which received universal condemnation.

9   Tenants are not necessarily the victims of the subletting arrangements – as *The Sowetan* reminded its readers. Intimidation of a landlord by the sub-tenants meant not only that tenants remained on low rents, but also that the owner was too afraid to evict them for fear of reprisal. In the context of low rentals that have been paid, this is presumably not an isolated case.

CHAPTER 10   THE PEOPLE BEHIND THE WALLS: INSECURITY, IDENTITY AND GATED COMMUNITIES

1   The term 'hostel' applies to the single-sex barrack-like dwellings that have housed migrant workers even before the apartheid era. Reflecting patterns of circulatory migration that had their roots in the twin processes of rural dispossession and controlled urbanization (Mabin, 1991), today they remain a symbolic remnant of apartheid urban planning.

2   It might also be argued that the crime paranoia has a racial dimension, fuelled by emigrating or potential émigré South Africans who find crime a more acceptable rationale for explaining their departure than the challenges posed by the change to a non-racial democracy.

3   There are two key sources for crime figures available on Johannesburg, those derived from the South African Police (SAP), compiled on the basis of reporting rather than real incidence, and those derived from victims' surveys. Johannesburg has been the focus of several victimization surveys, two conducted in 1993 and 1995, respectively, as part of the International Crime Victim Survey (ICVS), and one administered in July 1997 by the Institute of Security Studies (ISS) (Louw et al, 1998). The latter formed an initial component of a process to design a safer cities strategy for the GJMC (GJMC, 1997). Victim surveys are known to have their limitations, largely deriving from problems of definition and interpretation. However, in the Johannesburg context, when taken together with official police statistics, these two main sources point to similar trends. Both sources were used for the safety and security analyses undertaken for Johannesburg's medium-term planning framework (ISS, 1999, cited in Monitor, 2000b).

4   Most offenders are also young and, it is thought that 70 to 80 per cent of crime in Johannesburg is committed by 5 to 10 per cent of the young male population (Monitor, 2000b).

5   The controversy over the number of rapes that are reported in South Africa has risen to cabinet-level debate. Estimates range from 1 in 35, according to the NGO, People Opposing Women Abuse (POWA), and to nearly 1 in 3 according to the police (Monitor, 2000b).

6   In the northern complex, we held focus groups and interviews with women, all of whom were English-speaking whites, and with men who were all English-speaking but included one South African Indian. In the complex to the west of the city, residents spoke both English and Afrikaans, and both the male and female focus groups comprised one third African and two-thirds white discussants, as did the

individual interviews. It is difficult to assess how typical their views might have been, not least of all because people who choose to live in secure complexes may be a self-selecting group.

7 The methodology employed both in the case of the secure housing complexes and of the hostels was not designed to understand the extent or distribution of wealth or poverty within them, or between their residents and other groups. Rather, it was designed to analyse the social relations and institutional processes that accompany social exclusion and perceptions of these processes.

8 Most of the crimes raised by interviewees and discussants had happened to others, and not always necessarily in Johannesburg. In terms of their experiences within the complexes, in the north the only crimes reported were bicycle thefts; while in the west, individuals continued to suffer from constant car break-ins and vehicle thefts.

9 South African word for 'barbecue', which originates from the Afrikaans – literally meaning 'roasted meat' – but in general use.

10 A service in Johannesburg that has various branches across the city which pick up and deliver pre-ordered meals from a range of take-away restaurants in a particular area.

11 The opposition Democratic Party.

12 Both the municipality and private companies in Johannesburg used these single-sex institutions to accommodate male migrant workers from all over South Africa and beyond.

13 The development of the hostels was first put in the hands of the ANC-led National Housing Forum (NHF) and then the Independent Development Trust (IDT), in conjunction with provincial and local government housing departments.

References

Abbot, J (1996) *Sharing the City*, Earthscan, London

Abrahams, G (1998) 'Historical evolution of metropolitan government for Johannesburg' in *Metropolitan Government, 1994–1997*, Foundation for Contemporary Research, Cape Town

Abu–Lughod, J (1999) *New York, Chicago, Los Angeles: America's global cities*, University of Minnesota Press, Minneapolis

Adler, J, Beetge, M and Sher, S (1984) 'The "new" illegality: Squatters with urban rights but no houses', *Indicator South Africa* 2(2), pp8–10

Aglietta, M (1979) *A Theory of Capitalist Regulation: The US experience*, New Left Books, London

Allen, K, Gotz, G and Joseph, C (2001) 'Responding to crisis and change: *iGoli 2002* and a recent history of local government in Johannesburg', Report commissioned by the City of Johannesburg, Johannesburg

Alexander, E and Oldert, N (2000) *Profile's Stock Exchange Handbook: January 2000 to June 2000*, Profile Media, Johannesburg

Amin, A and Graham S (1999) 'Cities of connection and disconnection' in Massey, D and Pryke, M (eds) *Unsettling Cities: Movement/Settlement*, Routledge, London, pp7–38

Amis, P (1995) 'Making sense of urban poverty', *Environment and Urbanization*, 7(1), pp145–158

African National Congress (ANC) (1994) *The Reconstruction and Development Plan: A policy framework*, Umanyo, Durban

ANC (undated) '*iGoli 2002*: Moving beyond the form', Unpublished position paper Provincial Executive Committee, African National Congress

APS Planafrica (1998) 'Diepsloot/Olievenhoutbosch Integrated Development Framework', prepared for the Greater Pretoria Metropolitan Council, Khayalami Metropolitan Council (Midrand MLC) and the Northern Metropolitan Local Council by APS Planafrica in association with Plan Associates and Urban-Econ, 18 February 1998, Johannesburg

Ayres, R (1998) *Crime and Violence as Development Issues in Latin America and the Caribbean*, World Bank Latin American and Caribbean Studies, Washington, DC

Badcock, B (2000) 'The imprint of the post-Fordist transition on Australian cities' in Marcuse, P and van Kempen, R (eds) *Globalizing Cities: A new spatial order?* Blackwell Publishers, Oxford, pp211–227

Bailey, N (1994) 'Towards a research agenda for public–private partnerships in the 1990s', *Local Economy*, 8(4), pp292–306

Bailey, N with Barker, A and MacDonald, K (1995) *Partnership Agencies in British Urban Policy*, University College London Press, London

Batley, R (1996) 'Public–private relationships and performance in service provision', *Urban Studies*, 33(4/5), pp723–752

Beall, J (1996) *Urban Governance: Why gender matters*, UNDP Gender in Development Monograph Series, No 1, United Nations Development Programme, New York

Beall, J (1997a) 'Introduction' in Beall, J (ed) *A City for All: Valuing difference and working with diversity*, Zed Books, London, pp2–37

Beall, J (2000a) 'Life in the Cities' in Allen, T and Thomas, A (eds) *Poverty and Development into the 21st Century*, The Open University in association with Oxford University Press, Oxford

Beall, J (2000b) 'From the Culture of Poverty to Inclusive Cities: Re-Framing Urban Policy and Politics', *Journal of International Development*, 12, pp 843–856

Beall, J (2002a) 'Living in the present, investing in the future: Household security among the urban poor' in Rakodi, C and Lloyd–Jones, T (eds) *Urban Livelihoods: A People-centred Approach to Reducing Poverty*, Earthscan, London, pp71–95

Beall, J (2002b) 'Globalization and Social Exclusion in Cities: Framing the Debate with Lessons from Africa and Asia', *Environment and Urbanization*, 14(1), April, pp41–51

Beall, J, Crankshaw, O and Parnell, S (1999) *Urban Governance, Partnership and Poverty in Johannesburg*, Urban Governance, Partnerships and Poverty Research Working Papers, Working Paper No 12, School of Public Policy, University of Birmingham, Birmingham

Beall, J, Crankshaw, O and Parnell, S (2000) *Towards Inclusive Urban Governance in Johannesburg*, Urban Governance, Partnerships and Poverty Research Working Papers, Working Paper No 24, School of Public Policy, University of Birmingham

Beall, J, Crankshaw, O and Parnell, S (2002) 'Social differentiation and urban governance in Greater Soweto: A Case Study of post-apartheid Meadowlands', in Tomlinson, R, Beauregard, B, Bremner, L and Mangai, X (eds), *Emerging Johannesburg*, Routledge, London

Beall, J and Kanji, N (1999) 'Households, livelihoods and urban poverty', Urban Governance, Partnership and Poverty Working Paper No 3, International Development Department, University of Birmingham, Birmingham

Beall, J and Lawson, S (1999) 'Smart Johannesburg: Leading the African renaissance?' Audio cassette produced for the Masters Programme in Development Management, Open University, Milton Keynes

Beall, J and Lingayah, S (2001) 'A framework for evaluation of city challenge funds', Unpublished mimeo

Beare, M and Taylor, G (1996) 'Downtown downturn', *Millenium*, April, pp29–34

Beauregard, R (1995) 'Edge cities: Peripheralizing the center', *Urban Geography*, 16(8), pp708–721

Beavon, K (1997) 'Johannesburg: A city and metropolitan area in transformation' in Rakodi, C (ed) *The Urban Challenge in Africa: Growth and Management of its Large Cities*, United Nations University Press, Tokyo, pp150–191

Beavon, K (1998a) 'Johannesburg: Coming to grips with globalization from an abnormal base' in Lo, F and Yeung, Y (eds) *Globalization and the World of Large Cities*, United Nations University Press, New York, pp352–388

Beavon, K (1998b) 'Nearer my mall to thee: The decline of the Johannesburg central business district and the emergence of the neo-apartheid city', unpublished Seminar Paper No 442, presented to the Institute for Advanced Social Research, University of the Witwatersrand, Johannesburg

Beavon, K (2000) 'Northern Johannesburg: Part of the "rainbow" or neo-apartheid city in the making?' *Mots Pluriels*, 13, an electronic journal on the University of Western Australia website: www.arts.uwa.edu.au/MotsPluriels/MP1300kb.html

Beavon, K (2001) 'The role of transport in the rise and decline of the Johannesburg CBD, 1886–2001', Paper read at the CODATU seminar at the South African Transporation Conference, CSIR, Pretoria

Bekker, S and Humphries, R (1985) *From Control to Confusion: The changing role of administration boards in South Africa, 1971–1983,* Shuter and Shuter, Pietermaritzburg

Bessis, S (1995) 'From social exclusion to social cohesion: Towards a policy agenda', *Management of Social Transformations (MOST), UNESCO Policy Paper No 2,* UNESCO, Paris

Black, A (1991) 'Manufacturing development and the economic crisis: A reversion to primary production?' in Gelb, S (ed) *South Africa's Economic Crisis,* David Philip, Cape Town, pp156–174

Blakely, E and Snyder, M (1997) *Fortress America: Gated communities in the United States,* Brookings Institution Press, Cambridge, Massachusetts

Bollens, S (1998) 'Urban planning amidst conflict: Jerusalem and Johannesburg', *Urban Studies,* 35, pp729–450

Bollens, S (1999) *Urban Peace Building in Divided Societies: Belfast and Johannesburg,* Westview Press, Oxford

Bond, P (2000a) *Cities of Gold, Townships of Coal: Essays on South Africa's new urban crisis* Africa World Press, Trenton

Bond, P (2000b) *Elite Transitions,* Wits University Press, Johannesburg

Bozzoli, B (1987) 'Class, community and ideology in the evolution of South African society' in Bozzoli, B (ed) *Class, Community and Conflict: South African perspectives,* Ravan Press, Johannesburg, pp1–43

Brett, E (1996) 'The Participatory Principle in Development Projects: The Costs and Benefits of Cooperation', *Public Administration and Development,* 16(1), pp5–19

Budlender, D (1998) *The People's Voices: National speak out on poverty hearings,* South African NGO Coalition, Johannesburg

Business Day, Johannesburg

Caldeira, T (1996) 'Crime and individual rights: Re-framing the question of violence in Latin America' in Jelin, E and Hershberg, E (eds) *Constructing Democracy: Human rights, citizenship and society in Latin America,* Westview Press, Boulder, Colorado, pp197–211

Caldeira, T (2000) *City of Walls: Crime, segregation and citizenship in São Paulo,* University of California Press, Berkeley, California

Camerer, L, Louw, A, Shaw, M, Artz, L and Sharf, W (1998) *Crime in Cape Town: Results of a city victim survey,* Institute of Security Studies Monograph Series No 23, Institute of Security Studies, Pretoria

Cameron, R (1999) *Democratisation of South African Local Government,* Van Schaik, Pretoria

Campbell, C and Mzaidume, Z (2001) 'Grassroots participation, peer education and HIV-prevention by sex workers in South Africa', *American Journal of Public Health,* 91(12), pp1978–1986

Carney, D (ed) (1998) *Sustainable Rural Livelihoods: What contribution can we make?* Department for International Development, London

Carrim, N (1990) *Fietas: A social history of Pageview, 1948–1988,* Save Pageview Association, Johannesburg

CASE (1998a) 'Upgrading Gauteng's informal settlements', Report prepared for Gauteng Department of Housing and Land Affairs, Johannesburg

CASE (1998b) 'Determining our own development: A community-based socio-economic profile of Alexandra', Report prepared for the CFBN Foundation, Johannesburg

CASE (2001) *Towards the Formulation of Policy for Hostel Redevelopment,* Report for the Gauteng Department of Housing, Community Agency for Social Inquiry, Johannesburg

Cassim, F (1988) 'Growth, crisis and change in the South African economy' in Suckling, J and White, L (eds) *After Apartheid: Renewal of the South African economy*, James Currey, London, pp1–18

Castells, M (1989) *The Informational City: Information, technology, economic resturcturing and the urban-regional process*, Blackwell, Oxford

Castells, M. (1998) *The End of the Millenium*, Blackwell, Oxford

Community Development Forum (CDF) (undated) 'Diepsloot Integrated Development Programme', Unpublished Report, Diepsloot Community Development Forum Committee

Chambers, R and Conway, G (1992) *Sustainable Rural Livelihoods: Practical concepts for the 21st century*, IDS Discussion Paper 296, Institute of Development Studies, Sussex

Chaskelson, M, Jochelson, K and Seekings, J (1987) 'Rent boycotts and the urban political economy' in Moss, G and Obery, I (eds) *South African Review 4*, Ravan Press, Johannesburg, pp53–74

Chipkin, C (1993) *Johannesburg Style: Architecture and society 1880s–1960s*, David Philip, Cape Town

Chipkin, I (1997) 'Democracy, cities and space: South African conceptions of local government', Unpublished Masters thesis, the University of the Witwatersrand, Johannesburg

Chipkin, I (2001) 'A developmental role for local government' in Parnell, S, Pieterse, E, Swilling, M and Wooldridge, D (eds) *Developmental Local Government: The South African experiment*, UCT Press, Cape Town, pp61–95

Clague, C (ed) (1997) *Institutions and Economic Development: Growth and governance in less-developed and post-socialist countries*, The Johns Hopkins Press, Baltimore

Citizen, Johannesburg

City of Johannesburg (2001) *Social Capital and Social Exclusion in the City of Johannesburg*, Greater Johannesburg Metropolitan Council, Johannesburg

City Vision, Johannesburg

Clert, C (1999) 'Evaluating the concept of social exclusion in development discourse', *European Journal of Development Research*, 11(2), pp176–199

Coleman, J (1990) *Foundations of Social Theory*, Harvard University Press, Cambridge, Massachusetts

Coovadia, C (1991) 'The role of the civic movement' in Swilling, M, Humphries, R and Shubane, K (eds) *Apartheid City in Transition*, Oxford University Press, Cape Town

Crankshaw O and White, C (1995) 'Racial desegregation and inner city decay in Johannesburg', *International Journal of Urban and Regional Research*, 19(4), pp622–638

Crankshaw, O (1993) 'Apartheid, urbanisation and squatting on the southern Witwatersrand', *African Affairs*, 92(366), pp31–51

Crankshaw, O (1996) 'Exploding the Myths of Johannesburg's Inner City', Report prepared for the Inner City Housing Upgrading Trust, Johannesburg

Crankshaw, O (1997) *Race, Class and the Changing Division of Labour Under Apartheid*, Routledge, London

Crankshaw, O and Hart, T (1990) 'The roots of homelessness: Causes of squatting in the Vlakfontein squatter settlement south of Johannesburg', *South African Geographical Journal*, 72(2), pp65–70

Crankshaw, O and Parnell, S (1996) 'Housing provision and the need for an urbanisation policy in the new South Africa', *Urban Forum*, 7(2), pp231–236

Crankshaw, O and Parnell, S (1999) 'Interpreting the 1994 African township landscape' in Juden, H and Vladislavic, I (eds) *Architecture After Apartheid*, David Philip, Cape Town, pp439–443

Crankshaw, O and Parnell, S (forthcoming) 'Race, inequality and urbanisation in the Johannesburg region, 1946–1996' in Gugler, J (ed) *World Cities in Poor Countries*, Cambridge University Press, Cambridge

Crankshaw, O, Gilbert, A and Morris, A (2000) 'Backyard Soweto', *International Journal of Urban and Regional Research*, 24(4), pp841–857

Crush, J and James, W (1997) *Crossing Boundaries*, Institute for Democratic Alternatives in South Africa, Pretoria

CSS (1993) *Standard Industrial Classification of all Economic Activities (fifth edition): Report No 09–90–02*, Central Statistical Service, Pretoria

Davies, R (1964), 'Social Distance and the Distribution of Occupational Categories in Johannesburg and Pretoria', *South African Geographical Journal*, 46, pp24–39

Davies, R, O'Meara, D and Dlamini, S (1984) *The Struggle for South Africa: A reference guide to movement, organizations and institutions*, Zed Books, London

Davis, M (1990) *City of Quartz*, Verso Press, London

Davis, M (1998) *Ecology of Fear: Los Angeles and the imagination of disaster*, Metropolitan Books, New York

de Coning, C, Fick, J and Olivier, N (1987) 'Residential settlement patterns: A pilot study of socio-political perceptions in grey areas of Johannesburg', *South Africa International*, 17(3), pp121–137

de Haan, A (1998) 'Social Exclusion and South Asia', *International Institute for Labour Studies*, http://www.ilo.org/public/englishinst/papers/synth/socex/htm

Dear, M (2000) *The Postmodern Urban Condition*, Blackwell, Oxford

Devas, N and Rakodi, C (eds) (1993) *Managing Fast Growing Cities: New approaches to urban planning and management in the developing world*, Longman, Harlow

Devas, N, Amis, P, Beall, J, Grant, U, Mitlin, D, Rakodi, C and Satterthwaite, D (2001) *Urban Governance and Poverty: Lessons from a study of ten cities in the South*, University of Birmingham, Birmingham

DFID (1997) *Eliminating World Poverty: A challenge for the 21st century*, Department for International Development White Paper on International Development, Her Majesty's Stationery Office, London

Dieleman, F and Hamnett, C (1994) 'Globalisation, regulation and the urban system: Editor's introduction to the special issue', *Urban Studies*, 31(3), pp357–364

Douglas, M (1987) *How Institutions Think*, Routledge and Kegan Paul, London

Douglass, M and Friedmann, J (1998) *Cities for Citizens: Planning and the rise of civil society in a global age*, John Wiley and Sons, Chichester

Drakakis-Smith, D (1995) 'Third World cities: Sustainable urban development', *Urban Studies*, 32(4–5), pp659–677

Dudley, E (1993) *The Critical Villager: Beyond community participation*, Routledge, London

Dunn, S (ed) (1994) *Managing Divided Cities*, Ryburn, Saffordshire

Edwards, C (1998), 'Financing faster growth in South Africa: The case for reforming the financial sector', *Transformation*, 35, pp49–76

Emdon, E (1994) 'The Development Facilitation Act (DFA)', *Urban Forum*, 5(2), pp89–97

Evans, P (1996a) 'Introduction: Development strategies across the public–private divide', *World Development*, 24(6), pp1033–1037

Evans, P (1996b) 'Government action, social capital and development: Reviewing the evidence on synergy', *World Development*, 24(6), pp1119–1132

Everatt, D (1999) 'Yet another transition? Urbanization, class formation, and the end of national liberation struggle in South Africa', Comparative Urban Studies Occasional Paper Series No 24, Woodrow Wilson International Centre for Scholars, Washington, DC

Fainstein, S (1994) *The City Builders: Property, politics and planning in London and New York*, Blackwell, Cambridge Massachusetts

Fainstein, S, Gordon, I, Harloe, M (eds) (1992) *Divided Cities: New York and London in the contemporary world*, Blackwell, Oxford

Fajnzybler, P, Lederman, D and Loayza, N (1998) *Determinants of Crime Rates in Latin America and the World: An empirical assessment*, World Bank Latin American and Caribbean Studies, Washington, DC

Ferguson, J (1999) *Expectations of Modernity: Myths and meanings of urban life on the Zambian Copperbelt*, University of California Press, Berkeley, California

Fick, J, de Coning, C and Olivier, N (1988) 'Ethnicity and residential patterning in a divided society: A case study of Mayfair in Johannesburg', *South Africa International*, 19(1), pp1–27

Fihla, K (1999a) 'Forward' in Greater Johannesburg Metropolitan Council, *iGoli 2002: Making the city work*, GJMC, Johannesburg

Fihla, K (1999b) 'Implementing the *iGoli* plan', *Staff Matters*, 6, Greater Johannesburg Metropolitan Council Staff Bulletin

Financial Mail, Johannesburg

Fine, B (1999) 'The development state is dead: Long live social capital?' *Development and Change*, 30, pp1–19

Fox, J (1996) 'How does civil society thicken? The political construction of social capital in rural Mexico', *World Development*, 24(6), pp1089–1103

Frankel, P (1988) 'Urbanisation and Informal Settlement in the PWV Complex', Department of Political Studies, University of the Witwatersrand, Johannesburg

Friedlander, E (1996) *Look at the World through Women's Eyes: Plenary speeches from the NGO Forum on Women at Beijing 1995*, Women's Ink, New York

Friedman, S (2001) 'A quest for control: High modernism and its discontents in Johannesburg, South Africa', Unpublished Paper, Centre for Policy Studies, Johannesburg

Friedmann, J (1998) 'The new political economy of planning: The rise of civil society' in Douglass, M and Friedmann, J (eds) *Cities for Citizens*, John Wiley and Sons, Chichester, pp19–38

Fyfe, N (1998) 'Introduction: Reading the street' in Fyfe, N (ed) *Images of the Street: Planning, identity and control in public space*, Routledge, London, pp1–10

Garreau, J (1991) *Edge City: Life on the new frontier*, Double Day, New York

Gelb, S (1991) 'South Africa's economic crisis: An overview' in Gelb, S (ed) *South Africa's Economic Crisis*, David Philip, Cape Town, pp1–32

Giddens, A (1979) *Central Problems in Social Theory: Action, structure and contradiction in social analysis*, Macmillan, London

Gilbert, A (1992) 'Third world cities: Housing, infrastructure and servicing', *Urban Studies*, 29, pp435–460

Gilbert, A and Crankshaw, O (1999) 'Comparing South African and Latin American experience: Migration and housing mobility in Soweto', *Urban Studies*, 36(13), pp2375–2400

Greater Johannesburg Metropolitan Council (GJMC) (1997) 'Greater Johannesburg Metropolitan Council Land Development Objectives', Unpublished Reports (2 volumes), GJMC, Johannesburg

GJMC (1998a) '1998/1999 Municipal Budget', GJMC, Johannesburg

GJMC (1998b) 'Macro Summary: Historic results and five-year budget: rateable income and budget scenarios', Unpublished Document, GJMC, Johannesburg

GJMC (1998c) *Consolidated Financial Statement for Year Ended 30 June 1998*, GJMC, Johannesburg

GJMC (1998d) 'Greater Johannesburg Metropolitan Council Integrated Metropolitan Development Plan, 1997/98', Unpublished Report, GJMC, Johannesburg

GJMC (1998e) Memo from the Credit Control Task Team, 3 December 1998, GJMC, Johannesburg

GJMC (1999a) 'Financial Plan', GJMC, Johannesburg

GJMC (1999b) '*iGoli 2002*: Transformation and Implementation Plan', GJMC, Johannesburg

GJMC (1999c) *iGoli 2002: Making the city work*, GJMC, Johannesburg

GJMC (1999d) 'Notes from the GJMC Bite the Bullet Workshop', Metropolitan Centre, 19 January 1999, GJMC, Johannesburg

GJMC (1999e) 'Local Integrated Development Planning Process Tender Package', GJMC, Johannesburg

GJMC (1999f) *Local Integrated Development Plans (LIDPs) for Greater Johannesburg*, volume 1, GJMC, Johannesburg

GJMC (2001a) '*iGoli 2010*', Unpublished Document, GJMC, Johannesburg

GJMC (2001b) *Social Capital and Social Exclusion in the City of Johannesburg*, GJMC, Johannesburg

Gore, C and Figueiredo, J (eds) (1997) *Social Exclusion and Anti-Poverty Policy: A debate*, IILS Research Series 110, International Labour Organization, Geneva

Gotz, G and Wooldridge, D (2000) 'Local Government Innovation: A case study of the Greater Johannesburg Metropolitan Council's Inner City Office and three urban development projects', Unpublished Paper written for the Local Government Learning Network, Johannesburg

Gray, J (1996) *After Social Democracy*, Demos, London

Hadland, A and Rantoe, J (1999) *The Life and Times of Thabo Mbeki*, Zebra, Rivonia

Hall, T and P Hubbard (1996) 'The entrepreneurial city: New urban politics, new urban geographies', *Progress in Human Geography*, 20(2), pp153–174

Hamnett, C (1994) 'Social polarisation in global cities: Theory and evidence', *Urban Studies*, 31(3), pp401–424

Harrison, K (2001) 'Social capital and local government' in Parnell, S, Pieterse, E, Swilling, M and Wooldridge, D (eds) *Developmental Local Government: The South African experiment*, UCT Press, Cape Town, pp227–238

Harriss, J and de Renzio, P (1997) '"Missing link" or analytically missing? The concept of social capital, an introductory bibliographic essay', *Journal of International Development*, 9(7), pp919–937

Hart, D and Pirie, G (1984) 'The sight and soul of Sophiatown', *Geographical Review* 74(1), pp38–47

Hart, G (1968) 'An introduction to the anatomy of Johannesburg's southern suburbs', *South African Geographical Journal*, 50, pp65–72

Hart, G (1996) 'Resegregation within a process of desegregation: Social polarization in Johannesburg' in O'Loughlin, J and Friedrichs, J (eds) *Social Polarization in Post-industrial Metropolises*, Walter de Gruyter, Berlin, pp195–206

Hart, T (1975) 'The factorial ecology of Johannesburg', Occasional Paper No 5, Urban and Regional Research Unit, University of the Witwatersrand, Johannesburg

Hart, T (1976) 'The evolving pattern of élite white residential areas in Johannesburg, 1911–1970', *South African Geographical Journal*, 58(1), pp68–75

Hart, T and Browett, J (1976) 'A multi-variate spatial analysis of the socio-economic structure of Johannesburg, 1970', Occasional Paper No 13, Urban and Regional Research Unit, University of the Witwatersrand, Johannesburg

Harvey, D (1973) *Social Justice and the City*, Edward Arnold, London

Harvey, D (1989) *The Condition of Post-Modernity: An enquiry into the origins of cultural change*, Basil Blackwell, Oxford

Healey, P (1995) 'Discourses of integration: Making frameworks for democratic urban planning' in Healey, P, Cameron, S, Davoudi, S, Graham, S and Mandipour A (eds) *Managing Cities: The new urban context*, John Wiley and Sons, Chichester

Healey, P (1997) *Collaborative Planning: Shaping places in fragmented societies*, Macmillan, London

Healey, P, Cameron, S, Davoudi, S, Graham, S and Mandipour A (eds) (1995) *Managing Cities: The new urban context*, John Wiley and Sons, Chichester

Heller, P (2000) 'Moving the state: The politics of democratic decentralization in Kerala, South Africa and Porto Alegre', Paper presented at the International Conference on Democratic Decentralization, Thiruvananthapuram, India, 23–27 May

Hendler, P (1989) *Politics on the Home Front*, South African Institute of Race Relations, Braamfontein

Heymans, C (1993) 'Towards people's development', *Urban Forum*, 4, pp1–20

Hindson, D (1987) *Pass Controls and the Urban African Proletariat*, Ravan Press, Johannesburg

Hirschman, A. (1970) *Exit, Voice and Loyalty*, Harvard University Press, Cambridge Massachusetts

Homeless Talk, Johannesburg

Jackson, C (1999) 'Social exclusion and gender: Does one size fit all?' *The European Journal of Development Research*, 11(1), pp125–146

Jessop, B (1990) *State Theory: Putting the capitalist state in its place*, Polity Press, Cambridge

Johannesburg Stock Exchange (JSE) (1991) *The JSE Handbook*, Johannesburg Stock Exchange, Johannesburg

Jubber, K (1973) 'Some aspects of high-density flat living: With special reference to flatland, Johannesburg', Unpublished Masters thesis, University of the Witwatersrand, Johannesburg

Judd, D (1994) 'Urban violence and enclave politics: Crime as text, race as subtext' in Dunn, S (ed) *Managing Divided Cities*, Ryburn Publishing, Staffordshire, pp160–175

Kabeer, N (2000) 'Social exclusion, poverty and discrimination: Towards an analytical framework, *IDS Bulletin,* 31(4), pp83–97

Kane-Berman, J (2001) 'No major changes in crime trends' *Fast Facts*, 7, South African Institute of Race Relations, Johannesburg

Kanji, N (1995) 'Gender, poverty and economic adjustment in Harare, Zimbabwe', *Environment and Urbanization*, 7(1), pp37–56

Kasarda, J (1990) 'Urban industrial transition and the underclass', *Annals of the American Academy of Political and Social Science*, 501, pp26–47

Keenan, J (1984) 'The effect of the 1978–1982 industrial cycle on Sowetan household incomes and poverty levels', in Kraayenbrink, E (ed), *Studies on Urbanisation in South Africa*, South African Institute of Race Relations, Johannesburg, pp33–36

Keenan, J (1988) 'Reforming poverty: A socio-economic profile of Soweto households during the 'reform' era, 1978–1986', *African Studies*, 47(1), pp35–46

Kesteloot, C (2000) 'Brussels: Post-Fordist polarization in a Fordist spatial canvas', in Marcuse, P and van Kempen, R (eds) *Globalizing Cities: A new spatial order?* Blackwell Publishers, Oxford, pp186–210

Khosa, M (1991) 'Capital accumulation in the black taxi industry', in Preston-Whyte, E and Rogerson, C (eds) *South Africa's Informal Economy*, Oxford University Press, Cape Town, pp310–325

Khosa, M (1992) 'Changing state policy and the black taxi industry in Soweto' in Smith, D (ed) *The Apartheid City and Beyond: Urbanization and social change in South Africa*, Routledge, London, pp182–192

Khosa, M (ed) (2000) *Empowerment Through Service Delivery*, Human Sciences Research Council, Pretoria

Kihato, C (1997) '"Megacity" model is not the route the Greater Johannesburg should adopt', *Synopsis*, 1, Centre for Policy Studies, Johannesburg, pp5–7

King, A (1990) *Global Cities: Post imperialism and the internationalisation of London*, Routledge and Kegan Paul, London

Lauria, M (ed) (1997) *Reconstructing Urban Regime Theory: Regulating urban politics in a global economy*, Sage Publications, Thousand Oaks

Lawless, P (1991) 'Urban policy in the Thatcher decade: English inner city policy, 1979–90', *Environment and Planning C*, 9, pp15–30

Leduka, C (2000) 'The law and access to urban housing land in a sub-Saharan African city: Experiences from Maseru, Lesotho', Paper presented at a Conference on the Informal and Formal City, Nordic Africa Institute, Copenhagen, Denmark

Lenoir, R (1974) *Les Exclus: Un Francais Sur Dix*, Le Seuil, Paris

Levi, M (1996) 'Social and unsocial capital: A review essay of Robert Putnam's "Making Democracy Work"', *Politics and Society*, 24(1), pp45–55

Lewis, P (1966) 'A city within a city: The creation of Soweto', Special Issue of *The South African Geographical Journal*

Lipton, M (1977) *Why Poor People Stay Poor: Urban bias in world development*, Maurice Temple Smith, London

Lodge, T (1981) 'The destruction of Sophiatown', *Journal of Modern African Studies*, 19, pp107–132

Louw, A, Shaw, M, Camerer, L and Robertshaw, R (1998) *Crime in Johannesburg: Results of a victim survey*, Institute of Security Studies, Pretoria

Lupton, M (1993) 'Collective consumption and urban segregation in South Africa', *Antipode*, 25(1), pp32–50

Mabin, A (1991) 'The dynamics of urbanization since 1960' in Swilling, M, Humphries, R and Shubane, K (eds) *Apartheid City in Transition*, Oxford University Press, Cape Town

Mabin, A (1998) 'The creation of urban space: Contributions of South African cities to justice and injustice', Paper presented to the Conference on the Social Geography of Divided Cities, New York University, 26–28 February, New York

Mabin, A (1999) 'From hard top to soft serve: Demarcation of metropolitan government in Johannesburg' in Cameron, R (ed) *Democratisation of South African Local Government*, Van Schaik, Pretoria, pp160–199

Mabin, A (2001) 'Local government in the emerging national planning context' in Parnell, S, Pieterse, E, Swilling, M and Wooldrdge D (eds) *Developmental Local Government: The South African experiment*, UCT Press, Cape Town, pp45–59

Mackintosh, M (1992) 'Partnerships: Issues of policy and negotiation', *Local Economy*, 3(3), pp210–224

Maganya, E (1996) 'Community Development Forums and the development process' in Maganya, E and Houghton, R (eds) *Transformation in South Africa: Policy debates in the 1990s*, Institute for African Alternatives, Johannesburg

Mail and *Guardian*, Johannesburg

Mamdani M (1996) *Citizen and Subject: Contemporary Africa and the legacy of late colonialism*, Princeton University Press, Princeton

Mandy, N (1984) *A City Divided: Johannesburg and Soweto*, Macmillan, Johannesburg

Manor, J (1999) *The Political Economy of Democratic Decentralisation*, World Bank, Washington, DC

Marais, H (1998) *South Africa: Limits to change*, University of Cape Town Press, Cape Town

Marcuse, P (1995) 'Not chaos but walls: Postmodernism and the partitioned city' in Watson, S and Gibson, K (ed) *Postmodern Cities and Spaces*, Blackwell, Oxford, pp243–253

Marcuse, P and van Kempen, R (eds) (2000) *Globalizing Cities: A new spatial order?* Blackwell Publishers, Oxford

Mashabela, H (1988) *Townships of the PWV*, South African Institute of Race Relations, Johannesburg

Massey, D (1999) 'On Space and the City' in Massey, D, Allen, J and Pile, S (eds) *City Worlds*, Routledge, London, pp157–171

Massey, D and Denton, N (1993) *American Apartheid: Segregation and the making of the underclass*, Harvard University Press, Cambridge, Massachusetts

May, J (ed) (1999) *Poverty and Inequality in South Africa: Meeting the challenge*, David Philip, Cape Town

May, J, Carter, M, Haddad, L and Maluccio, J (1999) 'KwaZulu–Natal Income Dynamics Study (KIDS) 1993–1998: A longitudinal household data set for South African policy analysis', *Development Southern Africa*, 17(4), pp567–581

Mayekiso, M (1996) *Township Politics: Civic struggles for a new South Africa*, Monthly Review Press, New York

McCarney, P (1996a) 'Considerations of the notion of 'governance': New directions for cities in the developing world' in McCarney, P (ed) *Cities and Governance: New directions in Latin America, Asia and Africa*, University of Toronto Press, Toronto, pp1–22

McCarney, P (1996b) *Cities and Governance: New directions in Latin America, Asia and Africa*, University of Toronto Press, Toronto

McIlwaine, C (1999) 'Geography and development: Violence and crime as development issues', *Progress in Human Geography*, 23(3), pp453–463

McKinley, D (undated) 'Discussion document on *iGoli 2002*', Unpublished Document, South African Communist Party, Gauteng Provincial Executive Committee, Gauteng Province

Meintjies, H (1997) 'Punitive approach alone will not resolve electricity payment problems', *Synopsis*, 1(3), Centre for Policy Studies, Johannesburg, pp4-7

Meintjes, H and White, C (1997) '"Robbers and Freeloaders": Relations between communities and ESKOM in Gauteng townships', *Policy: Issues and Actors*, 10(5), Social Policy Series, Centre for Policy Studies, Johannesburg

Millward, C and Pillay, V (1996) 'The Economic Battle for South Africa's Future' in Maganya, E and Houghton, R (eds) *Transformation in South Africa?: Policy debates in the 1990s*, Institute for African Alternatives, Braamfontein, pp35–51

Minnaar, A (ed) (1993) *Communities in Isolation: Perspectives on hostels in South Africa*, Human Sciences Research Council, Pretoria

Mogase, I (1999) 'Message from the Mayor' in Greater Johannesburg Metropolitan Council, *iGoli 2002: Making the city work*, GJMC, Johannesburg

Monitor (2000a) 'Housing strategy in the City of Johannesburg', Unpublished Report prepared for the *iGoli 2010* Partnership, Monitor Company, Boston

Monitor (2000b) 'Resolve crime and security solutions: Safety and security sector report for the Greater Johannesburg Metropolitan Council', Unpublished Report prepared for the *iGoli 2010* Partnership, Monitor Company, Boston

Monitor (2000c) 'Solid waste sector: Summary report', Unpublished Report prepared for the *iGoli 2010* Partnership, Monitor Company, Boston

Moore, M (1993) 'Introduction on good government' *IDS Bulletin*, 24(1), pp1–6

Morris, M, Bozzoli, B, Cock, J, Crankshaw, O, Gilbert, L, Lehutso–Phooko, L, Posel, D, Tshandu, Z and van Huysteen, E (1999) 'Change and continuity: A survey of Soweto in the late 1990s', Department of Sociology, University of the Witwatersrand, Johannesburg

Morris, A (1994) 'The desegregation of Hillbrow, Johannesburg 1978–1982', *Urban Studies*, 31(6), pp821–834

Morris, A (1999) *Bleakness and Light: Inner-city transition in Hillbrow, Johannesburg,* Witwatersrand University Press, Johannesburg

Morris, P (1980) *Soweto: A review of existing conditions and some guidelines for change,* Urban Foundation, Johannesburg

Moser, C (1993) *Gender Planning and Development: Theory, practice and training,* Routledge, London

Moser, C (1996) *Confronting Crisis: A comparative study of household responses in four poor urban communities,* Environmentally Sustainable Development Studies and Monograph Series No 8, World Bank, Washington, DC

Moser, C (1998) 'The asset vulnerability framework: Reassessing urban poverty reduction strategies', *World Development,* 26(1), pp1–19

Moser, C and Clark, F (eds) (2001) *Victims, Perpetrators or Actors?: Gender, armed conflict and political violence,* Zed Books, London

Moser, C, Herbert, A and Makonnen, R (1993) *Urban Poverty in the Context of Structural Adjustment: Recent evidence and policy responses,* Urban Development Division Discussion Paper, World Bank, Washington, DC

Moser, C and Holland, J (1997) *Urban Poverty and Violence in Jamaica,* World Bank Latin American and Caribbean Studies, Washington, DC

Musiker, N and Musiker R (2000) *A Concise Historical Dictionary of Greater Johannesburg,* Francolin Publishers, Cape Town

Narayan, D, Chambers, R, Shah, P and Petesch, P (2000) *Voices of the Poor: Crying out for change,* World Bank, Washington, DC

Nattrass, N (1992) 'Profitability: The soft underbelly of South African Regulation/SSA Analysis', *Review of Radical Political Economics,* 24(1), pp31–51

Nattrass, N (2001) 'High productivity now: A critical review of South Africa's growth strategy', *Transformation,* 45, pp1–24

Nattrass, N and Seekings, J (1998) 'Changing patterns of inequality in the South African labour market' in Petersson, L (ed), *Post-Apartheid Southern Africa: Economic challenges and policies for the future,* Routledge, London, pp44–63

Nattrass, N and Seekings, J (2001) '"Two nations"? Race and economic inequality in South Africa today', *Daedalus* 130(1), pp45–70

Northern Metropolitan Council of Johannesburg (NMC) (undated) 'Diepsloot Integrated Development Project', Unpublished Report, NMC, Johannesburg

North, D (1990) *Institutions, Institutional Change and Economic Performance: Political economy of institutions and decisions,* Cambridge University Press, Cambridge

O'Loughlin, J and Friedrichs, J (eds) (1996) *Social Polarization in Post-Industrial Metropolises,* Walter de Gruyter, New York

O'Regan, C (1990) 'The Prevention of Illegal Squatting Act' in Murray, C and O'Regan, C (eds) *No Place to Rest: Forced removals and the law in South Africa,* Oxford University Press, Cape Town, pp162–179

Organization for Economic Cooperation and Development (OECD) (1995) *Women in the City: Housing, services and the urban environment,* OECD, Paris

OECD (1997) *Final Report of the ad hoc Working Group on Participatory Development and Good Governance: Part I,* Development Assistance Committee of the OECD, Paris

Oldfield S (2001) '"Embedded autonomy" and the challenges of developmental local government' in Parnell, S, Pieterse, E, Swilling, M and Wooldridge, D (eds) *Developmental Local Government: The South African experiment*, UCT Press, Cape Town, pp97–109

Olivier, J (1993) 'Preface' in Minnaar (ed) A. *Communities in Isolation: Perspectives on Hostels in South Africa*, Human Sciences Research Council, Pretoria

Ostrom, E (1996) 'Crossing the great divide: Coproduction, synergy and development', *World Development*, 24(6), pp1073–1087

Parnell, S (1991a) 'Race, class, gender and homeownership subsidies in contemporary South Africa', *Urban Forum* 2(1), pp21–40

Parnell, S (1991b) 'The ideology of African home-ownership: The establishment of Dube, Soweto, 1946–1955', *South African Geographical Journal*, 73, pp69–76

Parnell, S and Beavon, K (1996) 'Urban land restitution in post-apartheid South Africa: Questions from the Johannesburg inner-city', *GeoJournal* 39, pp13–19

Parnell, S and Hart, D (1999) 'Self-help housing as a flexible instrument of state control in 20th-century South Africa', *Housing Studies*, 14(3), pp367–386

Parnell, S and Pieterse, E (1998) 'Developmental local government: The second wave of post-apartheid reconstruction', *Africanus*, 29, pp61–85

Parnell, S and Pirie, G (1991) 'Johannesburg', in Lemon, A (ed) *Homes Apart*, Paul Chapman, London, pp129–145

Piazolo, M and Würth, M (1995) 'Productivity in the South African manufacturing industry', *South African Journal of Economics*, 63(2), pp173–196

Pieterse, E, Parnell, S and Wooldridge, D (1998) 'Emerging architecture of developmental local government and prospects for poverty reduction', Unpublished Paper presented at the UNCHS Regional Workshop on Mainstreaming Urban Poverty Reduction in Sub-Saharan Africa, Nairobi

Pirie, G (1984) 'Ethno-linguistic zoning in South African black townships', *Area*, 16(4), pp291–298

Pirie, G and da Silva, M (1986) 'Hostels for African migrants in greater Johannesburg', *GeoJournal*, 12(2), pp173–182

Pirie, G and Hart, D (1985) 'The transformation of Johannesburg's black western areas', *Journal of Urban History*, 11(4), pp887–410

Posel, D (1991) *The Making of Apartheid, 1948–1961: Conflict and compromise*, Clarendon Press, Oxford

Post, J (1997) 'Urban management in an unruly setting', *Third World Planning Review*, 19(4), pp347–366

Potts, D (1995) 'Shall we go home? Increasing urban poverty in African cities and migration processes', *The Geographical Journal*, 161(3), pp245–264

Price Waterhouse (1998) 'Organisation Review: Greater Johannesburg Metropolitan Council and Local Council, envisioning organisation design', Price Waterhouse, Ebony Financial Services and KMMT Brey, Johannesburg

Putnam, R (1993) *Making Democracy Work: Civic traditions in modern Italy*, Princeton University Press, Princeton

Putzel, J (1997) 'Accounting for the "dark side" of social capital: Reading Robert Putnam on democracy', *Journal of International Development*, 9(7), pp939–949

Rakodi, C and Lloyd–Jones, T (eds) (2002) *Urban Livelihoods: A People-centred Approach to Reducing Poverty*, Earthscan, London

Rebeiro, L and Telles, E (2000) 'Rio de Janeiro: Emerging dualization in a historically unequal city' in Marcuse, P and van Kempen, R (eds) *Globalizing Cities: A new spatial order?* Blackwell Publishers, Oxford, pp78–94

Roberts, S (1997) 'Monetary policy within macroeconomic policy: An appraisal in the context of reconstruction and development', *Transformation*, 32, pp54–78

Robinson, J (1992) 'Power, space and the city: Historical reflections on apartheid and post-apartheid urban orders' in Smith, D (ed) *The Apartheid City and Beyond: Urbanization and social change in South Africa*, Routledge, London, pp292–302

Robinson, J (forthcoming) 'City futures: The next phase of development studies?' Mimeo prepared for the Open University, Milton Keynes

Rodgers, G, Gore, C and Figueiredo, J (eds) (1995) *Social Exclusion: Rhetoric, reality, responses*, Institute for International Labour Studies, Geneva

Rogerson, C (1995) 'South Africa's Economic Heartland: Crisis, decline or restructuring?' *Africa Insight*, 25(4), pp241–247

Rogerson, C (1996) 'Dispersion within Concentration: The changing location of corporate headquarter offices in South Africa', *Development Southern Africa*, 13(4), pp567–579

Rogerson, C (2000) 'Re-examining the state of the manufacturing heartland', Unpublished Report for the Project on Spatial Guidelines for Infrastructure, Investment and Development, Coordinated by the CIU, Office of the Deputy-President

Rogerson, C and Hart, D (1989) 'The Struggle for the Streets: Deregulation and hawking in South Africa's major urban areas', *Social Dynamics*, 15, pp29–45

Rogerson, C and Rogerson, J (1997a) 'Intra-Metropolitan industrial change in the Witwatersrand, 1980–1994', *Urban Forum*, 8(2), pp194–223

Rogerson, C and Rogerson, J (1997b) 'The changing post-apartheid city: Emergent Black-owned small enterprises in Johannesburg', *Urban Studies*, 34(1), pp85–103

Rogerson, J (1995) 'The changing face of retailing in the South African City: The case of inner-city Johannesburg', *Africa Insight*, 25(3), pp163–171

Rogerson, J (1996) 'The geography of property in inner-city Johannesburg', *Geojournal*, 39, pp73–79

Rule, S (1988) 'Racial residential integration in Bertrams, Johannesburg', *South African Geographical Journal*, 70, pp69–72

Rule, S (1989) 'The emergence of a racially mixed residential suburb in Johannesburg: Demise of the apartheid city?' *Geographical Journal*, 155, pp196–203

Saff, G (1994) 'The changing face of the South African city: From urban apartheid to the deracialisation of space', *International Journal of Urban and Regional Research*, 18(3), pp371–391

Safier, M (1992) 'Urban development, policy, planning and management: Practitioners' perspectives on public learning over three decades', *Habitat International*, 16, pp5–12

South African Municipal Workers Union (SAMWU) (1999a) 'SAMWU slams latest Joburg proposal to give executives extra year's salary as "bonus" for privatising quickly!', COSATU website: www.cosatu.org.za/samwu/khetso.htm

SAMWU (1999b) 'SAMWU rejects the *iGoli 2002* restructuring plan for Johannesburg', COSATU website: www.cosatu.org.za/samwu/igoli1.htm

South African Non-Government Organization Coalition (SANGOCO) (1998) *Poverty, Housing and Urban Development in South Africa*, A Briefing Paper for the Poverty Hearings held by SANGOCO, Occasional Publications Series No 5, Johannesburg

Sapire, H (1990) *Report on the Social and Political Ecology of Free-Standing Settlements on the PWV*, Urban Foundation and the Centre for Policy Studies, Johannesburg

Sapire, H (1992) 'Politics and protest in shack settlements of the Pretoria–Witwatersrand–Vereeniging Region, South Africa, 1980–1990', *Journal of Southern African Studies*, 18(3), pp670–697

Sarakinsky, M (1984) *Alexandra: From 'freehold' to 'model' township*, Development Studies Group, University of the Witwatersrand, Johannesburg

Sassen, S (1991) *The Global City: New York, London, Tokyo*, Princeton University Press, Princeton, New Jersey

Sassen, S (1994) *Cities in a World Economy*, Pine Forge Press, Thousand Oaks, California

Satterthwaite, D (1997) 'Urban poverty: Reconsidering its scale and nature', *IDS Bulletin*, 28(2), pp9–23

Scheper-Hughes, N (1992) *Death Without Weeping: The violence of everyday life in Brazil*, University of California Press, Berkeley

Schmidt, D (1999) 'Organisational change in Greater Johannesburg Metropolitan Area' in Cranko, P and Schmidt, D (eds) *Organisational Change Theme Team*, Local Government Learning Network, Cape Town

Schönteich, M and Louw, A (2001) *Crime in South Africa: A country and cities profile*, Occasional Paper No 49, Institute of Security Studies, Pretoria

Schuurman, F (1997) 'The decentralisation discourse: Post-Fordist paradigm or neo-liberal cul-de-sac?' *European Journal of Development Research*, 9(1), pp150–166.

Seekings, J (1996) 'The decline of movement organisations', *Critical Sociology* 22(3), pp135–157

Seekings, J (2000) *The UDF: A history of the United Democratic Front in South Africa, 1983–1991*, David Phillip, Cape Town

Seekings, J and Nattrass, N (forthcoming) *From Race to Class: Inequality, unemployment and the social structure in South Africa*

Shaw, M and Gastrow, P (2001) 'Stealing the show? Crime and its impact in post-apartheid South Africa', *Daedalus*, 130(1), pp235–258

Sibley, D (1995) *Geographies of Exclusion: Society and difference in the West*, Routledge, London

Sibley, D (1998) 'The problematic nature of exclusion', *Geoforum*, 29(2), pp119–121

Simon, D (1992) *Cities, Capital and Development: African cities in the world economy*, Bellhaven Press, London

Simon, D (1999) 'Rethinking cities: Sustainability and development in Africa' in Kalipeni, E and Seleza, P (eds) *Sacred Spaces and Public Quarrels: African cultural and economic landscapes*, African World Press, Eritrea, pp2–41

South Africa (1998) *Local Government White Paper*, Department of Constitutional Development, Pretoria

South Africa (1998) *The People of South Africa: Population Census 1996, Census in Brief*, Report No 03–01–11, Statistics South Africa, Pretoria

Stadler, A (1979) 'Birds in the cornfields: Squatter movements in Johannesburg, 1944–1947' in Bozzoli, B (ed) *Labour, Townships and Protest: Studies in the social history of the Witwatersrand*, Ravan Press, Johannesburg, pp19–48

Stiefel, M and Wolfe, M (1994) *A Voice for the Excluded, Popular Participation in Development, Utopia or Necessity*, Zed Books, London

Stoker, G (2001) 'International trends in local government transformation' in Parnell, S, Pieterse, E, Swilling, M and Wooldridge, D (eds) *Developmental Local Government: The South African experiment*, UCT Press, Cape Town, pp35–44

Stren, R (1993) 'Urban management in development assistance: An elusive concept', *Cities*, May, pp125–138

Stren, R and White, R (eds) (1989) *African Cities in Crisis: Managing rapid urban growth*, Westview, Boulder, Colorado

Sunday Independent, Johannesburg

Swilling, M and Boya, L (1997) 'Local government in transition' in Fitzgerald, P McLennan, L and Munslow, B (eds) *Managing Sustainable Transition in South Africa*,

Oxford University Press, Cape Town, pp165–191

Swilling, M and Shubane, K (1991) 'Negotiating urban transition: The Soweto experience' in Lee, R and Schlemmer, L (eds) *Transition to Democracy: Policy perspectives 1991*, Oxford University Press, Cape Town, pp223–258

Swyngedouw, E (1992) 'The mammon quest: 'Glocalisation', interspatial competition and monetary order: The construction of new spatial scales' in Dunford, M and Kafkalas, G (eds) *Cities and Regions in the New Europe: The global–local interplay and spatial development strategies*, Belhaven Press, London

Taylor, P (1999) 'Democratizing cities: Habitat's global campaign on urban governance', *Habitat Debate*, 5(4), pp1–5

Tendler, J (1997) *Good Government in the Tropics*, The John Hopkins University Press, Baltimore

The Star, Johannesburg

Tomlinson, R (1996) 'The Changing Structure of Johannesburg's Economy' in Harris, N and Fabricius, I (eds) *Cities and Structural Adjustment*, UCL Press, London, pp175–199

Tomlinson, R (1999) 'From exclusion to inclusion: Rethinking Johannesburg's central city', *Environment and Planning A*, 31, pp1655–1678

Tomlinson, R, Attahi, K and Lamba, D (1998) 'Urban development and good governance: Case studies of Abidjan, Johannesburg and Nairobi', Unpublished Paper, Johannesburg

Turok, I (1994) 'Urban planning in the transition from apartheid part 2: Towards reconstruction', *Town Planning Review*, 65(4), pp355–374

United Nations Centre for Human Settlements (Habitat) (UNCHS) (1996) *An Urbanizing World: Global report on human settlements 1996*, Oxford University Press for UNHCS, Oxford

UNDP (1997) *Human Development Report*, United Nations Development Programme, New York

Urban Sector Network (USN) (1998) *Developmental Local Government*, USN, Johannesburg

Uphoff, N (1992) *Learning from Gal Oya: Possibilities for participatory development and post-Newtonian social science*, Cornell University Press, Ithaca, New York

Vanderschueren, F (1996) 'From violence to justice and security in cities', *Environment and Urbanisation*, 8(1), pp93–112

Vidler, E (1999) *City Economic Growth,* Urban Governance, Partnerships and Poverty Research Working Paper No 1, University of Birmingham, Birmingham

Villadsen, S and Lubanga, F (1996) *Democratic Decentralisation in Uganda: A new approach to local governance*, Fountain Press, Kampala

Viruly Consulting (2000) 'A sectoral perspective on property within metropolitan Johannesburg', Unpublished Report prepared for the *iGoli 2010* Project Office, Greater Johannesburg Metropolitan Council, Johannesburg

Wade, R (1987) *Village Republics: Economic conditions for collective action in South India*, Cambridge University Press, Cambridge

Watson, V (1998) 'Planning under political transition: Lessons from Cape Town's metropolitan planning forum', *International Planning Studies*, 3, pp335–350

Watson, V (2001) 'The usefulness of normative planning theories in the context of Africa', Paper Presented at the Oxford Planning Theory Conference, Oxford

Webster, E (1985) *Caste in a Racial Mould: Labour process and trade unionism in the foundries*, Ravan Press, Johannesburg

Weeks, A (1999) 'Unions and politics: *iGoli 2002*', *South African Labour Bulletin*, 23, pp52–55

Wheelan, P (2001) 'Local government finance reform' in Parnell, S, Pieterse, E, Swilling, M and Wooldridge, D (eds) *Developmental Local Government: The South African experiment,* UCT Press, Cape Town, pp241–258

White, C, Crankshaw, O, Mafokoane, T and Meintjes, H (1998) 'Social Determinants of Energy use in Low Income Households in Gauteng', Department Of Minerals and Energy Affairs, Pretoria

Wieczorek, J (1995) 'Sectoral trends in world employment and the shift toward services', *International Labour Review,* 134(2), pp205–226

Willis, M (2000) 'Meddling with the media': Democratic Left discussion zone website: www.democratic–left.org.uk/discuss/mwillis.html

Wilson, F and Ramphele, M (1989) *Uprooting Poverty: The South African challenge,* David Philip, Cape Town

Wilson, W (ed) (1996) *When Work Disappears: The world of the new urban poor,* Random House, New York

Wilson, W (1987) *The Truly Disadvantaged: The inner city, the underclass and public policy,* University of Chicago, Chicago

Wooldridge, D (1999a) 'Metropolitan Government: Lessons from the Greater Johannesburg experience', *SALGA Voice,* March, pp18–19

Wooldridge, D (1999b) 'The impact of the national framework for IDPs and PMS on municipal restructuring', Unpublished Paper, Johannesburg

Wooldridge, D (2001a) 'Introducing metropolitan government in South Africa' in Parnell, S, Pieterse, E, Swilling, M and Wooldridge, D (eds) *Developmental Local Government: The South African experiment,* UCT Press, Cape Town, pp133–146

Wooldridge, D (2001b) 'Hillbrow: The bleeding edge of South African urbanism?' in Greater Johannesburg Metropolitan Council, *Social Capital and Social Exclusion in the City of Johannesburg,* Report to GJMC, Johannesburg

World Bank (1991) *Urban Policy and Economic Development: An Agenda for the 1990s,* World Bank Policy Paper, The World Bank, Washington, DC

World Bank (1994) *Governance: The World Bank's experience,* Development in Practice, The World Bank, Washington, DC

World Bank (1997) *World Development Report 1997,* Oxford University Press, Oxford

Wratten, E (1995) 'Conceptualising urban poverty', *Environment and Urbanization,* 7(1), pp11–36

Xeketwane, B (1995) 'The relationship between hostels and the political violence on the reef from July 1990 to December, 1993: A case study of Merafe and Meadowlands hostels in Soweto', Unpublished Masters thesis, Faculty of Arts, University of the Witwatersrand, Johannesburg

Index

Page references in *italics* refer to figures and tables

unemployment 11, 31, 38, 39, 42, 46, 52, 57–8, 61, *143 see also* employment
United Democratic Front (UDF) 70, 72
United States 32, 61, 111, 114, 115, 175
upgrading hostels 186–7, 189, 190, 193, 194
upgrading squatter settlements 134–49
upgrading urban areas 109, 110–11, 113–19, 127–8
urban development corporations 116
urban governance *see* governance
Urban Management Programme 16, 18
urban poverty *see* poverty
urbanization 7, 8, 10, 199, 204

Village Main 52
violence
  in apartheid era 177–8
  in crime 120, 177, 178–9
  in hostels 186, 188, 190, 191–2
  insecurity results 179, 183, 191–2, 194
  political 140, 177–8, 186, 188
  and poverty 11
  and social exclusion 25, 120, 140, 141
  against women 25, 141, 177, 178–9, 182, 183, 190, 202

wage inequality 14, 36, 39, *44*
waste management *92,* 169–70, 174
water supply *92,* 104, 142, 153, 154–7, *158,* 167, 168, 174

welfare dependency 24
Westbury 51
Western Municipal Sub-Structure (WMSS) 78, *79*
White Paper on Local Government *74,* 75
white population
  gated communities 175, 176, 177, 195
  housing 48, 49, 50, 51, 52, 60, 112, 175
  in labour market 35–6, 37–8, 39, 40
  racial insecurity 113, 182–3, 195
  service provision *154,* 155, *156*
women
  in employment 40–1, *42,* 199
  in hostels 189, 190, 191, 193
  and violence 25, 141, 177, 178–9, 182, 183, 190, 202
  vulnerability 11, 141, 202
World Bank 8, 12, 16
Wynberg 54

xenophobia 20, 24, 141

Yeoville 50, 110, 115, 117, 118–27, 128

Zevenfontein 134, 142
zoning 51, 60, 73, 166
Zulu population 84, 176, 185, 186, 188–9, 195

ALSO AVAILABLE FROM EARTHSCAN
ON URBAN DEVELOPMENT

CITIES IN A GLOBALIZING WORLD
Global Report on Human Settlements 2001
United Nations Centre for Human Settlements (UNCHS)

'A comprehensive review of conditions in the world's cities and the prospects for making them better, safer places to live in an age of globalization... It will provide all stakeholders with reliable and timely information with which to set our policies right'
From the Foreword by **Kofi Annan**, Secretary General, United Nations

This major and influential report from the United Nations Human Settlements Programme (UN-Habitat) (formerly UNCHS) presents a comprehensive review of the world's cities and analyses the positive and negative impacts on human settlements of the global trends towards social and economic integration and the rapid changes in information and communication technologies.

The UNITED NATIONS HUMAN SETTLEMENTS PROGRAMME is the world's leading research and advisory body on the development of cities and other settlements.

Published in association with UN-Habitat

Pb • 1 85383 806 3 • £25.00
Hb • 1 85383 805 5 • £55.00
384 pages • 297x210mm • Maps, Figures, Tables, Index

To order, visit www.earthscan.co.uk
email: earthinfo@earthscan.co.uk • tel: +44 (0)1903 828 800
• fax: +44 (0)20 7278 1142

EARTHSCAN

Press Release

NEW BOOK EXPLORES JOHANNESBURG URBAN REALITY

Published by Earthscan on 26th August

'Johannesburg has become a litmus test for uniting divided cities and democratic urban governance everywhere.'

From the Introduction to the book

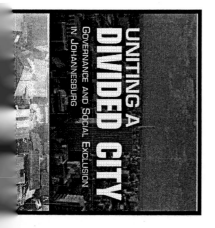

UNITING A DIVIDED CITY

GOVERNANCE AND SOCIAL EXCLUSION IN JOHANNESBURG

The authors, who live both in the UK and South Africa, investigate pragmatic approaches to urban economic development, service delivery, spatial restructuring, environmental sustainability and institutional reform in Johannesburg and explore the conditions and processes that could determine the city's transformation into a cosmopolitan metropole and magnet for the continent.

Moreover, they set Johannesburg as a paradigm of urban development and the solutions that they put forward can be applied to several cities around the world.

-Ends-

Contents: Johannesburg: An Exemplar of the Urban Challenge • Mapping Social, Economic and Environmental Complexity • Building Institutions for Democratic Urban Governance • Negotiating Urban Development Policy and Resources • Social Differentiation and Social Healing in Soweto • Strangers in the Night: Migrants and the Changing Face of Urban Community in the Inner City • Cementing Community Influence: Civic Participation in Johannesburg's Informal Settlements

... ... is Reader in Development Studies at the LSE, and formerly taught at UCL and University of Natal, South Africa. **Owen Crankshaw** is Senior Lecturer in Sociology, University of Cape Town, and has worked at the Centre for Policy Studies, Johannesburg. **Susan Parnell** is Associate Professor in Geography, University of Cape Town, and has taught at University of the Witwatersrand and SOAS, London, and Oxford

---

For further information, to request a review copy, or to interview the author please contact Martha Fumagalli: tel. 020 7278 0433, fax. 020 7837 6348 or e-mail. mfumagalli@kogan-page.co.uk

---

Notes to the editor

£18.95 ▪ Paperback ▪ 1 85383 916 7 ▪ 255 pages ▪ 234x153 mm £48 – Hardback – 1 85383 921 3

Available from all good book shops or direct from the publisher at:
Earthscan, 120 Pentonville Road, London N1 9JN
Tel. 01903 828800 Fax. 020 7837 6348
E-mail: orders@lbsltd.co.uk
or order on-line at www.earthscan.co.uk

Johannesburg Summit 2002 – the World Summit on Sustainable Development – will bring together tens of thousands of participants, including heads of state and government, national delegates and leaders from NGOs, businesses and other major groups to focus the world's attention and action towards meeting difficult challenges, including improving people's lives and conserving our natural resources in a world that is growing in population, with ever-increasing demands for food, water, shelter, sanitation, energy, health services and economic security.

Launched by Earthscan on 26th of August, the start date of the Summit, *Uniting a Divided City: Governance and Social Exclusion in Johannesburg*, describes the acute problems affecting the city such as urban explosion, social fracture, environmental degradation, escalating crime and violence, and rampant consumerism alongside grinding poverty.

/continued...

Earthscan Publications Ltd   120 Pentonville Road   London   N1 9JN
Telephone +44 (0)20 7278 0433   **Fax** +44 (0)20 7278 1142   **Email** earthinfo@earthscan.co.uk
Website www.earthscan.co.uk